FOOD LOVERS'
GUIDE TO
RALEIGH, DURHAM & CHAPEL HILL

Help Us Keep This Guide Up to Date

We would love to hear from you concerning your experiences with this guide and how you feel it could be improved and kept up to date. Please send your comments and suggestions to:

editorial@GlobePequot.com

Thanks for your input, and happy travels!

FOOD LOVERS' SERIES

FOOD LOVERS'
GUIDE TO
RALEIGH, DURHAM & CHAPEL HILL

The Best Restaurants, Markets & Local Culinary Offerings

1st Edition

Johanna Kramer

Guilford, Connecticut

To buy books in quantity for corporate use
or incentives, call **(800) 962-0973**
or e-mail **premiums@GlobePequot.com**.

Editor: Amy Lyons
Project Editor: Lynn Zelem
Layout Artist: Mary Ballachino
Text Design: Sheryl Kober
Illustrations by Jill Butler with additional art by Carleen Moira Powell and MaryAnn Dubé
Maps: Alena Joy Pearce © Morris Book Publishing, LLC

ISBN 978-0-7627-7976-5

Printed in the United States of America
10 9 8 7 6 5 4 3 2 1

All the information in this guidebook is subject to change. We recommend that you call ahead to obtain current information before traveling.

Contents

Recipes, 255

Lemongrass-Grilled Hanger Steak with Cucumber Salad & Spicy Peanut Sauce (Chef Charlie Deal of Jujube), 289

Buttermilk Pie (Executive Chef Jay Pierce of Lucky 32 Southern Kitchen), 291

Appendices, 293

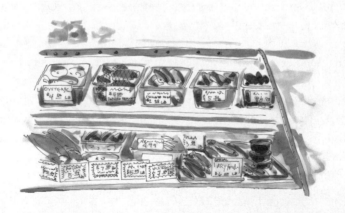

About the Author

Johanna Kramer is a North Carolina–based freelance writer who specializes in writing about food and food-related events through her popular blog, Durhamfoodie. She writes for magazines such as *SavorNC* and *Edible Piedmont*. She also hosts special events and develops business opportunities for *Edible Piedmont*, a member of the Edible Communities Publications, the recipient of the 2011 James Beard Award for Publication of the Year.

Johanna's Durhamfoodie blog features local food events, cookbook reviews, artisanal product reviews, and on-the-spot reporting through her Twitter feed. Her tweet-up venues—a meet-up of food lovers sponsored by local eateries—sell out within minutes of being posted online. Most recently, Johanna was invited to put her taste buds to work as a judge of California artisanal beers at the Good Food Awards in San Francisco. She is also very committed to the farm-to-fork movement, working closely with the Carolina Farm Stewardship Association (CFSA) promoting its annual farm tours through social media and public relations events and most recently instructing farmers on how to use social media to promote their individual produce, thanks to a grant from the Golden Leaf Foundation.

Born in Montreal, Canada, Johanna spent her first two years living on a farm in Athelston, Quebec, where her mom and dad had a large vegetable garden and made her baby food from scratch. The family moved back to Montreal and then to Toronto, where they lived in Bloor West Village, a culturally diverse community whose main street consisted of small family-run markets, butcher shops, and bakeries. During high school, Johanna held a part-time job at the exclusive Boulevard Club, learning how to run a professional kitchen from a manager whom Johanna still considers a mentor 15 years later. After earning a degree in Hospitality and Marketing from George Brown College in Toronto, Johanna moved to North Carolina and studied at the Central Carolina Community College's Natural Chef Culinary Program. Today, writer, blogger, and social-media expert Johanna Kramer is happiest at home in her kitchen cooking for her family—and posting menus online that make her Durhamfoodie followers wish they were invited for dinner.

Acknowledgments

There does not seem to be an appropriate place to start thanking all the people who have helped me on the journey to writing my first book. The extra help researching and sharing thoughts and opinions on particular restaurants quite possibly put a strain on my friendships, but oftentimes that was appeased by an invitation to join me for breakfast, lunch, or dinner all in the name of research.

Without a doubt, this book would not have come to fruition without the love and support, the encouragement and the backing of my wonderful family. My mother, Linda Scovill, especially stepped up to the plate, and inadvertently and effectively became the best assistant any writer could ask for. She researched, edited, and helped me keep track of where I was and what still needed to be completed. Her unconditional love, sound advice (she is a former editor and publisher) when I was feeling the stress, and many, many much-needed "mummy hugs" helped me plow through some really tough days.

My partner and best friend, David Jung, let me cry on his shoulder when I went through moments of self-doubt, scream and yell, and just downright throw a childish temper tantrum when I was frustrated, and yet always managed to bring a smile back to my face and make me feel loved. I love you, babe!

Thank you to my boss and more importantly good friend, Fred Thompson, publisher of *Edible Piedmont,* for his patience and understanding. He knows firsthand what it takes to write a book—he's written several—and generously afforded me the time to write my own.

A huge thank you goes to my wonderful, dear-to-my-heart group of fabulous friends, many of whom I didn't see for several months. They saw me through the excitement, panic attacks, serious doubting moments, and of course, the euphoric relief I felt on the day I finally sent in my manuscript. Thank you Carrie Nickerson, Christie Vasquez, Andrea Weigl, Paul Reid, and Matt Lardie. A very special mention to Susan Frederick Rains and Gabrielle Kassa for helping to research restaurants, test recipes, and really bringing me through some tough times—you guys are the best.

I must say I ate very well during the time it took to research and write this book, and I have to thank the many marketing and public relations professionals and chefs who took the time to set me up with breakfasts, lunches, and dinners and all kinds of treats in between. Sasha Travers for inviting me to tastings at Tonali, Guglhupf, and Bull Street Market; Susan Reda for a delightful lunch at Il Palio; Martin Armes for the Winter menu tasting at Carolina Crossroads; Chef de Cuisine Carrie Shleiffer and Pastry Chef Deric McGuffey, for what turned into a fabulously delicious 4-hour feast at G2B Gastro Pub and Beer Garden; Theresa Chiettini and Colin Bedford for a delightful lunch at The Fearrington Granary and the most exquisite fine-dining experience at The Fearrington House;

and my good friend Jay Pierce for the many menu tastings he has invited me to at Lucky 32.

When I started the initial task of writing this book and determining what restaurants to include, or at least the ones I may have missed after writing my first outline, I must thank Greg Cox, restaurant critic for the *News and Observer,* for taking the time to meet with me over coffee and read through my entire list and offer his suggestions and tips. Andrea Weigl, food editor at the *News and Observer* and dear friend, helped with my restaurant outline, but also answered some of the many questions that popped up during the process, even when she was 9 months pregnant. Thank you—and congratulations on your beautiful baby girl.

I want to thank Globe Pequot Press and my Editor Amy Lyons for the opportunity to write this book; even when I was behind on deadline, you helped me through and gave me the guidance I needed. Every first-time book writer needs a stand-behind-you editor.

Thank you to the wonderful people at the Convention and Visitors Bureaus in the "Triangle." Sam Poley in Durham for the in-depth listings and national accolades of restaurants, Patty Griffin in Chapel Hill for food event listings, and Ryan Smith in Raleigh.

This book would not have been possible without the many talented chefs we are so lucky to have in this area. For your hard work, dedication, and endless creativity, I thank you. For feeding me, for introducing me to new foods, and for making Raleigh, Durham, and Chapel Hill the dining destinations they have become. You feed our hearts and souls, one meal at a time, and for that I, along with everyone else, say "Thank you!"

Introduction

I have always been fortunate to be surrounded by good food and I've been a "foodie" in training ever since I took my first bites. Those bites were boiled and pureed vegetables from my parents' garden, and scratch-made baby food even included pressure-cooked beef tongue; it is no wonder I have an adventurous palate today.

As I was growing up, home-cooked meals were important to our family. Even when mum went back to work, my brother and I could always count on coming home to delicious smells wafting from the slow cooker—beef stew being a personal favorite. On Sundays, my dad would spend the afternoon at the stove whipping up a hearty batch of soup, and to this day, those memories always come back every time I make my own batch of soup for the family.

My parents were avid gardeners. My mum had scarlet runner beans and cucumbers growing up trellises on the sunny side of our house or on the fence around the yard. In the small plot at the end of our garden, my dad enjoyed nurturing earthbound vegetables such as beets and potatoes—and true to his German heritage, bunches of curly-leaf, green kale. Each spring we watched as the rhubarb buds peeked through the last of the snow knowing that my

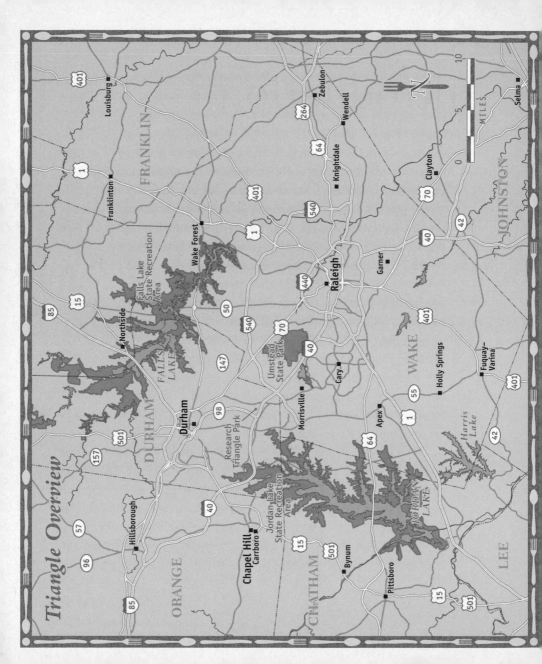

mum would soon make us all an apple and rhubarb crumble when the stalks were ruby-red ripe. When crab apples were in season, the whole family would jump in the car and drive over to the tree-lined streets by my grandparents' home to pick bags of the fresh fruit. The 3-day canning process that ensued always produced the best-tasting crab-apple jelly I've encountered to this day.

I learned early on that cooking was a family affair: Meals were shared around the dining room table each evening. My mum and I would make chocolate-chip cookies so often that her 1964 edition of *The Joy of Cooking,* which she gave to me, still falls open to the page where the recipe is located; and every winter on especially crisp, cold days, my dad and I made peanut brittle and placed the cookie sheet covered with our sugary syrup and peanut mixture out on the snow-covered patio to harden.

In my later teens, I worked part-time in a snack bar at the prestigious Boulevard Club in Toronto, Canada. Here I learned knife skills, flavor profiles, large-batch cooking, and how to run multiple stations and expedite tickets as a short-order cook. It was my first restaurant experience, and under my boss Ann Lino, a true love of the industry was born. She is still a mentor to me today.

My passion for the hospitality industry eventually landed me back in school to obtain my Hospitality and Tourism degree from George Brown College in Toronto, and upon my return to North Carolina I accepted a position with Georgios Hospitality Group in marketing and sales for all eight restaurants that were under this group at the time.

From that point forward, I immersed myself in the culinary scene that was beginning to take shape in Durham and all around the region known as the Triangle. I attended culinary school and started hosting the Triangle Foodie Tweet-ups with *News and Observer* food writer Andrea Weigl. I promote the Carolina Farm Stewardship Association's Farm Tours and Sustainable Agriculture Conference and work on business development for the local food magazine, *Edible Piedmont*.

All this has led me to where I am today and explains why cooking for my family, blogging about food events, artisan products, recipes, and cookbooks, and promoting the Raleigh, Durham, and Chapel Hill dining scene have become my passion.

Raleigh, Durham, and Chapel Hill are often referred to as "the Triangle" because of the invisible lines that connect the three cities. Research Triangle Park or "RTP" as it is referred to, located at the core of this imaginary triangle, is a mecca for major corporations, employing a great number of area residents. Drawing from the large pool of university graduates (the Triangle is home to three major universities; NC State, Duke, and UNC Chapel Hill) as well as PhDs from all over the US and the world, RTP has become a nationally recognized business community with leading-edge research in pharmaceuticals and information technology. Over the years, the Triangle has come to include many of the surrounding areas, including Apex, Cary, Carrboro, and Morrisville, while "RTP" is still associated with the original designated area and is often referred to as "the Park."

As our population has grown, so has our appetite for good food, and as our appetites have grown, so has the number of aspiring young chefs opening new and innovative restaurants. Seasoned chefs have continued to excel, and the two combined have placed the Triangle on the culinary map as a dining destination.

From one tip of the Triangle to the others, the number of popular restaurants has grown astronomically over the last decade and those with nationally acclaimed chefs at their helms equally so. The numbers of local nominees and regional winners for the various James Beard Awards are a testimony to the quality of the food world here. The James Beard Awards were established in 1990 and are often called "the Oscars of Food." The awards honor the great chefs, restaurants, wine professionals, journalists, cookbook authors, restaurant designers, and other food professionals in the United States. In 2011 Gene Hammer and Bill Smith of Crook's Corner were awarded an America's Classic award, given to "restaurants with timeless appeal beloved for quality of food that reflects the character of their community," while Lantern's Andrea Reusing won "Best Chef Southeast," and Edible Communities, of which *Edible Piedmont* is a part, won "Publication of the Year." And when the James Beard Foundation announced their semifinalist nominees in 2012, it was no surprise to see, once again, several Triangle establishments on the list: Magnolia Grill (although sadly now closed), for Outstanding Restaurant; Scott Howell, Ashley Christensen, Aaron Vandermark, and Vivien Howard for Best Chef Southeast; and Sean Lilly Wilson from Fullsteam Brewery for outstanding wine and spirits professional. Although none of them were nominated as finalists, they are considered winners by local residents.

I could continue to list the chefs, restaurants, food writers, and cookbook authors who have been nominated or won the various food awards, but that alone could be a stand-alone book. As for other noteworthy mentions, there is no denying Andrea Weigl's substantial contributions to the food community or her award for Best Newspaper Food Coverage from the Association of Food Journalists, acknowledging just that. Andrea has become a beacon to the food community, making sure to pass along all the most up-to-date restaurant and food-event news on her blog Mouthful, while writing interesting and thought-provoking stories for the local daily newspaper, the *News and Observer*.

An important aspect of how these chefs have come to the forefront is their commitment to supporting local agriculture. The number of farms using sustainable and organic practices within North Carolina is prolific—spurring the growth of the "Farm to Table" concept both at home and in the restaurant. As the farming industry continues to grow with the support of organizations

North Carolina Barbecue

What can you say about North Carolina barbecue that hasn't already been said in countless articles and cookbooks for decades? There is always going to be a debate about which is the best barbecue: Eastern or Western.

All North Carolina barbecue is very slow-cooked pork, generally for a minimum of 16 to 18 hours at a low temperature, usually between 250 and 300°F. The slow cooking allows the meat to age without drying out. After the meat is thoroughly cooked, it is pulled from the bones and pulled apart into smaller chunks and then chopped further with a cleaver. Real NC barbecue is never served sliced.

Eastern-NC style barbecue has only the vaguest hint of vinegar with the possible addition of a few spices. The vinegar mixture is applied as a moistening agent after the hog has been barbecued. Western-NC style barbecue is not made from the whole carcass of the hog but from pork shoulders only, and while being cooked, it is braised with a tomato-based sauce that is added to the vinegar base, sometimes with a small amount of sugar added.

Typically, barbecue is served with coleslaw and hush puppies, washed down with jugs of strong, sweet iced tea, and banana pudding for dessert.

To understand more about North Carolinians' fascination with barbecue, read about it from the Master of North Carolina Barbecue: Bob Garner. His two original books on NC barbecue have been recently combined, updated, and expanded into one volume: *Bob Garner's Book of Barbecue: North Carolina's Favorite Food.*

like the **Carolina Farm Stewardship Association** (p. 14), **Animal Welfare Approved** (p. 13), and **Piedmont Grown** (p. 16), and as people continue to purchase from local farmers' markets and track those purchases through the **10 Percent Campaign** (p. 17), the number of restaurants utilizing seasonal ingredients on their menus and community members cooking with seasonal ingredients at home will continue on its upward trend.

The farmers' markets have not only become a place to pick up our weekly or biweekly groceries but also a place to catch up with friends, meet and talk to farmers, and learn how to incorporate new ingredients into our everyday cooking. On any given weekly visit to the market, you are bound to see several local chefs shopping too, and this is evident in the seasonal changing menus you will encounter on your dining experiences around town; many restaurants change their menus weekly, some daily, to reflect the seasonal bounty at hand.

The bounty of the season has not only found its way to the plate but also to the glass. The importance of a quality cocktail has grown in popularity and is equally significant when talking about the Triangle food culture. The importance and art of replicating a classic cocktail, using seasonal ingredients, house-made sodas and mixers, have slowly found their place among us at popular establishments like the Whiskey in Durham, the Crunkleton in Chapel Hill, and Foundation in Raleigh. These establishments, with their talented and passionate "mixologists," meticulously and expertly hand-craft each cocktail to perfection.

The "Farm to Table" movement is not the only emerging culinary trend. As our multicultural communities have grown, so has the number of ethnically diverse restaurants offering many new and diversified culinary experiences. Across the Triangle, the Asian, Latino, and Indian communities also enter the restaurant business. Our food-loving residents support restaurants featuring Thai, Korean, and Chinese cuisines; the authentic South American taquerias and bodegas continue to move into the area as a direct result of a growing Hispanic population. The popularity of each is proven by the numbers of people who line up daily to savor a spicy curry or authentic taco. Even *Gourmet* magazine traveled to the area in 2007 to report on the many popular taquerias.

The Triangle food scene is much more than only the individual chefs and restaurateurs, it is the passionate home of chefs, local food writers, bloggers, and cookbook authors who collectively make the Raleigh, Durham, and Chapel Hill culinary scene so special. Undoubtedly, the food community is much like a family. We care about our food, our farms, our chefs, and how our food is prepared; lovingly, tenderly, and obsessively, nurturing each to its full potential.

You will notice the introductions to Raleigh, Durham, and Chapel Hill are each significantly different. Each city has its own distinct personality, one that is very obvious as you get to know the area.

I hope you enjoy this book as much as I did writing it. The culinary diversity of the

Triangle is a celebration of a multitude of cooking styles, from regional Southern cuisine and the multicultural influences to twists on the traditional, there is something for everyone to embrace and enjoy.

To summarize, the Triangle has become a mecca for foodies, a place where chefs and restaurant owners are respected to the highest degree—for their culinary creativity, their commitment to elevating the traditions of the past, and the commitment to forging relationships with area farmers and bringing us the best available local and seasonal ingredients. It is a multicultural pool of diverse eateries, bringing traditional foods from around the world to our doorstep and teaching us new ways to incorporate unique flavors into our menus.

Restaurants come and go, and many in this book may have changed. Please research ahead of time before dining at any of these establishments.

How to Use This Book

The listings in this book are organized geographically in chapters devoted to Raleigh, Durham, and Chapel Hill. The entries are further arranged according to the following categories:

Foodie Faves

Raleigh, Durham, and Chapel Hill are fast becoming a destination for good food, with nationally acclaimed and award-winning chefs and restaurants that range from world-class upscale steak houses to authentic BBQ shacks. Farms and farmers' markets are plentiful, allowing chefs to showcase seasonally available ingredients, with several restaurants in this section changing their menus on a daily or weekly basis. Although this section does not include every "wonderful" restaurant in the area, I've tried to include a range of solid eateries at all price points that are sure to please even the most discerning palates. These summaries are not reviews, rather an attempt to describe the atmosphere, ambience, and notable dishes in an effort to help you choose your next destination for a pleasant dining experience.

Landmarks

The landmark eateries chosen for this section are those that have stood the test of time based on their distinct characteristics and the permanent mark they have left on the community. Several of these restaurants are small family-run establishments, passed down from one generation to the next, and range from long-standing steak houses to old-time corner-store grills. Some are renowned for their traditional country cooking and Southern charm, while others are widely known for their upscale dining in historic surroundings. The one thing they all have in common is the desire to welcome diners into their "homes" and offer them a memorable dining experience.

Brewpubs & Microbreweries

North Carolina is home to more brewpubs and microbreweries than any other state in the American South.

The NC Brewers Guild (ncbeer.org) has an active membership of almost 50 brewpubs and production breweries throughout the state, with almost one-quarter of them in Raleigh/Durham/Chapel Hill or surrounding Triangle communities. Additionally, specialty and traditional cocktail lounges are popping up as more "mixologists" are using seasonal ingredients to concoct their handcrafted libations.

Specialty Stores, Markets & Producers

From community-run co-ops to custom butchers and bakers, this section was designed to showcase those establishments offering a single unique concept. They may offer artisan chocolates or handmade sausages while others offer wine and cheese or delectable baked goods. Also listed are gourmet food markets that offer everything from grocery staples (like meats, produce, dairy, and paper products) to sandwiches, salad bars, hot meals, and prepared entrees.

Price Codes

Landmark Restaurants and Foodie Faves generally follow a pricing guide, giving you a relative idea of what to pay per entree. Price listings are for dinner only. Lunch prices are generally lower.

$	**less than $10**
$$	**$10 to $20**
$$$	**$20 to $30**
$$$$	**$30 to $40**

Getting Around the Triangle

For a wealth of information about public transportation around the Triangle, including Raleigh, Durham, Chapel Hill, Hillsborough—plus more local communities—visit the Triangle Transit Authority (TTA) at (919) 485-RIDE (7433) or triangletransit.org. Otherwise, after each introduction to Raleigh, Durham, and Chapel Hill, read how to get around these cities by public transportation.

Recipes and Sidebars

The recipes at the end of the book offer insight into the kitchens of some of our top chefs and local restaurants, with brief explanations leading into each one. Recipes showcase local flavors, many highlighting the abundance of locally and seasonally available fruits and vegetables.

I am grateful to the many chefs who enthusiastically shared these with you, and I hope you enjoy them as much as I have. The sidebars scattered throughout are brief explanations of local specialties and specific ingredients indigenous to this region of the South.

Food Organizations

Animal Welfare Approved, animalwelfareapproved.org. Are you concerned about where the food on your table came from and how it got there? Animal Welfare Approved advocates for standards for rigorous and progressive animal care requirements, and its label is only given to participating family farms that put each individual animal's comfort and well-being first. As a consumer, you can ask your local grocery stores to buy from farmers using sustainable farming methods. Animal Welfare Approved has its label on eggs, dairy, and meat products.

Carolina Farm Stewardship Association (CFSA), PO Box 448, Pittsboro, NC 27312; (919) 542-2402; carolinafarmstewards .org. CFSA's mission is to "advocate, educate and build connections to create sustainable food systems centered on local and organic agriculture." The most popular public events hosted by the CFSA are the Farm Tours held once in the spring and once in the fall. It is the Piedmont's biggest sustainable farm tour, often touted as the largest in the United States! Local food stores sell "buttons" in advance. Load up the car with family and friends, choose the farms on the map that you'd like to visit and follow the directions. Bring a cooler for the farm-fresh products that you can buy to take home. The tour is self-guided and farms and sites are located throughout the Triangle in Alamance, Chatham, Durham, Orange, and Person counties. The 2012 Spring Farm Tour featured 40 small sustainable farms, and the cost per carload in advance was $25 ($30 on the day of the tour). Maps to the farms are available in PDF format online. Also, the CFSA has a popular blog called The Sweet Potato that you can sign up for at carolinafarmstewardsblog.org. Many different writers contribute.

Chop NC, chopnc.com. CHOP NC is Culinary Historians of Piedmont North Carolina, an organization welcoming the participation of all those who love food, history, and the traditions of the kitchen, the farm, and the table. To receive notices about events, sign up at chopnc.com. As well, read the Chop NC blog at chopnc.com/blog.

NC Brewers Guild, general inquiries admin@ncbeer.org; ncbeer .org. The NCBG is a nonprofit whose membership is comprised of brewers, vendors, retailers, and craft beer enthusiasts focused on promoting North Carolina beer. North Carolina lays claim to the largest number of craft breweries in the American South, with more than 20 brewpubs and 20 packaging breweries. The NCBG was formed following the "Pop-the-Cap" initiative of 2005 that did away with the 6 percent alcohol cap on beers in North Carolina. Anyone can become an "enthusiast" member of the NCBG for $30 a year. The website also promotes beer-related events and festivals. The home page of NC Beer appears to be a blog, even though it's not labeled as such.

NC Choices, ncchoices.com. NC Choices is the Center for Environmental Farming Systems' initiative to promote the advancement of local, niche, and pasture-based meat supply chains through educational and networking experiences for producers, processors, food professionals, and buyers to enhance consumer access to NC grown pasture-based meat products. Check out the website for the occasional workshop on whole-animal butchery.

Piedmont Grown, piedmontgrown.org. Its mission is to promote local food systems through the certification of food and farm products grown or raised in 37 counties in the North Carolina Piedmont Region. Piedmont Grown wants to link consumers to local farm-fresh foods, build local markets for farmers and food entrepreneurs, and grow healthy and prosperous communities. The Piedmont Grown program incorporates Piedmont farmers and other local food businesses including artisan food producers, retailers, wholesalers, institutional food service directors, and distributors. Individual consumers can join Piedmont Grown. Check out the membership details and benefits on the website.

Slow Food Triangle, slowfoodtriangle.org. Slow Food Triangle supports and celebrates local food and the people who grow it and/ or make it. A membership-based organization, Slow Food Triangle supports farmers and food artisans who farm responsibly and bring their produce to market for people like you and me to buy. Slow Food Triangle supports farmers and food artisans in the counties of Chatham, Durham Franklin, Granville, Harnett, Johnston, Orange, Person, and Wake. The cost of a membership begins at $60. To become a member of the local chapter, first join Slow Food USA, which you can do through the Slow Food Triangle website.

Southern Foodways Alliance (SFA), Center for the Study of Southern Culture, PO Box 1848, Barnard Observatory, University, MS 38677; (662) 915-5993; southernfoodways.org. The SFA is a member-supported nonprofit based at the University of Mississippi designed to celebrate the diverse food cultures of the changing American South by producing documentary films, collecting oral histories, and staging symposia on food writing. Southern Six-Pack is its popular blog (southernfoodways.blogspot.com), and the SFA also produces a quarterly online newsletter called Gravy. Membership is available beginning at $75 for individuals.

10 Percent Campaign, ncsu.edu/project/nc10percent/index .php. To help North Carolina's agrarian economy, many businesses and residents are participating in the 10 Percent Campaign. The campaign promotes the growth, distribution, and purchase of locally produced food in the state. In 2007, the Center for Environmental Farming Systems (CEFS) began searching for ways to build a sustainable statewide food economy. Funding from the Golden Leaf Foundation and partnerships with state universities enabled 10 Percent to launch in July 2010. The goal of 10 Percent is simple: To encourage consumers to commit 10 percent of their food dollars to support local food producers, businesses, and communities. Consider this: North Carolinians, on average, spend about

$35 billion a year on food. If individuals spent 10 percent, or $1.05 per day, locally, about $3.5 billion would be available in the local economy. Many local farmers' markets, restaurants, and city and county governments across the state have already signed on.

Keeping Up with Food News

There is no shortage of writers and journalists and simply everyday people who enjoy writing about food and drink in the Triangle area. In the past few years, print media have remained remarkably strong with the emergence of new "city" magazines that promote individual cities, including the food scene in each. Our largest daily newspaper, the *News and Observer,* has a robust subscriber base in the tri-city area that is supported by readers of print and online with blogs covering the vibrant food scene through profiles, trends, recipes, the farm-to-fork movement, and agriculture. As you plan your visit to the Triangle, check out these publications and blogs for up-to-the-minute happenings in the ever-changing world of food and drink in the Piedmont region of North Carolina.

The News and Observer, newsandobserver.com. Check out the food stories in our daily newspaper and link to them online at news-andobserver.com. Here's who to follow:

Mouthful: Where to shop, what to eat, what to cook by Andrea Weigl. (@andreaweigl)

Greg's Corner: Restaurant Reviews by Greg Cox. (@ggcox)

Weekend Gourmet: Writer, food stylist, and cookbook author Fred Thompson writes this biweekly column. (@fredthompsonNC)

Sunday Dinner: A monthly column about food and life in the South by Tar Heel Debbie Moose, cookbook author, editor, freelance writer, and award-winning essayist. (@debbiemoose)

On Wine: By Catherine Rabb who teaches culinary students at Johnson & Wales University in Charlotte, NC. She holds a sommelier certification from the Court of Master Sommeliers.

The Independent, indyweek.com. The *Independent* is a popular weekly tabloid that offers a variety of food news from around the tri-city area. It also includes an online Triangle Dining Guide. Of course, the *Independent* also offers progressive news stories on local issues as well as a roundup of the entertainment scene weekly.

Beer Hopping: Julie Johnson shares her love and passion for all things beer. She is well versed on the subject, having been the editor and co-owner, and now contributing editor, of the Durham-based national publication *All About Beer.*

Other Food and Drink Columns: The following columns are written by local journalists on a rotation basis, all of which can be found archived online: **First Bite** (reviews); **Now Serving** (foodie news and events), **Guidance for Gourmands** (local recipes), **Blessed Is the Pour** (wine); **Feed with Care** (explores

issues such as food allergies); **Object of Desire** (products); and **Meet-and-Three** (stories about local restaurateurs).

All About Beer, allaboutbeer.com; @allaboutbeer. Celebrate the world of beer culture through this award-winning, national bimonthly magazine, which has been published for over 20 years from Durham. Dan and Julie Bradford run this publication and the very active website is the go-to location for all things beer related—travel, local and international events, brewery openings, learn-about-beer articles, beer reviews, beer festivals (see pp. 27, 28, 30), and much more information all aimed toward the pursuit of beer pleasure.

Edible Piedmont, ediblepiedmont.com. One of the highly successful Edible Communities publications and winner of the James Beard Foundation Award for Publication of the Year 2011, quarterly magazine *Edible Piedmont*, led by publisher Fred Thompson and his wife, editor Belinda Ellis, brings the local food scene to life from the foothills of North Carolina to the coast, a region known as the Piedmont. *Edible Piedmont* features local foods and the stories of producers and growers in this region, including recipes.

Our State North Carolina, ourstate.com/topics/food. Published since 1933, this is the granddaddy of all magazines in North Carolina, featuring travel, history, people, places, and food. Food features and recipes are found online at their website.

SavorNC, savorncmagazine.com. A relative newcomer in the publication network in North Carolina, SavorNC promotes wine, food, decor, and travel from the mountains to the coast.

City Magazines

Independently published city magazines, generally with a controlled circulation, feature stories that pertain to each community such as Raleigh, Cary, Durham, and Chapel Hill. Local food articles feature in each of these publications as well. Check out the following publications online:

Raleigh Metro Magazine, metronc.com/foodandwine. A monthly magazine for Raleigh and its outlying communities.

Cary Magazine, carymagazine.com/category/channel/restaurant-row. A lifestyle magazine for Western Wake County, published six times a year.

Durham Magazine, durhammag.com/dining. This bimonthly city magazine is all about living well in Durham.

Chapel Hill Magazine, chapelhillmagazine.com/dining. Sister publication to the *Durham Magazine, Chapel Hill Magazine* is published bimonthly and highlights living the good life in Chapel Hill and surrounding communities, such as Carrboro and Hillsborough.

Blogs

Of course, where would we be today without the blogger? Food blogs are proliferating exponentially as social media have gained ground in the recognition of the fact that we all enjoy eating, and therefore like to read about food and anything food-related. Here are a few of the popular bloggers, some of whom you will note above write for traditional print media as well:

Carpe Durham, carpedurham.com. A "group" food blog about eating and drinking in Durham. If you want to know the location on a particular day for a favorite food truck, Carpe Durham has a beta food truck mapper that resets daily and tracks truck locations as their operators tweet location updates.

Cranky Diners, crankydiners.com. Blogs unbiased restaurant reviews and food-related things generally in the Raleigh, Durham, and Chapel Hill area.

DeMandy, demandy.com. Amanda Steinhardt proclaims herself a food-obsessed marketer turned blogger who writes about food and recipes in the Triangle. Her day job is with Burt's Bees. Mandy hosts the Social Media Supper Club, an informal gathering of foodies who tweet about meeting up for meals.

Durham Foodie, johannakramer.com. Follow Johanna Kramer's musings about food and food-related events; she is also the author of this book.

Eat It, North Carolina, eatitnorthcarolina.com. This food blogger must live to eat as she and her husband cover cities and towns across the state!

Food . . . Celebrating Our Market's Bounty, chapelboro.com. Susan Reda, a native North Carolinian who lives in Chapel Hill, writes about local food, farms, and recipes. Her blog appears online in the *Chapelboro* newspaper, the community portal for the Chapel Hill, Hillsborough, and Orange County community.

The Gourmez, thegourmez.com. Written by Becca Gomez Farrell, a Durham-based writer who feels she is only perched in the Bull City until her next move.

Green Eats, greeneatsblog.com. Matt Lardie is chronicling his journey through the world of sustainable agriculture in North Carolina through trends, events, news, commentary, and recipes. He even claims to throw in a "healthy dose of sarcasm."

The Masala Wala, masalawala.wordpress.com. Restaurant reviews around the Triangle by Jyotsna, a recent transplant to Chapel Hill from Boston. Of Indian descent, she is learning about Southern food culture and sharing her experiences online.

Moose Musings, debbiemoose.com/wordpress. Debbie Moose (yes, that is her real name) writes about life in general, the South, and "anything you can put into your mouth!" She is a prolific writer and observer of life.

Nancie McDermott, nanciemcdermott.wordpress.com. A Southerner by birth, Nancie grew up on Southern food until she served with the Peace Corps in Thailand and developed a passion for Asian cuisine. Nancie writes about ingredients, recipes, traditional dishes, food people, cookbooks, and culture in Asia and the American South.

Triangle Food Guy, trianglefoodguy.blogspot.com. Sean Lennard is our Raleigh man-around-town working hard to keep up with reviews on the ever-changing restaurant scene in our capital city. He also runs an online catering company.

Varmint Bites, varmintbites.com. Dean McCord, a Raleigh-based father of four, has an opinion on almost every aspect of the local food scene that he shares on his blog. You can visit his blog site to find out why his blog is called Varmint Bites. Hint: It has nothing to do with a possum or coon!

Events & Festivals

Throughout the Triangle, there must be at least one food-related event each weekend, often beginning on a Friday evening. The hardest part for most area residents and visitors alike is to choose which foodie event to attend. By far, the two best ways to find out what's happening in a particular city or town in this area is to check the local free paper, the *Independent,* online at indyweek.com, or the local Convention and Visitor Bureaus, which are listed below. Highlighted in this section are the largest and most popular events around the Triangle that strongly feature food. Each site has its own web link, and I invite you to check these out for the exact dates for this coming year: **Raleigh:** *visitraleigh.com;* **Durham:** *durham-nc .com;* **Chapel Hill:** *visitchapelhill.org.*

February

Krispy Kreme Challenge, krispykremechallenge.com. Fancy a dozen free doughnuts? As a challenger or a casual runner in the Krispy Kreme Challenge, they are yours for signing up, along with a racer T-shirt. All the proceeds from the Krispy Kreme Challenge go to the NC Children's Hospital, which provides care to patients from all 100 counties in North Carolina, regardless of a family's ability to pay for services. The Challenge started in December 2004 as a dare between a few NC State University

(NCSU) undergraduate students. All challengers attempt to complete the entire race, which includes eating all 12 doughnuts, in under one hour. Casual runners are not required to finish the race, and entrants need not eat all the doughnuts to compete! This race sells out in advance online; NCSU student $20; nonstudents $27; you can register online.

Vintage 2012, trianglewineexperience.org. A charity event featuring iconic wines and sublime foods, like-minded wine buffs, and a top-notch auction of awesome goodies. For tickets visit triangle wineexperience.org.

March

Empty Bowls/Urban Ministries of Durham, 410 Liberty St., Durham; (919) 682-0538; umdurham.org. Empty Bowls Durham is an event associated with Urban Ministries of Durham (UMD) and held each spring as a fund-raiser to provide three warm and nutritious meals daily to upward of 600 people. The idea for Empty Bowls initiated with an art teacher in Michigan in 1990 and has since become a grassroots movement, spreading as each community starts its own independent cause to help feed the community's hungry. Potters from around the Durham community unite to donate hand-thrown soup bowls to the UMD, and tickets are sold in advance of the springtime event, generally held in Durham in early March. Many community sponsors get involved including artists, musicians, restaurateurs, florists, church groups, and individuals plus an army of local community volunteers. In March 2012, over $32,000 was raised!

April

World Beer Festival Raleigh. Held in downtown Raleigh and its bordering streets, this beer festival sells out each year. Beer, street vendors, bands. Tickets sold for each of the two 4-hour sessions. Single admission $40 in advance and $50 day of the event, if available! Buy your tickets online at allaboutbeer.com/gather-for-beer/world-beer-festival-nc/buy-tickets or etix.com. Check out the VIP package as well for $75.

May

Doughman, doughman.org. The 2012 DOUGHMAN, Durham's favorite quadrathlon, marks its fifth anniversary. This year, celebrate the five tastes: sweet, salty, sour, bitter, and umami. The goal is to raise money for SEEDS, an educational community garden that teaches respect for ourselves, each other, and the earth through gardening and growing food. Find out how to register for the race and volunteer opportunities at doughman.org.

Hillsborough Hog Day, hillsboroughchamber.com/hog-day. Friday evening 6 p.m. to 10 p.m. and Saturday 9 a.m. to 6 p.m. in the River Park behind the Courthouse, downtown Hillsborough. For 30 years, Hillsborough Hog Day has offered family fun, good food, live music, crafters, merchandise vendors, games, and rides, and the area's largest classic auto show. The festival starts on Friday night, when pig cooking teams from all over the state roll into town, but you don't get to taste until Saturday's Barbecue Tasting Judges have declared the top five barbecue cooking teams. Admission is free! But come early, as you will be vying with thousands of people for seats near the music and queues for fresh barbecue. For a complete schedule visit their website.

August

Beer, Bourbon & BBQ, beerandbourbon.com/cary/show-info. A festival recipe for an awesome two days of "beer sippin', bourbon tastin', music listenin', cigar smokin', and barbecue eatin'." The price of admission buys you a sampling glass so you can enjoy everything that you wish to. Eat great barbecue and listen to live music all day.

September

Bluegrass, Biscuits and Big Fish, (919) 942-7818. Share an evening of Southern music and food on the lawn of the Horace Williams House (610 E. Rosemary St., Chapel Hill) hosted by the Preservation

Society of Chapel Hill. Proceeds of the event will benefit the Preservation Society's Founders' Fund. Tickets are $25 in advance; $35 at the door. Call (919) 942-7818 or e-mail chpreservation @mindspring.com.

BugFest, bugfest.org. Jones Street, The Plaza, Edenton Street (all downtown Raleigh locations) and all four floors of the NC Museum of Natural Sciences are filled with "buggy" fun. Last year's theme was spiders, which included delectable dishes featuring creepy crawlers as a major ingredient at Cafe Insecta!

TerraVITA's Grand Tasting on the Green, terravitaevent.com. This Chapel Hill food and wine event will take place on the Green at Southern Village. Tickets are all-inclusive (all alcoholic and nonalcoholic beverages, as well as food samplings are included) and can be purchased for $65 each, or excluding alcohol $55. The Sustainable Classroom tickets can be purchased separately for $35 or a Combined Tasting & Classroom ticket, including both events, can be purchased for $90.

October

Pittsboro Pepper Festival, theabundance foundation.org/events/pepper-festival. Join over 500 folks to sample dishes and drink made from different varieties of sweet peppers, including pepper beer! Local chefs participate and local wines and beers are featured. Live music and dance. Held in Pittsboro at the Briar Chapel Community Park. Tickets are $30.

World Beer Festival Durham. Held at the Durham Bulls Athletic Park, this 1-day event features two 4-hour sessions that allow visitors to taste and sample the different beers in 2-ounce pours. Visitors have the opportunity to choose among 300 different types of beer from over 100 different breweries around the world. The event also features live music from local bands. Offered in two sessions (12 to 4 p.m. or 6 to 10 p.m.) for $45 each in advance or $50 at the door. You get a little plastic "glass" (2 ounces) in which to sample your brews.

Food Events Beyond the Triangle

February

National Truffle Fest, Asheville; (919) 845-8880; trufflefest .com. The National Truffle Fest (NTF), brings together food enthusiasts and connoisseurs to experience a wide range of truffle varieties in dishes prepared by leading chefs using top quality American and European truffles. Enjoy truffles in many exotic preparations along with special pairings of fine wines and spirits at participating Asheville restaurants. World-renowned truffle experts host seminars and presentations and leading North American chefs offer cooking demonstrations. All proceeds from the festival directly benefit the Frankie Lemmon School and Development Center while at the same time raising awareness for the North American Truffle Association. Western North Carolina has an expanding truffle industry with specialty farms throughout the region.

April

BBQ Capital Cook-Off, Historic Uptown Lexington, 207 E. 3rd Ave., Lexington; (336) 249-0383; uptownlexington.com. What could be more fitting than to host a BBQ cook-off in a town that claims to be first in the world for barbecue! Lexington hosted the second BBQ Cook-Off in April 2012, and there were over 50 competitive teams and judges from across the United States. Teams served up their best pork, chicken, brisket, and ribs in hopes of winning the substantial Grand Prize of over $15,000—plus there are many more treats in store from local and regional barbecue restaurants; be sure to save enough room for a generous helping of good old-fashioned banana pudding. Lexington is also well known for Childress Vineyards, the Bob Timberlake Gallery, and the RCR Racing Museum. Admission is free to the BBQ Capital Cook-Off and includes all the entertainment venues. Children are welcome. Event begins on a Friday evening and runs through Saturday, when the slow-roasted pork is judged and the winner announced; then the music begins!

Charlotte Food & Wine Festival, Charlotte; (704) 338-9463; charlottewineandfood.org. Started in 1989 with good intentions to raise money for community groups that were child-centered, the Charlotte Food & Wine Festival has grown into one of the largest events of this kind in the southeastern United States, raising over $3.2 million dollars to date. There are vintner dinners, gala dinners, educational sessions, and a live auction with participation through individually purchased tickets for each event; events sell out fast. The weekend draws chefs from around the world and pairs them with Charlotte's top chefs for the weekend. The Festival is held every even-numbered year and for 2012, the Charlotte Ritz-Carlton was the host hotel.

North Carolina Herring Festival, Jamesville; (252) 217-5363; ncherringfestival.com. Who would have thought that the simple herring could warrant a festival all of its own! Well, for the past 60 years, the town of Jamesville in eastern NC has celebrated the arrival of spring right around the Easter weekend. This festival celebrates the annual "run" of herring to the spawning area of Roanoke River. The festivities take over the whole town from Friday evening's band concert to the Easter egg hunt on Saturday to the sunrise service on Easter Sunday. Not to be missed is the street dance and fireworks on Saturday evening.

North Carolina Pickle Festival, Mount Olive Chamber of Commerce, 123 N. Center St., Mount Olive; (919) 658-3113; ncpickle fest.org. If you're not from North Carolina, then you probably don't know that Mount Olive is famous for Mount Olive Pickles, an 80-year-old company located in Mount Olive at the corner of Cucumber and Vine Streets, and the expression, "That's Picklicious!" In 1987, Mount Olive began to honor the humble pickle with a festival all of its own. The festival has grown from the original three square blocks of festivities to today's Pickle Festival, which encompasses all downtown Mt. Olive and features live entertainment, an antique car show, petting zoo, vintage farm equipment, various vendors, and, of course, lots of pickles to eat. For family fun you can join in the treasure hunt and look for a specially marked hidden jar of pickles! There is a 5K run and a Festival Canned Food Drive.

Pleasure Island Chowder Cook-Off, 1121 N. Lake Park Blvd., Carolina Beach; (910) 458-8434; pleasureislandnc.org/chowder-cook-off. The NC Pleasure Island Chowder Cook-Off is a family-oriented event featuring great food, good music, and family fun at Carolina Beach Lake Park. While chefs from North Carolina restaurants prepare seafood chowders, visitors can keep themselves amused at a variety of beach-related activities in anticipation of a bowl of the freshest seafood chowder. Make sure you arrive early while the chowder is abundant; hours for the chowder tasting and voting are 11:30 a.m. to 4 p.m. Admission for adults is $5; children 12 and under are free.

October

North Carolina Oyster Festival, Ocean Isle Beach; ncoyster festival.com. For the past 31 years, the coastal waters of Brunswick County have produced an abundance of oysters and now over 50,000 people annually attend the NC Oyster Festival to pay homage of this mighty mollusk. The Brunswick Chamber of Commerce hosts the festival, which also features live entertainment, festival food (yes, including oysters cooked and raw), a road race, and a surfing contest. Not to be missed is the NC Oyster Shucking Championships, featuring amateur and professional shuckers and the Oyster Stew Cook-Off. There is plenty of seafood and Low Country cooking, including jambalaya, chowders, fried fish, oysters, and shrimp. Bring the kids because there is a kids' area where they can learn all about marine life in the Atlantic Ocean.

Farmers' Markets

Your food life in the tri-city area of Raleigh, Durham, and Chapel Hill would not be complete without a weekly visit to one of the farmers' markets. Not only can you buy locally raised vegetables, fruits, and meats, but you're also likely to meet friends and work colleagues who, like you, have made this shopping trip de rigueur for a Saturday morning. Each market has its own set of rules about whose produce it accepts, generally based on mileage from Raleigh, Durham, or Chapel Hill/Carrboro. For instance, vendors at the Chapel Hill/Carrboro Farmers' Market must produce everything that is sold, and they must produce it all within a 50-mile radius of Chapel Hill/Carrboro. Likewise, Durham Farmers' Market vendors must drive 70 miles or less and only sell what they produce. So it may  be that a trip to more than one farmers' market is on the weekly "honey-do" list. Leave time to watch cooking demonstrations by local chefs . . . with taste rewards afterward.

Wake County

Campus Farmers' Market, The Brickyard in front of D. H. Hill Library, North Carolina State University, Raleigh; campusfarmersmkt .wordpress.com. Open: Wed 10 a.m. to 3 p.m., September through November and February through April.

Cary Downtown Farmers' Market, 744 E. Chatham St., Chatham Square; caryfarmersmarket.com. Open: Sat 8 a.m. to 12:30 p.m., April through November; Tues 3 to 6 p.m., April through November.

Inter-Faith Food Shuttle Young Farmer Market, Tryon Road and Dover Farm Road, Raleigh; facebook.com/IFFSYoungFarmerMarket. Open: Sat 9 a.m. to 1 p.m.

Midtown Farmers' Market, The Commons at North Hills, Raleigh; midtownraleighfarmersmarket.com. Open: Sat 8 a.m. to noon, April through November.

North Raleigh Farmers' Market, Falls River Town Center; northraleighfarmersmarket.com. Open: Sat 8 a.m. to noon, year-round.

Raleigh Downtown Farmers' Market, Fayetteville Street, City Plaza; raleigheatlocal.com. Open: Wed 3 to 6 p.m., April through October.

Saturday Market, Rebus Works, 301-2 Kinsey St., Raleigh; rebus works.us. Open: Sat 9 a.m. to 2 p.m., April through November. This Saturday market deserves a special visit because it is also an artists' collective featuring local artists, food artisans, crafters, food trucks, brewers, and more.

State Farmers' Market, 1201 Agriculture St., Raleigh; ncagr .gov/markets/facilit/farmark/raleigh. Open: Mon through Sat 5 a.m. to 6 p.m., year-round.

Western Wake Farmers' Market, 1226 Morrisville Carpenter Rd., Carpenter Village, Cary; westernwakefarmersmarket.org. Open: Sat 8 a.m. to noon, year-round; Tues 3:30 to 6:30 p.m., year-round.

Durham County

Durham Farmers' Market, The Pavilion at Durham Central Park; durhamfarmersmarket.com. Open: Sat 8 a.m. to noon, April through November, and 10 a.m. to noon, December through March; Wed 3:30 to 6:30 p.m., mid-April through September.

South Durham Farmers Market, Greenwood Shopping Center, 5410 NC 55 (Corner of NC 55 and Sedwick), southdurhamfarmers market.org. Open Sat 8 a.m. to noon, year-round.

Orange County

Carrboro Farmers' Market (outskirts of Chapel Hill), Carrboro Town Commons; carrborofarmersmarket.com. Open: Sat 7 a.m. to noon, year-round; opening time adjusted seasonally; Wed 3:30 to 6:30 p.m., mid-April through mid-October. Carrboro Farmers' Market also operates in Chapel Hill's Southern Village, Market Street, Southern Village Green. Open: Thurs 3:30 to 6:30 p.m., May through August.

Chapel Hill Farmers' Market, A Southern Season parking lot; thechapelhillfarmersmarket.com. Open: Sat 8 a.m. to noon, April through November and Sat 10 a.m. to noon, December through March; Tues 3 to 6 p.m., May through September.

Eno River Farmers' Market, Margaret Lane, Public Market House, Hillsborough; enoriverfarmersmarket.com. Open: Sat 8 a.m. to noon, April through October; Sat 10 a.m. to noon, November through March; Wed 4 to 6 p.m., May through September.

Hillsborough Farmers' Market, 625 Hampton Point Rd. (Home Depot parking lot); hillsboroughfarmersmarket.org. Open: Sat 8 a.m. to noon, April through September; Sat 10 a.m. to noon, November through March; Wed 4 to 7 p.m., May through October.

Food Trucks

The food truck phenomenon has grown to include cities all over the country and has been the subject of many articles, TV shows, and the like. No exception here in the Triangle. For the last several years, our area has grown from just a few trucks on the road to enough to draw crowds by the hundreds, with more being introduced on a regular basis. **Carpe Durham** (p. 22) even offers a beta food truck tracker that tracks the locations of the trucks based on their tweets. Regular "food truck rodeos" can be found throughout the Triangle, bringing together several trucks to feed the hungry masses that arrive in droves. Almost all the trucks have a Facebook page and Twitter handle to follow for location updates.

American Meltdown, @AmericanMLTDWN; americanmeltdown .org. Looking for that gourmet melt? Look no further than American Meltdown, your one-stop truck for locally inspired melted cheese sandwiches. From a 1940s incarnation of the patty melt (a local beef burger topped with melted cheddar cheese and grilled onions on fresh sourdough bread) to the decadent hangover (melted pimiento cheese topped with a fried egg and salsa verde on country white bread), you are in for a treat.

BAGUETTEABOUTIT, @Baguetteaboutit; baguettaboutit.com. Follow the BAGUETTEABOUTIT truck and you are in for something special. Premium ingredients (they use Giacomo's sausages); creative sauces, and quality bread leave nothing to be desired. Build your own creation choosing from six different types of sausages and a myriad of toppings or opt for the Betcha (bratwurst with beer-garden mustard), It's Greek Tu Me (chicken and spinach sausage with tzatziki sauce), or the South of the Border (chorizo and a spicy habañero hellfire sauce). All sandwiches are $6.50, and specials are tweeted daily.

Big Deez Dogs, @BigDeezDogs. "Southern Style" hot dogs with all-beef franks and Hillshire Farms CheddarWurst, but no lettuce, tomatoes, or mayonnaise for your dogs. Instead, your topping choices include homestyle beef chili, mustard, onions, or slaw. And if you're familiar with the Sabrett hot dog carts in New York City, Big Deez Dogs offers genuine Sabrett's onion sauce.

bikeCOFFEE, @bikeCOFFEE; cocoacinnamon.com. From a small bike cart, Areli and Leon are serving up some of the best coffee available in the Triangle. They serve a rotating selection of carefully selected, sustainable grown coffees from local and national roasters. The menu of coffees and teas can be overwhelming, there is so much to choose from, but let them know what you like; sweet or spiced to strong or mild, and know that a hand ground, gourmet "cup o joe" is only moments away. Look for their coffee shop, Cocoa Cinnamon, to open soon in downtown Durham.

Blue Sky Dining, @BlueSkyDiningNC. Blue Sky Dining seems to have a different business model from most of the other trucks around the Triangle. It's a mobile caterer/busy family take-out option, and every day a different meal is offered. The daily meals are posted online at the start of the week and made up of a meat dish, two sides, and a dessert for a set price, usually around $9. Meals are also posted on Twitter and Facebook. Call and order before noon for dinner pickup.

Boxcarr Farms, Local in Motion, @boxcarrfarms; boxcarrfarms .com. With 30 acres of beautiful farmland, the Boxcarr Farms, Local in Motion food truck offers a menu that is seasonally and locally inspired; bringing the freshest local ingredients straight to the public and preparing it in both innovative and traditional ways while being respectful to the land, animals, and environment. Because the seasons change, so does the menu. Look for tasty options like North Carolina shrimp and grits with mushrooms, bacon, and scallions, and eggs Benedict with hollandaise with your choice of braised smoked ham or a vegetable alternative (braised greens, roasted vegetables, etc.) to grilled sandwiches with goat cheese, roasted peppers, and caramelized onion jam. Seasonal soups and salads are also available along with vegetarian options. If you catch them late at night, do indulge in the fritto misto (tempura-fried seasonal vegetables), veg tart, or fresh pasta. For daily special and location, follow @boxcarrfarms on Twitter.

Bulkogi Korean BBQ, @NCBulkogi. A Korean taco truck with high-quality food at street-level prices with a little bit of Korea in every bite. The menu consists of tacos, burritos, steak 'n' cheese, kimchee "bul-dogs," kimchee quesadillas, and Korean BBQ, fried dumplings, or spicy pork.

Cafe Prost, @cafeprost; cafeprost.com. Not just your typical pretzel, Cafe Prost's traditional German "Swabian"-style pretzels have very thin "arms" and a "fat belly" that are crisp on the outside with a soft and chewy center. Always freshly baked using natural ingredients, they have flavors that range from the traditional lightly salted pretzel to a savory peppered cheddar with hot and mild minced peppers and melted cheddar cheese to a sweet pretzel with slivers of almonds served with your choice of honey or Nutella. These fabulous knots of dough are addictive and can easily be consumed breakfast, lunch, and dinner.

Captain Poncho's Tacos. Known as the "real deal" when it comes to made-on-the-spot Mexican food, including just-pressed tortillas. Situated in a parking lot next to an abandoned tire depot, Captain Poncho's Taco Truck has random hours.

Chick-N-Que, @Chick-N-Que; chicknque.com. This family-run food truck is fast becoming a favorite among BBQ lovers for their perfectly cooked, and expertly seasoned BBQ chicken. After an overwhelming response to their chicken at a football party, Chik-N-Que began taking special orders in January 2009 and has since expanded to both the truck and a successful catering operation. Try the original Chick-N-Que sandwich, based on an old family recipe; it is similar to NC Eastern-style barbecue and is a crowd pleaser. For a change, check out "The Big Bird," 100 percent ostrich steak topped with grilled green peppers and onions with smoked provolone on a warm pita, or indulge in "the Bird's Nest," a large bed of seasoned crinkled fries topped with a scoop of chick-n-que and melted cheddar cheese. Owners, Ernest and Queen have made their truck a family affair; it's likely you will be served by them, their kids, and even their parents.

Chirba Chirba Dumpling Truck, @chirbachirba; chirbachirba .com. Chirba Chirba Dumpling Truck is a mobile restaurant based out of Durham that features tasty street eats—mainly Chinese-style dumplings—from a big yellow food truck. Chirba Chirba launched in August of 2011 with a "dumpling raid" on **Fullsteam Brewery** (p. 201) surprising patrons with steamy juicy buns and edamame (or as Team Chirba calls them, "mao dou," literally "fur bean," Mandarin for edamame). The four owners are University of North Carolina alumni with a common passion for China and making and sharing Chinese food. They tweet and Facebook their location daily and stake out local bars like Motorco Music Hall, where they host or attend community sponsored events that, according to the Chirbs, are driven by things such as delicious street food. Chirba Chirba Dumpling Truck sells Asian dumplings, which can be filled with meat, seafood, or vegetables, spices, and other various ingredients and can be steamed, boiled, or fried. You can choose a sampler tray of dumplings with a sauce of choice, with an option of a side for an additional cost. In Mandarin, "chirba chirba" means "eat eat." See Chirba Chirba Dumpling Truck's recipe for **Pork Dumplings** on p. 283.

Crossroads Kettle Corn, @XRdsKettleCorn. Kettle corn is the name of the game, and you don't want to miss out. Also look for butter-flavored popcorn, boiled NC peanuts, along with assorted drinks. Wherever there is a large crowd gathering, Crossroad Kettle Corn is there.

Dang Good Dogs, @DangGoodDogs; danggooddogs.com. Whether they are boiled, steamed, deep fried, or grilled, these delicious "dogs" are cooked to order and made using only the finest and freshest ingredients. Look for all-beef hot dogs, veggie dogs, and sausages with all the traditional fixins'.

Don's Classic Ices, @DonsClassicIces. Homemade, fresh, semi-healthy (lots of agave and organic options) Italian ices. Flavors include classics like blueberry and strawberry and fancier options like organic kalawi peach, tart cherry vanilla, and more. Patrons are encouraged to sample.

Farmhand Foods Sausage Wagon, @FarmhandFoods; farmhand foods.com. All-local sausage sandwiches served on fresh-baked rolls from Durham's **Guglhupf Bakery** (p. 164). Local favorites include the spicy Italian sausage with fennel chow chow and mustard, smoky Polish sausage, pimiento cheese, and pickles or the delicious vegetarian option with smoked shiitakes with goat cheese, arugula, and leek pesto.

Joey D's NY Dogs, @JoeyDsNYDogs. Regular hot dogs, foot-long hot dogs as well as bratwurst and spicy *kabanosi*, Italian, and Polish sausage; plus a large array of condiments to dress up the dog.

Klausie's Pizza, @KlausiesPizza. Deep-dish pizza, cooked in square cast-iron pans accented with generous portions of sauce and cheese.

KoKyu, @KoKyuBBQ; kokyubbq.com. With a dedicated following on Twitter, food truck owners David Filippini, aka "Flip," and wife Sarah sell out regularly to an eager crowd of hungry Durhamites. With a flair for bold, spicy flavors, their Korean short-rib *takos*, sliders, or quesadillas are my go-to favorites. I guess I have a je ne sai quoi for their Korean BBQ. But ask around and the debate begins about what are the truly most sought after menu items. Are they the duck fat tater tots topped with a generous sprinkling of rosemary and black pepper; the vinegary pork sliders finished with refreshing avocado and cilantro; or the savory array of *takos?* Or are they the ever changing, mouthwatering specials that Flip conjures up from a seemingly bottomless pit of creativity? Whatever the verdict is, to each their own little piece of heaven. To Get "TaKo'd", follow the truck on Twitter, or find them on a permanent basis at Motorco Music Hall several nights a week, and every Sunday for the venue's Bloody Brunch from noon to 4 p.m.

Kona Chameleon, @konachameleon; konachameleon.com. This "bean wagon" runs on biofuels to deliver a deliciously sustainable coffee experience. All the coffee served is made from locally roasted beans that are certified organic and fair trade.

LoYo On The Go, @LoYoOnTheGo; localyogurt.com. If you can't get to any of the two **Local Yogurt** (p. 209) locations, look for their mobile unit around Durham to enjoy the same delicious flavors and toppings you can find at their stores.

Monuts Donuts, @MonutsDonuts; monutsdonuts.com. Monuts Donuts offers fresh, handcrafted doughnuts with unique flavor combinations using seasonal and local ingredients. Sold off a "food trike" at the **Durham Farmers' Market** (p. 37) and other locations around town, be sure to seek them out—these are some of the best doughnuts in town. Although they make a great glazed doughnut, look for interesting flavors like hibiscus cinnamon, cheddar apple and bacon, maple bourbon bacon, or sweet potato and brown butter. They can be preordered by the dozen from their website for pickup at the market or ordered in large quantities for your next special event.

Old North State BBQ, @ONSBBQ; onsbbq.com. For some state-of-the-art BBQ, follow this truck on Twitter for locations around the Triangle. Look for such items as the Flaming Pig BBQ sandwich with slaw in a chipotle sauce, Hoosier Daddy (fried pork tenderloin sandwich with lettuce, tomato, onion, pickle, and mayo), or indulge in the BBQ platter (BBQ, slaw, hush puppies, and choice of side).

Only Burger, @OnlyBurger. Named one of the best food trucks in the South by *Southern Living,* **Only Burger** (see p. 175) uses Montana-raised antibiotic- and growth-hormone-free beef ground daily by a local butcher. For a vegetarian choice, try the fried green tomato, egg, and pimiento cheese breakfast burger. Fries are meal-worthy in themselves.

Parlez-Vous Crepe, @ParlezVousCrepe. Having learned the art of crepe-making while in Beaune, France, owner Jody Argote has taken her love of French cuisine to bring us delicate and delicious made-to-order crepes using local ingredients. Options include savory and sweet concoctions so that there is always something for everyone to enjoy.

The Parlour, @ParlourDurham. The Parlour is the Triangle's own ice-cream shop on wheels, and the wheels are a modified mini school bus! Enjoy a scoop of NC dairy-fresh ice cream in a cone or a cup, or design your own sundae from an array of handmade toppings. The Parlour also offers ice-cream sandwiches, milk shakes, and floats. Vegan options are also available. For a list of weekly flavors go to theparlourdurham

.com/flavors or check out the schedule at theparlourdurham.com/schedule. A Saturday morning at the Durham Farmers' Market will be all the more enjoyable with a salted caramel ice-cream cone.

Pie Pushers, @PiePushers. This is a pizza truck serving freshly made pizzas using local and seasonal ingredients. Owners Mike Hacker and Becky Cascio like to call their crust "Durham-style." It is a hand-tossed thin crust, a little crunchy, but still wonderfully fluffy at the same time. The dough is a recipe of Mike's and his mother's, one they have been mastering and tweaking over the past decade. Specialties include pies like the State of Nirvana (pesto, roasted chicken, caramelized red onions, spinach, blue cheese, and mozzarella), or the Dan's Zza (tomato sauce, pepperoni, salami, sausage, mushrooms, caramelized red onions, bell peppers, fresh garlic, and mozzarella). They also serve garlic knots, wings, and salads as well as whole pies. Supporting local farmers and artisans is an important aspect of what Mike and Becky bring to their work, and it shows in the masterful creations they come up with—these are pies worth waiting in line for!

Slippin Sliders, @SlippinSliders. Gourmet sliders made with local and seasonal ingredients. Try the West Coast slide, with Cajun remoulade, cheddar cheese, caramelized onions, bacon, lettuce, tomato, and pickles. Check out the veggie options, too.

Sympathy for the Deli, @Sympathy4Deli, sympathyforthedeli.com. Sympathy for the Deli is a mobile deli featuring "classic sandwiches with a soulful flair." All deli meats are made using locally sourced and sustainably raised meats that are hand cured, smoked, or roasted in Durham. The menu is an array of delicious sandwiches including the classic hot pastrami or traditional Reuben with sauerkraut, swiss cheese, and Russian dressing.

Triangle Raw Foods, @TriangleRawFood; trianglerawfoods.com. A food truck with a twist: all its food is raw, dairy-free, meat-free, and gluten-free. And it's hot stuff in the Triangle! TRF is now offering a weekly food service throughout the Triangle. Check its website for the following week's selections. In addition to the new delivery service, TRF parks its truck at events all around the Triangle and has the schedule for current stops posted online. If you're thinking of going raw, try something from the food truck first. My personal favorite is the carrot and zucchini pad thai (see recipe on p. 275) or Indian carrot pâté with sunflower seeds, almonds, carrots, garlic, ginger, cumin, coriander, curry, tamari, black pepper, sea salt, and paprika.

Valentino's, @ValentinosTruck. Owner Steve Valentino offers Italian-inspired dishes that remind you of sitting around the dining room table with family for Sunday night supper. Popular items include his meatballs, sausage and peppers, ravioli, and eggplant parmesan. For a spin on the traditional, Steve makes a pork and cheese popper with a beer batter. The Valentino truck is often set up at **Big Boss Brewing Co.** (p. 128).

Will & Pop's, @WillAndPops. Not your everyday grilled cheese sandwiches. Extras grilled in your sandwich include guacamole, mango chutney, bacon and tomato, pulled pork, hot pepper jelly, and more. Daily soups are made from scratch with local and seasonal meats and vegetables.

Learn to Cook

For those of you who enjoy eating out and cooking at home, consider going to one of the local cooking schools that offer short courses—often an evening or half-day—to brush up on a particular skill (like braising) or to learn about how to plan and prepare a regional menu. It's been my experience that you can find either a "hands-on" course or a "demonstration" course. For instance, I recently spent an evening at **Scratch Baking** (p. 185) in Durham as a participant in Pie 101. I didn't know what to expect, but it turned out to be an evening demonstration course by pastry chef Phoebe Lawless. It was, in fact, a great way to learn about making pastry. In another instance, Scot Howell of

Nana's hosted a small group of five on the secrets of braising. It was very much a hands-on class—under Scott's direction, we all had to prepare the meal we were actually going to eat. So my advice to you is to ask a lot of questions about any course you sign up for so that you know what to expect. Many area restaurants randomly offer cooking classes or demonstrations without a lot of publicity. The best way to find out about these events is to call a favorite restaurant and ask if they offer these kinds of opportunities.

The Art Institute of Raleigh-Durham, 410 Blackwell St., Ste. 200, Durham; (919) 317-3050; artinstitutes.edu/raleigh-durham. Indulge in your passion for food by studying for a Culinary Arts Management BA degree and graduate to an entry-level management position in restaurants and hotels within the food services industry.

C'est Si Bon Cooking School, 1002 Brace Ln., Chapel Hill; (919) 942-6550; cestsibon.net. C'est Si Bon offers classes for everyone—mom, dad, and the kids, plus one-on-one cooking classes or team-building efforts for office workers. The cooking school is situated on 3 acres, with a wood-fired bread oven, aromatic herb garden, and seasonal vegetable garden, and free-roaming chickens and turkeys. Check the website for classes and gift certificates.

Chef's Academy, 2001 Carrington Mill Blvd., Morrisville; (919) 246-9044; thechefsacademy.com. The Chef's Academy is a hands-on training college offering associate degrees in culinary arts, pastry arts, and hospitality and restaurant management. It is the Culinary

Division of Harrison College (Indiana) with a second campus in Morrisville, situated between Raleigh and Durham.

Culinary Lessons at A Southern Season (CLASS), A Southern Season, Hwy. 15-501 at Estes Dr., University Mall, Chapel Hill; (919) 929-7133; southernseason.com/class. A Southern Season is a specialty food and wine shop (p. 253) offering many cooking classes featuring local chefs of note. Class schedule is online. Join "Fridays Uncorked" between 5 and 8 p.m. to enjoy wines in a casual, self-directed tasting.

Durham Spirits Company, 311 E. Trinity Ave., Durham; (425) 463-5430; durhamspiritscompany.com. Each cooking class is a combination of hands-on and demonstration learning. Take classes at the school or get together a small group of friends for a private class in either your kitchen or the school's kitchen. "Mixology" classes are offered so you can learn how to mix the perfect cocktail, or you can learn more about tasting wine and beer. Check the website for the class schedule.

Food Tours

As a visitor to the area or as a local resident, you may get confused by the choices of where to eat or you may not cross over into another county often enough to know the current hot spots for dining. Raleigh, Durham, and Chapel Hill all reside in different counties, Wake, Durham, and Orange respectively. East to west, that takes in about 30 miles. Enter food tours—generally walking tours that take in a 2- to 3-mile radius on foot and feature a concentrated look at restaurants and specialty shops whereby you meet the chefs and sample the wares. Check out the tour companies listed here and move beyond your own neighborhood to find a new favorite restaurant. In fact, sign up for several different tours as your free time and budget allow.

Taste Carolina Gourmet Food Tours, 500 Reynolds Ave., Durham; (919) 237-2254; tastecarolina.net. For visitors and locals alike, walking around different cities in the Triangle area can whet your appetite for the six to eight restaurants you'll stop at on these tours, where you can talk with chefs and owners and sample locally sourced foods. Along the way, a professional guide will chat with you about local history and folklore. Walking tours are every Saturday year-round in Raleigh, Durham, Chapel Hill/Carrboro, Hillsborough, Greensboro, and Winston-Salem. Tours are 2 to 3 miles and cost between $40 and $70. Check the website for details.

Triangle Food Tours, (919) 319-5674; trianglefoodtour.com; trianglefoodtour@gmail.com. This is the original food tour company in the Triangle featuring a diverse number of experiences, all relating to food and drink. At time of writing, a quick check of the website showed that all tours were sold out a month in advance!

Walking tours include Raleigh, Durham, Chapel Hill/Carrboro, Cary, and Lafayette Village. Special monthly "Dine With Chef" events are prix-fixe dinners at a local restaurant, prepared and hosted by the chef. Tickets are about $30 for the walking tours and can be bought online. The Dine With Chef dinners vary in price.

Road Trips

Traveling beyond the Triangle also yields wonderful places to eat, while allowing you to see other parts of the immediate area. The following eateries are all day trips for the area and are within 60 to 70 miles from the Triangle.

Angelina's Kitchen, 23 Rectory St., Pittsboro; (919) 545-5505; angelinaskitchenonline.com; Greek; $ Greek food cooked with in-season produce bought from local Chatham County farmers. A typical Greek menu is offered as well as packaged dinners for a family dash-and-dine-at-home. Call ahead to order.

Chef and The Farmer, 120 W. Gordon St., Kinston; (205) 208-2433; chefandthefarmer.com; American/Farm to Table; $$$. Husband-and-wife team Ben Knight and Vivian Howard were devastated when they had to close their restaurant, often touted as a destination in itself, due to a fire in 2011. In spite of the fire setback, Chef Vivian was nominated as a James

Beard Foundation semifinalist in the Best Chef, Southeast category. Reopened in May, Chef and The Farmer continues its commitment to serving local and seasonally inspired fare.

The Eddy Pub, 1715 Saxapahaw-Bethlehem Church Rd., Saxapahaw; (336) 525-2010; theeddypub.com; American/Farm to Table/Pub; $$. A restored mill—named after NC native and former "rodbuster" Eddie Williams—that pays homage to simple pub food with daily specials to provide a more refined experience. Dishes use local ingredients that change with the season—but you will always find pub favorites such as fish-and-chips and shepherd's pie. North Carolina brews are favored here, with a rotating selection to reflect the season and the menu.

Elliotts on Linden, 905 Linden Rd., Pinehurst; (910) 215-0775; elliottsonlinden.com; American/Farm to Table; $$$. Situated in the golf capital of the Southeast US, Pinehurst's Elliotts on Linden (EOL) serves the best and freshest locally produced agrarian products available from the small farms that dot the countryside around the Pinehurst/Southern Pines area of North Carolina. Chef-Owner Mark Elliott adheres to the principle of everything local. Carnivores will delight in the freshest meat, especially lamb dishes. And, if you really want to explore where your meat came from, sign up for the EOL NC Farmers Series: It will be a true farm-to-fork experience!

The Fearrington House Restaurant, 2000 Fearrington Village Center, Pittsboro; (919) 542-2121; fearrington.com/house/

restaurant; American/Farm to Table; $$$$. A member of the Relais & Chateaux group, this classic restaurant has been ranked one of the top 50 restaurants in the US for almost all the 30 years it's been in existence. Don't arrive just in time for dinner, but plan for a walk through the exquisite gardens and the shops of the village. You will also catch sight of the Belted Galloway cows, also known as "Oreo cows," in the adjacent pastures. Of course, staying overnight at the Fearrington Inn, adjacent to the restaurant, would be a perfect end to an evening of fine dining.

The Granary, 2000 Fearrington Village, Pittsboro; (919) 542-2121; fearrington.com/village/granary; American; $$. If your pocketbook can't accommodate eating at the main restaurant, Fearrington also offers The Granary, a neighborhood gathering place with more modest prices yet outstanding contemporary American cuisine prepared by Chef Colin Beford. Wine Director Maximilian Kast offers Thursday evening wine classes where attendees learn about and taste wines from all over the world while enjoying light hors d'oeuvres.

Mother Earth Brewing, 311 N. Heritage St., Kinston; (252) 208-2437; www.motherearthbrewing.com; Brewery/Brewpub; $. Located in downtown Kinston and walking distance to **Chef and The Farmer** (p. 54), this popular brewery is as much a destination as the restaurant. Diners often stop in for a pint before and after dinner. The on-site tavern is comfortable yet chic with a bit of big city flair. Beers on tap always include a selection of their year-round brews plus a rotating selection of seasonal and cask-conditioned ales. A trip to Kinston North Carolina is not complete without a stop at Mother Earth Brewing.

On the Square, 115 E. Saint James St., Tarboro; (252) 823-8268; onthesquare.com; Asian/European/Latin American; $$$. Located in the historic mill town of Tarboro, On the Square owners Inez and Stephen Ribustello are a classic example of a sommelier and chef marriage in life and in business. Menus feature European, Asian, and Latin American–inspired flavors, using seasonal ingredients. The award-winning wine list offers 500+ selections, displaying regional and vintage breadth and depth.

Saxapahaw General Store, 1735 Saxapahaw-Bethlehem Rd., Saxapahaw; (336) 376-5332; saxgen store.com; Cafe; $. An eco-conscious store and cafe, Saxapahaw General Store touts itself as "Your local five-star gas station." Stock up on local produce or fine wine or stop by for breakfast, brunch, lunch, or dinner.

Skylight Inn, 4618 Lee St., Ayden; (252) 746-4113; Barbecue; $. Barbecue heaven! Owner Pete Jones serves "Eastern NC" barbecue, slaw, corn bread, and sweet tea or soft drinks. That's all, folks, there is nothing else on the menu. Want to know the difference between Eastern and Western NC barbecue? Eastern barbecue is sauceless and the whole hog is used, both white and dark meat. Western barbecue adds tomato sauce and generally only the pork shoulder (dark meat) is used. Best read *Bob Garner's Guide to North Carolina Barbecue* for the real lowdown on NC barbecue.

SoCo Farm and Food, 6538 Slabtown Rd., Wilson; (252) 243-8441; soconc.com; Farm to Table/Southern; $$$. The concept: A B&B, working farm, and a food destination—the now-realized dream of Chef Jeremy Law and his wife Kimberly. Southern classic food is served once a day, farmhouse style—8 to 14 people seated around one table. For a tranquil weekend away, stay overnight at the B&B. And, if you are traveling with your horse, there is a stable with room for six horses!

Raleigh

Already dubbed "the best American city" by *Business Week* based on criteria like amount of green space, school performance, and number of professional sports teams, Raleigh has now attained a new level of stardom as one of the "Tastiest Towns in the South" in a recent survey by *Southern Living*. Readers were asked to vote for their favorite city based on several criteria, including diverse cuisine, food culture, cultural identity, sustainable practices, and number of food events. The multicultural community offers a growing number of ethnic dining options, including Thai, Vietnamese, Indian, and Korean as well as an increasing number of supermarkets to match. A preference for sourcing locally and knowing where our food comes from is a high priority throughout the Triangle when it comes to dining out or eating at home. The number of chefs making this a precedent has grown dramatically with the likes of Ashley Christensen of **Poole's** (p. 102), Chad McIntyre of **Market** (p. 91), and Jason Smith of **18 Seaboard** (p. 78), all of whom take seasonally available ingredients and prepare them simply but expertly. The 30,000-square-foot Raleigh Farmers'

Market and multiple local markets have made it possible to utilize seasonal ingredients and bring more awareness to sustainable living. Of equal importance is the number of food-related events taking place each year, but for a real treat, head on over to the NC State Fair, North Carolina's largest event, and indulge yourself in deep-fried chocolate bars, burgers sandwiched between Krispy Kreme doughnuts, or any number of the hundreds of food vendor that participate each year.

Greater Raleigh—made up of Raleigh plus several other surrounding cities including Cary, Apex, and Morrisville—has not always been the dining destination it is today. But as new and up-and-coming chefs have moved into the area over the last few years, it is easy to conclude that along with the neighboring cities of Durham and Chapel Hill, it has placed itself on the gastronomic map.

The growing city of Cary, affectionately known as the "Central Area for Relocated Yankees" because of the number of Northern transplants who have made their home here, is a mere 20 minutes west of downtown Raleigh and home to some of the best dining options around. Making their culinary mark as some of the top chefs in the area are Chef Scott Crawford of **Herons** restaurant (p. 84) and Executive Chef Jay Pierce of **Lucky 32 Southern Kitchen** (p. 89). Asian fusion takes its place at **An** (p. 63), while the growing Indian population has made Cary a destination for authentic southern and northern Indian cuisine.

Approximately 25 minutes southwest of downtown Raleigh, the small strip that makes up downtown Apex is experiencing a rejuvenation that is giving restaurants like **Salem Street Pub** (p. 106) and **Anna's Pizzeria** (p. 64) a reason to make the drive. If ethnic diversity is what you are craving, take the time to drive to Morrisville, 25 minutes west of downtown Raleigh, to enjoy Indian, Mediterranean, Chinese, and African cuisine, just to name a few options, right in the middle of Research Triangle Park.

When you talk about the restaurants that make their home in the Greater Raleigh area, there are no defining foods or flavors that sum up the experience. Instead, it's an eclectic variety of chefs raising the bar on Southern country favorites like fried chicken or contemporary Italian cuisine. There are a diverse number of ethnic dining options that showcase our growing international population and introduce us to a vibrant subculture of food. Whether you are pampering yourself with a fine-dining experience, seeking a romantic outdoor cafe, casual local pub, or authentic Asian cuisine, dining is a superlative mix of diverse and varied options allowing everyone to satisfy every craving.

Getting Around

There are several options for getting around the central area of Raleigh. However, you will still need a car to drive yourself to the many outlying eateries mentioned in this book.

Raleigh Rickshaw, 418-B S. Dawson St., Raleigh; (919) 523-5555; raleighrickshaw.com. Hours of operation are Tues and Wed 6 to 11 p.m., Thurs and Fri 5 p.m. to 3 a.m., Sat 10 a.m. to 3 a.m., and Sun 10 a.m. to 11 p.m., or by reservation. Contact Donald Mertrudo at Donald@raleighrickshaw.com.

R-Line (Downtown Raleigh Circulator), (919) 485-RIDE (7433); yourhere.com. Visit the website to download the R-Line map and real-time projections, godowntownraleigh.com/_files/docs/map_online.pdf. You can also access the information at www.m.yourhere.com by clicking on the "R-LINE" tab. This eco-friendly free circulator service connects you to restaurants, retail and entertainment venues, museums, hotels, and parking facilities in downtown Raleigh. Buses are scheduled to run every 10 to 15 minutes. Hours of operation are Mon through Wed 7 a.m. to 11 p.m., Thurs through Sat 7 a.m. to 2:15 a.m., Sun 1 p.m. to 8 p.m.

Showtime Trolley, (919) 828-7228; godowntownraleigh.com/go/showtime-trolley. This free trolley ride operates every 15 to 20 minutes on Thurs, Fri, and Sat from 5:30 until 11:30 p.m. Look for the Trolley Stop signs along the route that runs between Glenwood Avenue, City Market, and other downtown nighttime hot spots. The Showtime Trolley is great for those who are pairing up dinner with a show at the performing arts center. However, at time of writing, there was some construction to various roads in downtown Raleigh that impacted the route. So double-check that the trolley will go where you want it to and go online for the latest update.

Triangle Segway, (919) 828-1988; by reservation only (800) 979-3370; trianglesegway.com. Offers guided Segway tours and stand-up paddleboarding lessons. The Segway tours are fully narrated and get you up close to points of interest in Raleigh. Training, helmets, and a wireless audio pack are provided. Age and weight guidelines apply so check out the website first. All the tours are outlined on the website as well. Alas, no foodie tours yet!

Foodie Faves

Abyssinia Ethiopian, 2109-146 Avent Ferry Rd., Raleigh; (919) 664-8151; abyssiniarestaurant.net; Ethiopian; $$. The alluring flavor of the food will keep you coming back to this small Ethiopian restaurant, located in close proximity to NC State. The *kitfo,* tender chopped prime beef, is well seasoned as is the *yebeg wat,* pieces of lamb that have been slowly simmered in spicy red pepper sauce with garlic, onion, and butter. All dishes are served with spongy *injera* bread for scooping (yes, you get to eat with your hands) and your choice of house salad and side. Look for plenty of vegetarian options too.

An, 2800 Renaissance Park Pl., Cary; (919) 677-9229; ancuisines .com; Asian Fusion; $$$. A blend of Southeast Asian and European flavors influence the menu at this high end Asian fusion restaurant. For an extravagant beginning to dinner, feast on the Emperor

Seafood Tower, a spectacular presentation of Maine lobster, snow crab claws, shrimp cocktail, and various fish. This is definitely meant for more than one person. Other notable appetizers include the pot stickers, Thai-style chicken wings, and the popular Maine lobster appetizer, which pairs succulent lobster with sweet melon, Belgian endive, and a spicy cream for a delicious combination. Cocktails are fun and creative and include a Tom Yum Martini that is worth the indulgence—Ketel One, Malibu Coconut, basil, jalapeño, lime, and lemongrass simple syrup. The menu offers an excellent selection of fresh sushi as well as enticing land and sea options. From *nigiri* to sashimi and miso sea bass to beef filet, the chefs are expert in their culinary skills and artful presentation. The beautiful outside terrace is ideal for dining on fair weather days in the spring, summer, and fall. An is open for lunch Mon through Fri and dinner Mon through Sat.

Anna's Pizzeria, 100 N. Salem St., Apex; (919) 267-6237; annaspizzeria.com; Pizza; $$. A busy, family-friendly restaurant located in historic downtown Apex that serves New York–style pizzas and Italian dishes. Popular pizzas include cheese only or the spinach pizza that is also topped with two kinds of white cheese; the crostini pizza is garlic bread topped with fresh mozzarella, tomatoes, roasted red peppers, and basil. Takeout and delivery are available.

Asian Grill, 6611 Falls of Neuse Rd., Raleigh; (919) 232-9488; asiangrillnc.com; Chinese; $$. Featuring authentic Shanghainese cuisine, this small restaurant located in Falls Village is often packed with guests clamoring for the renowned soup dumplings made with homemade dough, a flavorful broth, and your choice of filling. Fresh and never frozen, the steamed dumplings are brought to the table in a bamboo basket with a side of black rice vinegar. Other traditional dishes include the fish fillet served in a delicate white wine sauce with black mushrooms, homemade noodle dishes, twice-cooked Shanghai pork, and several fish casseroles. There is also a decent selection of Chinese-American dishes offered. For lunch, look for a great selection of bento boxes, with your choice of dishes like hibachi chicken, basil beef, or shrimp in lobster sauce. All are served with steamed rice and rotating sides.

Bali Hai Mongolian Grill, 2414 Wake Forest Rd., Raleigh; (919) 828-3103; 811 Ninth St., Durham; (919) 416-0200; balihainc.com; Mongolian; $. The approach to your meal at this pan-Asian restaurant is simple and efficient. Pile your choice of meats and vegetables into a bowl, choose a house sauce and level of spiciness, then wait and watch as your meal is grilled to perfection by a smiling and energetic staff. Sauces include: a house sauce (an exotic blend of Asian spices); ginger; soy sauce; sweet and sour; spicy sauce with a unique mix of pepper spices (with the house-sauce base spiced to your preference, 1 for mild, 10 for super spicy); a combination of the sweet and sour and spicy; or curry. This hidden gem is a favorite among locals looking for an inexpensive lunch or dinner.

Battistella's, 200 E. Martin St., Raleigh; (919) 803-2501; batti stellas.com; Cajun/Creole; $$$. Located in Raleigh's City Market, in a former 1920s hotel, Battistella's is a comfortable, inviting restaurant serving up excellent New Orleans classics and upscale Southern cuisine. The interior, made up of subtle, cozy colors, exposed brick walls with remnants of the original wallpaper still visible, and black-and-white photographs depicting New Orleans street scenes, easily transports you back to the French Quarter. New Orleans native Chef Brian Battistella shows off his heritage with classics like oyster po' boys, Louisiana crawfish étouffée, and New Orleans BBQ shrimp, pan-seared in a rich, peppery butter sauce with lemon and toasted garlic and beautifully balanced with the addition of rosemary. Upscale Southern creations like pimiento cheese fritters with goat cheese and green tomato "chow chow" or Southern-fried Georgia quail, served over Creole hash browns with smoky onions, sweet peppers, oyster mushrooms, and a green onion hollandaise sauce, round out the menu, showcasing Brian's love of the Southeast. Great emphasis is placed on sourcing many of their ingredients locally, and a chalkboard next to the kitchen detailing the farms used is proof of that commitment. Battistella's is open for lunch and dinner, Tues through Sat, and brunch on Sun.

Beasley's Chicken + Honey, 237 S. Wilmington St., Raleigh; (919) 322-0127; ac-restaurants.com/beasleys; American/Fried Chicken; $–$$. The much-anticipated second restaurant from **Poole's Diner** (p. 102) Chef-Owner Ashley Christensen opened in August 2011. Housed in a renovated Piggly Wiggly building,

Beasley's keeps it simple and delicious. The main star here is her perfectly fried Springer Mountain Farms chicken drizzled with (local) honey. There's also chicken potpie with milk gravy and cornmeal crust, fried chicken and waffles, and a couple of other non-bird options that change seasonally, including Market salad with smoked tomato, charred red onion, and marinated Sea Island red peas, goat cheese, and red wine vinaigrette. They offer an excellent selection of local, seasonal sides for $3.50 each. The Hook's 3-year cheddar pimiento mac-n-cheese custard is off the hook! I'm still reeling over the German Johnson thick-cut tomatoes with malt mayo. Ashley is a stickler for perfection and searched for one of the best bartenders in New York City to develop the craft cocktail menu at Beasley's and her two other new ventures. The same care went into selecting her pastry chef—these cakes and pies are incredible. Ashley designed Beasley's, along with her neighboring restaurant **Chuck's** (p. 67) and **Fox Liquor Bar** (p. 130) to be as sustainable as possible. No beer cans or bottles here—the whole building uses one draft beer system throughout, significantly reducing waste and recycling. Beasley's is open 7 days a week for lunch, dinner, and late-night eating.

Bella Mia, 2025 Renaissance Park Pl., Cary; (919) 677-3999; bellamiacoalfire.com; Italian/Pizza; $$. The pizza here is Neapolitan-style; thin puffy crusts that are light and airy thanks to a coal-fired pizza oven that reaches temperatures of 900°F. The Delancey St. pie is wonderful—tomato sauce, fresh mozzarella, house meatballs, caramelized onions, and Gaeta olives, as is the Bleecker St., topped with Parmigiana Reggiano, fresh mozzarella, piled with arugula and prosciutto. High-quality ingredients and fresh local toppings make these pizzas, named after streets in New York City, stand out as some of the best in the Triangle, so much so that *News and Observer* restaurant critic Greg Cox named it the 2010 restaurant of the year.

Bella Monica, 3121-103 Edward Mills Rd., Raleigh; (919) 881-9778; bellamonica.com; Italian; $$. Bella Monica is a family-friendly neighborhood trattoria known for top-notch Italian cuisine in a cozy and casual environment. The menu reflects what one might expect from a traditional Italian kitchen: bright flavors, fresh ingredients. The *antipasto piatto,* a combination of sopressata, provolone picante, olives, herbed mushrooms, roasted peppers, and tapenade and pesto crostini just begs to be shared among friends  while the roasted portobello mushrooms with feta cheese, sun-dried tomato, and rosemary are a delectable starter for a romantic dinner for two. Gourmet flatbreads are made with the requisite crisp crusts and blistered edges; the bianco—ricotta cheese, mozzarella, Parmesan, and olive oil—is simple and delicious. Entrees, an extension of "Nana's" kitchen, include pastas, seafood, and meats including a pork piccata with a luscious lemon and caper sauce with just the right amount of citrus to lend a sense of brightness to the dish. Open for lunch and dinner daily. Closed Sun.

The Berkeley Cafe, 217 W. Martin St., Raleigh; (919) 821-0777; berkeleycafe.net; American; $. This small dive has been serving Raleigh residents for almost 30 years. The menu consists of burgers, salads, sandwiches, and late-night munchies, but it's the burgers that draw the crowds back time and again. Selections ranging from the Old Fashioned, with mustard, slaw, and chili, to the Luau Lisa, topped with grilled pineapple and honey mustard, or the Walter Mitty burger with sautéed peppers, onions, mustard, A1, and Worcestershire sauce are so flavorful and juicy they require several napkins to wipe the drippings off your chin. Several vegetarian options are also available. Ask about the daily specials or call ahead for take-out orders.

Bloomsbury Bistro, 509 W. Whitaker Mill Rd., Raleigh; (919) 834-9011; bloomsburybistro.com; American; $$$. With a seasonal menu that changes every 6 weeks, Chef John Toler uses only fresh ingredients to create French, globally inspired haute cuisine at this elegant neighborhood bistro. Innovative menu selections may include roasted leg of venison, osso buco, and Carolina mountain trout. The ragout of slow-cooked Black Angus brisket and mixed mushrooms, "French-onion style," over cabbage, potato colcannon with gruyère, baby carrots, and an enticing sherry-scented beef broth is delightfully rich and hearty. Knowledgeable staff will happily offer pairing suggestions from a solid wine list while the dessert menu will entice you with several luscious creations.

Brewmasters' Bar and Grill, 301 W. Martin St., Raleigh; (919) 836-9338; brewmastersbarandgrill.com; Burgers/Pub; $. Brewmasters' Bar and Grill is a no-nonsense, must-see destination for the beer lover, with an extensive draft beer list and some of Raleigh's best pub grub. All of Brewmasters' burgers are great, but my favorite is the Hangover Burger. With avocado, bacon, fried egg, pepper jack cheese, and Bloody Mary aioli, this burger will cure what ails you. Try it with a little hair of the dog from their excellent beer list. Brewmasters' also has many vegetarian options, a welcome change from most pubs. This is a family-friendly place, especially in the early evening. There are lunch specials every weekday and Trivia Thursday night at 8 p.m. The Grill is located in the Warehouse district, on the corner of Dawson and W. Martin Streets. The historic building has been a restaurant since the 1940s—according to their website, soldiers stopped there before shipping out to WWII.

Buku, 110 E. Davie St., Raleigh; (919) 834-6963; bukuraleigh .com; International; $$$. Located at the corner of Wilmington and Davie Streets in the heart of downtown Raleigh, Buku offers global cuisine inspired by the street vendors found around the world. The atmosphere is urban chic, providing an upscale vibe that matches the elevated street food found on the menu. The menu is a collec-tion of unique and flavorful dishes, incorporating various regional traditions. Look for Polish beer-braised chicken; butternut squash pierogies in brown butter sauce; Colombian arepas with corn, chile, *queso fresco,* tomato, and avocado salsa; and a Japanese-inspired Buku sushi roll with crab, avocado, cucumber, and roe, topped with spicy tuna tartare. Not to be missed is the Sunday brunch buffet where a collection of serving stations offer every-thing from made-to-order Belgian waffles and omelets to a roasted meat carving station, fresh cut fruits and salads, to desserts and pastries. "Weekday Getaways," offered from 1:10 to 6:10 p.m. Monday through Friday, include a daily drink and food special while Friday nights feature a flight of wines from a different regions of the globe. Sample a trip around the world without having to board a plane by stopping into Buku for your world tour of food.

Busy Bee Cafe, 225 S. Wilmington St., Raleigh; (919) 424-7817; busybeeraleigh.com; American; $. Voted one of the top 100 beer bars in the US by *Draft* magazine, it's understandable why beer afi-cionados regularly flock to this downtown restaurant and beer bar. With draft beer selections changing daily and a cask that changes weekly, every visit is sure to offer something new. Intriguing is the bourbon barrel–aged beer procured exclusively for the bar by owners Chris Powers and David "Woody" Lockwood. The menu is a collection of small plates, salads, and sandwiches, many of which change with the season. Dinner entrees are available after 5 p.m., and brunch is offered on both Saturday and Sunday along with the regular lunch menus, 11 a.m. to 3 p.m.

Caffé Luna, 136 E. Hargett St., Raleigh; (919) 832-6090; cafeluna
.com; Italian; $$. This upscale Italian restaurant in the heart of
downtown delights guests with Tuscan-inspired
dishes, a well thought out wine list, and warm
and friendly service. The *prosciutto e melone*—
cured Parma ham with fresh melon—is a nice
start to a meal with the sweet melon offsetting
the slightly salty ham, creating a perfect balance
of flavors. Pasta dishes are in abundance: the
tortelli crostacci—fresh pasta stuffed with lobster, crabmeat, and
prawns sautéed in cream—is decadent, and the *linguini pescatore,*
chock-full of calamari, shrimp, mussels, clams, and scallops sautéed
in olive oil and tomato is a must for seafood lovers. The elegant
setting is perfect for special occasions and events and can accom-
modate more than 200 people. Reservations are recommended.

Capital Club 16, 16 W. Martin St., Raleigh; (919) 747-9345;
capitalclub16.com; European/German; $$. Named for the historic
building it's housed in, Capital Club 16 offers traditional German
and American fare in a bright, 1930s vintage atmosphere. To start,
choose from a large selection of small plates and appetizers, such
as beef brisket horseradish minis; potato pancakes with house-made
applesauce, caramelized onions, and greens; or the currywurst brat
grilled to perfection and served sliced in curry ketchup with fries.
Entree selections include herb roasted chicken, skillet macaroni
and cheese, and the butcher's plate. Vegetarians will delight in the
Crispy Garden Skillet—pan-seared seasonal vegetables over crispy

rice topped with a fried egg and served with a side of sweet and spicy paprika dressing. The bar, built from reclaimed wood from one of Manhattan's landmarks (Lüchow's Restaurant), offers a good selection of local craft beer and imported European wines. Brunch and lunch menus are also available.

Carolina Ale House, 7981 Skyland Ridge Pkwy., Raleigh; (919) 957-4200; 2240 Walnut St., Cary; (919) 854-9444; 4512 Falls of Neuse Rd., Raleigh; (919) 431-0001; 512 Creekside Dr., Raleigh; (919) 835-2222; 11685 Northpark Dr., Wake Forest; (919) 556-8666; carolinaalehouse.com; American/Burgers/Pub; $$. See write-up in the Durham chapter, p. 151.

Centro, 106 S. Wilmington St., Raleigh; (919) 835-3593; dostaquitos centro.com; Mexican; $$. Centro's atmosphere is a kaleidoscope of color that is bright and cheery with an artsy bistro vibe. Expect high-quality Mexican food made with fresh ingredients like the *chilaquiles verdes con borrego en barbacoa*—añejo tequila–stewed leg of lamb over green *chilaquiles* with creamy salsa verde, or the carnitas made with crispy, tender grass-fed pork sautéed in a special homemade tomatillo and jalapeño sauce and served with whole black beans, rice, vegetables en escabeche, and fresh corn tortillas. Over 30 types of tequila are available along with several creative cocktails. Try one of the tequila flights or the Antiguo Mexicano, a Mexican Old Fashioned with Jimador Añejo, orange bitters, Angostura bitters, agave, and muddled orange.

Char-Grill, 618 Hillsborough St., Raleigh; (919) 821-7636; 3211 Edwards Mill Rd., Raleigh; (919) 781-2945; 4621 Atlantic Ave., Raleigh; (919) 954-9556; 9601 Strickland Rd., Raleigh; (919) 845-8994; 1125 W. NC Hwy. 54, Durham; (919) 489-6900; 3635 SW Cary Pkwy., Cary; (919) 461-7112; 1155 Timber Dr. East, Garner; (919) 662-4290; chargrillusa.com; Burgers; $. What began in 1960 as a small burger joint on Hillsborough Street has grown to nine locations with franchise opportunities available. Hungry diners place their orders by filling out an order form, sliding it through a slot and watching as the cook grills up hamburgers, hot dogs, and chicken sandwiches over charcoal flames, made right when you order. The burgers are so juicy and delicious it's no wonder their char-grilled flavor won them a mention in "Great American Bites: 51 Best Burger Joints" in *USA Today*.

Chubby's Tacos, 2444 Wycliff Rd., Raleigh; (919) 781-4480; 10511 Shadowlawn Dr., Raleigh; (919) 846-7044; 12513 Old Creedmoor Rd., Raleigh; (919) 846-6565; chubbystacos.com; Mexican; $. See write-up in the Durham chapter, p. 152.

Chuck's Burger, 237 S. Wilmington St., Raleigh; (919) 322-0126; ac-restaurants.com/chucks; Burgers; $–$$. Next door to her Beasley's Chicken + Honey, local celeb chef Ashley Christensen's new burger joint is anything but standard. The space is clean and simple—white walls hung with bright red papier-mâché bulls. Order at the counter and they bring your food out to you. Each half-pound, house-ground burger is made with care—100 percent chuck, grilled to perfection and topped with a variety of locally sourced ingredients. One of the local faves is the Dirty South Burger: smoked pork shoulder and Anson Mills Sea Island red pea "chili," crispy tobacco onions, roasted tomato slaw, Ashe Mountain cheddar, and yellow mustard. Belgian fries come with your choice of four or five different aiolis, and milk shakes can be spiked with bourbon, spiced rum, etc. Try the salted peanut butter with roasted banana shake. Chuck's is open 7 days a week for lunch and dinner, till midnight Thurs through Sat.

Coquette Brasserie, 4351 The Circle at North Hills, Raleigh; (919) 789-0606; coquetteraleigh.com; French; $$. For a true Parisian-style dining experience, step into Coquette. The floor is a checkerboard of black and white tiles, while Parisian streetlamp–style chandeliers and seasonal outdoor dining are reminiscent of a true Paris brasserie. The traditional menu features time-honored French classics like escargots, salads, and simple fish, *fruits de mer,* and meat entrees. *Moules frites* arrive in a delicate broth made of white wine with a hint of garlic and the delicately salted *frites* are accompanied by homemade mayonnaise. The all-French wine list is extensive and the knowledgeable servers are happy to offer pairing suggestions. Come in and experience excellent service, wonderful wine, and true Parisian-style dining.

FIGS

North Carolina is probably as far north in the US where you can successfully grow figs. Figs grown here are called "common figs" because they do not require a pollinator, usually small wasps that do not survive in our climate. Varieties favorable to our NC growing conditions are Celeste, Brunswick, NC Brown Turkey, Greenish, Marseille, and Magnolia. Of these, Magnolia is the most cold resistant. Figs grow on a tree or a bush, and the fruit is smooth on the outside and soft on the inside with lots of edible seeds: You can eat the whole fig raw, skin and all. If you are a fig lover and not into growing your own fig tree or bush, keep a watch out at the farmers' markets for fresh figs August through September, the time of year that they are available here. But get there early as they sell out fast! North Carolina has a fine breakfast tradition of fig preserves served over warm scratch-made biscuits.

Dalat Oriental, 2109 Avent Ferry Rd., Raleigh; (919) 832-7449; Vietnamese; $. Located in the Mission Valley Shopping Center, this casual Vietnamese restaurant has an extensive menu featuring meat, vegetarian, and vegan dishes. The *banh mi* is a Vietnamese sub served on freshly baked bread with homemade mayonnaise, lightly pickled carrots and daikon radish, crispy cucumbers, green onions, hot peppers, and cilantro; choose from several fillings, including grilled chicken, BBQ pork, spicy beef, or grilled tofu. Other menu options include *pho,* vermicelli dishes, and rice dishes.

The *pho* is made with a rich and flavorful broth and tender meat and arrives at the table with a heaping plate of sprouts, Thai basil, jalapeño peppers, and lime wedges. Located in close proximity to NC State, Dalat is a favorite among students on a tight budget.

Dos Taquitos, 5629 Creedmoor Rd., Raleigh; (919) 787-3373; dostaquitosnc.com; Mexican; $$. When you walk into Dos Taquitos you are immediately reminded of a Mexican marketplace: Everywhere you look there is something interesting to see. At night, the space is dimmed and almost completely lit by candles throughout. It's quirky, cozy, and fun. The food is not entirely authentic Mexican, but try the enchilada stuffed with cactus and cabbage, or the lamb *birria,* or the carnitas plate. For dessert, sample buñuelo—a family recipe of fried pastry dough served with ice cream, honey, chocolate sauce, cinnamon, and whipped cream! There is a small bar stocked with a large selection of tequilas, from white and gold to Reposado and Añejo. The enormous outdoor eating area is enclosed during the chillier months. Open for lunch and dinner.

Draft Carolina Burgers and Beers, 510 Glenwood Ave., Raleigh; (919) 834-2955; draft raleigh.com; American/Burgers; $$. Located in the popular Glenwood South district, Draft Carolina Burgers and Beers is the place to go for burgers and beer. The menu, with a focus on locally sourced ingredients, has a solid choice of appetizers, pizzas, sandwiches, and salads, but it's the burgers you really need to get your hands around. With 15 different specialty burgers, and a choice of ground beef, Kobe, bison, chicken, lamb, turkey, and veggie, there is something for everyone to enjoy. You can build your own burger; toppings range from bacon or portobello mushroom to over 10 different varieties of cheese. If you're feeling adventurous, go for the Breakfast Burger: a fresh ground beef patty topped with a sausage patty, hoop cheddar, country ham, oven-roasted tomatoes, pepper bacon, and fried egg, stacked high on a toasted everything bagel, whew! The draft and bottled beer selection is extensive, with several North Carolina options, including a rotating variety of their signature Mash House brand. Several TVs are located around the bar as well as flat screens at each booth where you can change the channels—perfect if you want to watch a game or entertain the kids while dining. A separate billiards room with additional seating is an ideal setting for a private party.

18 Seaboard, 18 Seaboard Ave., Raleigh; (919) 861-4318; 18seaboard.com; American; $$$. As a native North Carolinian, Chef-Proprietor Jason Smith offers delicious upscale contemporary American fare inspired by local and seasonal ingredients. Choose to dine alfresco on the second-floor open-air mezzanine looking out at incredible views of downtown Raleigh or in the sleek modern dining room surrounded by white flowing draperies and exposed brick walls—either is perfect for a business lunch or celebration dinner. The menu is an eclectic variety of starters, salads, pastas, and entrees. Start your meal with chilled potato–wild ramp soup or refreshing spinach salad, or head straight to the entrees and indulge in the cracklin' pork shank with blue-cheese grits, spinach, and green tomato marmalade. Offerings from the hardwood-fired grill include Atlantic salmon, yellowfin tuna, and bone-in rib eye. Choose from several house-made sauces to enhance your selection including cranberry-pistachio vinaigrette, mint and cucumber butter, maple pumpkin butter, and the 18 Seaboard Worcestershire. Open for lunch Mon through Fri and dinner every day.

518 West, 518 W. Jones St., Raleigh; (919) 829-2518; 518west .com; Italian; $$. Located in the heart of Glenwood South, this sleek and modern, contemporary Italian restaurant offers a menu inspired by the flavors of Italy and the Mediterranean. Look for a tantalizing array of fresh pastas, wood-fired pizzas, fresh seafood, and steaks. Start with the lightly breaded and fried calamari or the wood-grilled shrimp marinated with freshly squeezed citrus and herbs, wrapped in prosciutto, then grilled and served over sautéed spinach with grated Romano. Fresh pastas come in several variations including a rich spaghetti Bolognese or lemon linguini loaded with shrimp, scallops, and tomatoes in white wine with lobster butter and clam broth. For a shared meal, enjoy various small plates, salads, and pizzettes. Save room for tiramisu made with house-made ladyfingers, espresso, and chocolate ganache, and enjoy.

Five Star, 511 W. Hargett St., Raleigh; (919) 833-3311; heat seekershrimp.com; Chinese; $$. Located in the heart of Raleigh's warehouse district, Five Star's unmarked heavy wooden door doesn't even hint at the multilevel interior that is abuzz with late evening diners enjoying the authentic and modern Asian cuisine that Five Star is so well known for. The diversified menu will taunt you to try almost everything, but you can't go wrong with Five Star General's chicken or the crispy sesame beef or the yellowfin tuna with spicy Szechuan sauce and stir-fried vegetables. Late-night weekends turn Five Star into a social gathering environment. Five Star Restaurant is open 7 days a week from 5:30 p.m. until midnight.

Flights (in the Renaissance Raleigh Hotel), 4100 Main at North Hills St., Raleigh; (919) 278-1478; flightsnorthhills.com; American; $$$. Located in the Renaissance Hotel, Flights offers upscale dining in a warm and relaxed environment. The eclectic menu features a variety of soups, salads, pastas, and entrees for lunch and dinner. Start your meal with a pan-seared crab cake or she-crab soup with jumbo lump crabmeat in a creamy broth accented with Amontillado sherry. Enjoy inventive entrees like the fried Cornish hen, BBQ braised local pork shank, lobster and grits, or crispy rosemary-infused wild salmon. All entrees are paired with sides that complement the dishes perfectly. Flights is conveniently located in North

Raleigh, making it an ideal location for a business meeting or special event.

Fonda y Birrieria Jalisco, 1600 Ronald Dr., Raleigh; (919) 790-1999; fondaybirrieriajalisco.com; Taqueria; $. Tucked away in a hidden strip mall, this authentic taqueria offers a bright and inviting atmosphere in which to enjoy the bold flavors of Mexican cuisine. The menu offers traditional tacos, *sopes,* enchiladas, and fajitas. Among their signature dishes is the *birria*—a rich savory stew made with dried chiles and *cabrito* (goat meat) that offers the comfort of a warm blanket on a cold and rainy day. A variety of tacos like *al pastor,* asada, chorizo, and tripe arrive loaded into fresh corn tortillas with the necessary accoutrements of cabbage, radish, cilantro, and lime. Round out your meal with a refreshing Mexican beer or thirst-quenching margarita.

Fork and Barrel, 6675 Falls of Neuse Rd., Raleigh; (919) 322-0190; forkandbarrelnc.com; American/Burgers/Pub; $$. This upscale yet casual American restaurant in North Raleigh is the ideal spot for a casual working lunch, satisfying dinner, or watching your favorite sports team on game day. The decor consists of dark woodwork, beer signs, old movie posters, and several stone accents, providing a comfortable and relaxed environment. The beer growlers displayed in a glass case near the entrance are a sign they take their beer seriously and the selections prove it; they offer about 20 different draft beer options. The menu is upscale pub grub with several creative global influences. Look for plentiful appetizers, salads, sandwiches, and entrees, including tuna tacos, turkey burgers, and red-curry pork with sweet potato ravioli. The grilled salmon with a salad of avocado, tomato, red onion, jicama, and black beans arrives dressed in a tasty charred jalapeño vinaigrette—the reason this dish has become a personal favorite.

Glenwood Grill, 2603 Glenwood Ave., Raleigh; (919) 782-3102; glenwoodgrill.net; American; $$$. The decor is elegant but casual and the food beautifully executed at this neighborhood gem located in the Five Point district. Inspired by the coastal Carolinas and the American South, Chef John Wright prepares enticing appetizers and entrees with a Southern flair. Luscious entrees include Frog Island NC crab cakes with creamed corn and arugula salad with blue cheese, pecans, and Granny Smith apples dressed with balsamic vinaigrette. Classic shrimp and grits get a makeover with the addition of pan-seared scallops, roasted corn, and tomatoes, mushrooms, and maple-pepper bacon over crawfish cheese grits, and the popular carpetbagger features succulent filet mignon topped with Parmesan fried oysters on a bed of parsnip whipped potatoes. Other a la carte options include pork tenderloin, Scottish organic salmon, and a burger topped with pimiento cheese, horseradish, fried green tomatoes, and crispy shallots. The wine list is extensive and the staff knowledgeable and professional. Glenwood Grill is open for lunch Mon through Fri and dinner Mon through Sat. Closed Sun.

Hayashi Japanese Restaurant, 13200 New Falls of Neuse Rd., Ste. 105 (Wakefield Crossings Shopping Center), Raleigh; (919) 544-0508; hayashijapaneserestaurant.com; Japanese; $$. Hayashi is a full-service restaurant open for lunch and dinner from Mon to Sat and offers takeout. You can choose to eat in the privacy of a tatami room or the village atmosphere of the main dining room, or sit at the sushi bar and watch your Japanese-style sushi being made right before your eyes. While I rarely indulge in deep-fried dishes, my favorite dish here is the *katsu* dinner—a prime pork cutlet crusted with tempura flakes and deep fried. It is served with shredded cabbage, steamed rice, miso soup, and *katsu* sauce, a delicate blend of applesauce, tomatoes, onions, and carrots.

Hayes-Barton Cafe & Dessertery, 2000 Fairview, Five Points, Raleigh; (919) 856-8551; hayesbartoncafe.com; American/Burgers; $. Tucked away in the back of Hayes-Barton Pharmacy, this 1940s-inspired restaurant, with walls adorned with photos of old movie stars and WWII memorabilia, is best known for its top-notch desserts worthy of overindulgence. Towering slices of carrot and coconut cake are some of the best in the city while the key lime pie and lemon meringue pie are sweet, creamy, and slightly tart. For lunch or dinner, American comfort food is served by an attentive staff. Enjoy classics like meat loaf, chicken pot pie, mussels, and filet mignon. The coq au vin—delicately braised boneless chicken breasts cooked in a savory red wine sauce with bacon, pearl onions, and mushrooms—is hearty and comforting while the award-winning "Buckhead" certified Angus filet served blackened with Gorgonzola au jus or simply seasoned with button mushroom demi-glace is rich and flavorful. Open for lunch Tues through Sat and dinner Wed through Sat. Cash only.

Herons, 100 Woodland Pond Dr., Cary; (919) 447-4400; the umstead.com; American; $$$. There is no denying the elegance of the Umstead Hotel and Spa situated on 12 acres of stunning natural beauty on the SAS Campus in Cary. Matching that is the ambience of the hotel with its fresh flower arrangements, art-adorned walls, luxurious guest rooms, and celebrated spa. From the hotel's signature restaurant, Executive Chef Scott Crawford and Chef de Cuisine Steven Greene create seasonal, Southern-infused American dishes. For lunch, consider the delicately seared salmon with broccoli, hon shimeji mushrooms, and five-spice consommé, with the tendrils of spicy steam tickling your nose with each bite, or redefine your image of an American classic by ordering the Umstead BLT: warm ciabatta, crispy pork belly, fried egg, and truffle aioli. Dinner is a welcoming assault on the senses times two: vision and taste. Surrounded by curved ceilings, remarkable artwork and stunning views of the terrace, lake, and lawns, the food is a further extension of the pleasing environment, offering thoughtful, classic, and contemporary cuisine. Chef Crawford and his team source local and seasonal ingredients, including fruits, vegetables, and herbs from their own farm. Celebrate the quality of ingredients with favored entrees like duck consommé, with duck and mushroom dumplings, baby bok choy, and pomegranate purée; vanilla-spiced sea bass, with fingerling potatoes, braised tatsoi, fennel confit, and parsnip-lobster bisque; or filet of natural beef, with salsify, poached egg, crispy broccoli, king trumpet mushrooms, and truffle BBQ. The sophistication of each dish is artfully, skillfully, and lovingly pre-pared, and not soon forgotten. The restaurant offers an intimate dining environment for lunch, dinner, and weekend brunch. Guests can sit inside and enjoy a full view of the kitchen or sit outside on the terrace during the spring, summer, and fall to enjoy a serene dining experience. With several accolades from publications like *Food & Wine, Condé Nast Traveler,* and *Southern Living,* Chef Crawford will continue to tempt the palate for a long time to come.

Hibernian Irish Pub and Restaurant, 311 Glenwood Ave., Raleigh; (919) 833-2258; 1144 Kildaire Farm Rd., Cary; (919) 460-6599; hibernianpub.com; Pub; $$. Hibernian Pub serves a mix of traditional Irish dishes and American comfort food, all with a heaping helping of Southern friendliness. It's hardly a stop at an Irish pub if you don't try the bangers and mash—you won't be disappointed. The Hibernian has an excel-lent selection of Irish beers and whiskeys, as you might imagine. There are food and drink specials every day. Cary location: Trivia Tuesday at 9 p.m.; Pub Run Wednesday at 7 p.m.; live music Friday and Saturday night.

Humble Pie, 317 S. Harrington St., Raleigh; (919) 829-9222; humblepierestaurant.com; American; $$. This restaurant and tiki bar, located in the downtown warehouse district, is known for an extensive tapas menu that offers a variety of creative small plates, all under $15. It is best to come with a group of people in order to maximize the number of tasty dishes you can try. Share tempura asparagus, crisp wild mushroom risotto, sesame seared ahi tuna, or braised short rib tostadas. A brunch menu is also available and best enjoyed on the patio when weather permits.

J. Betski's, 10 W. Franklin St., Raleigh; (919) 833-7999; jbetskis .com; European/German/Polish; Lunch: $; Dinner: $$. As one of Raleigh's most beloved restaurants, J. Betski's celebrates owner John Korzekwinski's German and Polish heritage. With doppel bocks, pilsners, and wheat beers on draft, and a lot more hard-to-find and unexpected bottles from Germany, Austria, and Poland, this is the place for an authentic experience. They also have great cocktails— I love the Beet Jammer (roasted beet–infused vodka, apple cider, and Blenheim's spicy ginger ale). But the real star is the food and its nuanced flavors as prepared by Chef Todd Whitney. German and Polish dishes are elevated using fresh, local ingredients: mushroom and cabbage pierogies with sage brown butter, house-made kielbasa, bratwurst, pork schnitzel, duck, spaetzle, fresh fish, and pub plates for sharing. And dessert . . . check out the chocolate-hazelnut torte with sea salt, caramel, and crispy bacon.

Jibarra, 327 W. Davis St., Raleigh; (919) 755-0556; jibarra.net; Mexican; $$. Located in a renovated depot building of the warehouse district, Jibarra is vibrant and upbeat and serves Mexican food with upscale flair. Order the Los Cuatro to sample all four of the guacamole appetizers, including the *a la jaiba* with crabmeat and jicama. Entrees are loaded with bold and innovative flavors. Try the *pollo con mole casero,* a pan-roasted chicken breast with a 22-ingredient mole or the *chilorio de camorro,* a chile-oregano-cumin marinated Kirobuta pork osso buco. Make sure to check out the extensive margarita list.

KoMo KoMo, 1305 NW Maynard Rd., Cary; (919) 462-3555; komokomonc.com; French/Korean; $. Located in a typical Cary strip mall, KoMo KoMo, offers Korean- and French-inspired dishes in a bright, welcoming, and relaxed environment. Neutral colored walls, a scattering of tables, and a wood banquette dotted with a colorful array of pillows are a warm and inviting backdrop in which to enjoy beef *bulgogi bibimbap,* a traditional Korean rice bowl, topped with garlic, ginger, soy, and onion-marinated beef or a classic French bouillabaisse, a seafood stew of mussels, shrimp, calamari, scallops, and seasonal fish in a saffron tomato broth. Along with the various Korean and French options, also look for fresh salads, soups, and sandwiches. KoMo KoMo is open for lunch and dinner.

La Farm Bakery, 4248 SW Cary Pkwy., Cary; (919) 657-0657; lafarmbakery.com; Bakery/Cafe; $. Master baker Lionel Vatinet uses centuries-old traditions and techniques to make a huge selection of artisan breads, pastries, and tarts at this authentic French bistro in the heart of Cary. Breakfast is served daily until 11 a.m., and the french toast with Amish maple syrup with fresh strawberries and whipped cream is a decadent way to begin the day. The lunch menu offers soups, salads, quiches, sandwiches on fresh-baked bread, and the prosciutto asparagus tartine, as featured in *Food & Wine* magazine, with Asiago, Parmesan, fresh mozzarella, olive tapenade, roasted tomatoes, shallot butter, artichokes, mild goat cheese, prosciutto, asparagus, and a balsamic drizzle. Don't forget to leave with fresh bread to take home.

Lilly's Pizza, 1813 Glenwood Ave., Raleigh; (919) 833-0226; lillys pizza.com; Pizza; $$. Located in historic Five Points, Lilly's Pizza is consistently voted the Triangle's Best Pizza by the readers of the *Independent Weekly*, and with good reason. Pizzas are made from organic whole-wheat flour, organic vegetables, and all chicken and beef toppings are antibiotic- and hormone-free. Creatively named pies include "Sir Walter," "Mr. Greenjeans," and my favorite, "Dante's Inferno" (barbecue sauce, mozzarella cheese, bacon, onions, roasted red peppers, Parmesan cheese, and barbecued chicken). You can also create your own pizza, whether it be vegetarian, vegan, or a meat version. Offering a large selection of salads, pastas, and calzones, Lilly's delivers their entire menu starting at 4 p.m. daily.

Little Hen, Shoppes at Woodcreek, 5160 Sunset Lake Rd., Apex; (919) 363-0000; littlehennc.com; American/Farm to Table; $$$.

Little Hen, a family business owned by Regan and Dawn Stachler, is a farm-to-table restaurant located in the town of Holly Springs, serving New American cuisine in a modern farmhouse setting. Little Hen is committed to working directly with local farmers, all of whom practice sustainable, organic methods. A seasonal menu changes almost daily and features the freshest ingredients, including the popular house-ground burger and local Okfusee Farm pork chop. The Big Board, a delightful tasting for two, offers a selection of meats prepared in different styles, and four or five side dishes; this is quickly becoming their signature menu item. There is also a selection of local cheeses and cured meats ideal for sharing. The wine list features a range of varietals from unique wineries while local craft beer is available on tap and in bottles. Vegetarian and vegan options are available, and they happily accommodate guests with food allergies.

Lucky 32 Southern Kitchen, 7307 Tryon Rd., Cary; (919) 233-1632; lucky32.com; Farm to Table/Fried Chicken/Southern; $$. Executive Chef Jay Pierce's effort to build a menu based on authentic, sustainable, locally sourced Southern flavors is a testament to his love of the Southern foodways. Whistle bite sliders—house-cured pork belly with Pig and Whistle sauce and green tomato chow chow are perfect for sharing or enjoyed as a small meal. The array of side dishes like collard greens, mac and cheese, pintos, and chow chow that accompany the herb-crusted Carolina catfish or salt and pepper rib eye reflect the traditional meat-and-three meal found in diners all over the South. The Wednesday Skillet-Fried Chicken Night has fast become a local favorite, and for good reason. Panfried in Cane Creek Farm's locally rendered pork fat, the chicken arrives crispy on the outside while remaining moist and juicy on the inside. Served alongside creamy whipped mashed potatoes, giblet gravy, collard greens, and a hunk of cornbread, it's a meal that is both familiar and comforting. In addition to the regular menu, a rotating seasonal menu based on regional themes debuts about every 6 weeks. See Jay Pierce's recipes for **Whipped North Carolina Sweet Potatoes** and **Buttermilk Pie** on pp. 256 and 291.

Margaux's Restaurant, 8111 Creedmoor Rd., #111, Raleigh; (919) 846-9846; margauxsrestaurant.com; American/French/Seafood; $$. The multilevel dining room with its stone fireplace, modern decor, and energetic ambience offers consistently high-quality food in an upscale, contemporary setting. The eclectic menu draws from Mediterranean, Pacific Rim, and Low Country influences and often includes dishes using game meats like kangaroo, antelope, and boar. Aside from a few select "vintage" dishes like the mustard-seared calf's liver with red wine vinegar, caramelized onions, and crispy bacon strips that have remained on the menu since Margaux's opened in 1992, the menu changes daily. A creative appetizer menu will tempt you with delicacies like fresh-shucked North Carolina oysters or escargots with garlic butter and fresh herbs to Vietnamese fresh shrimp spring rolls with jumbo lump crabmeat, pickled vegetables, peanut pesto, and chile jam. Entree options are intriguing and range from antelope rack of ribs or kangaroo with port cherry gastrique to roast rockfish with artichoke roast garlic puree, grilled vegetables, Tuscan tapenade, and lobster. For a sampling of several dishes, opt for the 3-course prix-fixe menu, an absolute steal at $19.95 if you dine between 5:30 and 6:30 p.m., Tues through Fri. See Chef Andrew Pettifer's recipe for **Pamlico Sound Crab Cakes & Shrimp atop Pickled Green Bean & Artichoke Salad** on p. 264.

Market Restaurant, 938 N. Blount St., Raleigh; (919) 754-0900; eatatmarket.com; American/Farm to Table; $$. In the historic Mordecai neighborhood of downtown Raleigh, Chef-Owner Chad McIntyre offers West Coast–inspired cuisine using local and seasonal ingredients. His commitment to serving only the freshest food is evident as you look around the restaurant; vegetables, herbs, and even fruit trees are growing alongside and behind the restaurant, beehives can be seen on the roof, and bottles of various house-made pickles decorate the shelves. He has even designed and built the first ever solar powered draft beer system. The atmosphere is comfortable and relaxed, and a patio on the side offers a delightful setting to enjoy a beautiful Carolina day. To start, dig into a bowl of kale chips, oven-baked crispy kale, or crack fries (and yes, these are worthy of the name)—hand-cut fries tossed in truffle oil and fresh herbs, topped with Asiago cheese and served with house-made ketchup. Using only seasonal ingredients, the menu changes every few months. Tomato season may mean stuffed vine-ripe tomatoes filled with a mixture of orzo, almonds, fresh herbs, and *queso fresco,* then drizzled with jalapeño vinegar and blood orange–infused olive oil, while shrimp season may combine fresh North Carolina shrimp with local chorizo over herbed polenta. Fish tacos are a must here: seasonal fish is lightly fried and served on fresh corn tortillas, topped with salsa and *queso fresco* and a side of colorful slaw. They are light yet filling and perhaps one of my favorite lunch items. A great selection of local beers is available along with a nice selection of wines. The Bloody Mary fan will be pleasantly surprised by the house-made mix and the pickled okra that accompanies the drink. If you are a fan of chocolate, be sure to indulge in one of the chocolate desserts; the chocolate used to make these desserts comes from award-winning Escazu Artisan Chocolates, located right next door. See Chef Chad McIntyre's recipe for **Market's Ketchup** on p. 266.

Martin's Curry Rice, 9549 Chapel Hill Rd., Morrisville; (919) 380-7799; martinscurryrice.com; Indian; $. Located in a nondescript strip mall, Martin's Curry Rice offers Indian-inspired "Farm Fresh Fusion food in five minutes!" The counter service concept is simple: choose your protein (chicken, beef, fish, egg, or tofu), vegetables, and sauce (red, green, or yellow), then wait as your meal is stir-fried and served in a bowl over a bed of rice. Chef Martin's commitment to sourcing local ingredients means your food is always fresh. Most of the fresh vegetables, like bell peppers, squash, kale, and other seasonal produce, are sourced from **Western Wake Farmers Market** (p. 37), and if you happen to be at the market Saturday morning, you will most likely find Martin selling ready-to-eat meals like beef or vegetarian samosas, yellowfish curry, or pork vindaloo. All menu items can be made vegetarian or vegan with gluten-free options also available. During the week, follow Martin on Facebook and Twitter to find out where his Curry Truck is located. During the week he is often in Cary, and on Saturday night you can find him at **Fullsteam Brewery** (p. 201).

Maximillians Grill, 8314 Chapel Hill Rd., Cary; (919) 465-2455; maximilliansgrill.com; American; $$. Chef-Owner Michael Schiffer and Executive Chef Edward Krynicki team to bring a unique combination of gourmet and fusion cuisine to Triangle restaurant-goers. On the hot list of must-go-to restaurants, Maxmillians has a trademark dish in Voodoo Tuna, seared delicately with a peppercorn crust and served with a spicy ginger-cumin-garlic sauce, shrimp, and cilantro on top of Mahogany fire noodles. Maximillians Grill is an exquisite dining location for a special occasion—its ambience of low lighting and dark paneling encourages intimate conversation over superb food for an evening to remember. Open for dinner Mon through Sat.

Mura, 4121 Main at North Hills St., Raleigh; (919) 781-7887; mura northhills.com; Japanese/Seafood; $$. Mura's sleek modern decor, renowned Kobe beef, and excellent sushi make it a great place for a business lunch or special dinner. The lunch menu includes several sushi combinations, hibachi-style entrees, and bento boxes filled with your choice of teriyaki chicken, steak, or salmon, served on a bed of rice, salad, tempura, and a chef's choice sushi roll. For dinner, try the seared yellowfin summer wraps or the Cukani roll (*kani* crab, avocado, red tobiko, and cream cheese rolled in a peeled cucumber). The Kobe beef is a must, and the red miso–braised short rib entree with Korean barbecue sauce, blue potato puree, and tempura green beans is excellent. Sushi happy hour is offered Mon to Fri (buy one sushi roll, get another at half price).

NC Seafood Restaurant, 1201 Agriculture St., Raleigh; (919) 833-4661; ncseafood.com; Seafood; $. The NC Seafood Restaurant serves fantastic fried Calabash–style and broiled NC seafood at amazing prices, and unless you are actually at the beach, you can't beat it. (Named after a small Eastern North Carolina town, "Calabash-style" refers to any lightly breaded and fried seafood). The Calabash plates are a great deal—a large is truly large enough for two people to have a very filling meal. The atmosphere is very casual; orders are taken at a counter, or if they are busy, someone will walk through the line to take your order; there are no servers. All food is cooked to order and ready in less than 10 minutes, making it a great place for families. Meals come in carry-out containers (no plates here), and you can take your order to go or dine on tables inside or picnic benches outside. Popular menu items include the lightly breaded and tender fried shrimp and the moist and flaky flounder. All "Calabash-style" meals come with the requisite home fries, hush puppies, and slaw.

Neomonde Mediterranean Cafe & Market, 3817 Beryl Rd., Raleigh; (919) 828-5244; neomonde.com; Bakery/Cafe/Middle Eastern; $. Now in its 35th year, Neomonde began as a traditional Lebanese bakery in 1977 but soon expanded to include a deli and market featuring a range of Lebanese/Mediterranean cuisine. You can also buy nuts, spices, and Middle Eastern grocery items. With three locations in the Raleigh area, Neomonde is famous for its fresh pita bread and for the delicious, fresh, traditional Lebanese food based on family recipes. One of my favorites is the chicken salad tossed with golden raisins, walnuts, and spices. Order at the counter, pick up ingredients for dinner, or grab something to go.

NOFO at the Pig, 2014 Fairview Rd., Raleigh; (919) 821-1240; nofo.com; American; $. Located in the Five Points area of Raleigh, NOFO is a combination gift shop, market, and bistro. At the bistro, look for Southern inspired cuisine, including soups, salads, sandwiches, entrees, and daily blue-plate specials like black bean burgers or fish tacos. The market features specialty grocery items such as fine chocolates, novelty candies, beer and wine, cookies, crackers, nuts, sauces, pickles, condiments, whole-bean coffees, and tea. If you are looking for a unique gift item, the gift shop has an eclectic mix of furniture, books, kitchen and household items, toys, and more. NOFO is a truly unique experience.

Nur Grocery & Deli, 2233 Avent Ferry Rd., Ste. 108, Raleigh; (919) 828-1523; nurdeli.com; Deli/Middle Eastern; $. Tucked away in the Mission Valley Shopping Center close to North Carolina State University, Nur Grocery and Deli specializes in Middle Eastern foods at affordable prices with fast and friendly service. On the grocery side of the store, shelves are lined with an excellent selection of authentic Middle Eastern pantry staples. Look for couscous, rice, flour, canned goods, and hard-to-find spices. In the refrigerator section you will find *halloumi*, a traditional cheese from Cyprus made from goat's and/or sheep's milk, while from the freezer section you can pick up Armenian meat pies. For a quick lunch or dinner on the go, stop by the deli case and order from a menu made up of sand-wiches, salads, platters, and authentic sides. Middle Eastern offerings include a hummus and pita plate, gyros, kofta, and falafel or spinach and cheese pies. An American menu with cheeseburgers, Philly cheese-steaks, and fries is also available. Open since 1980, Nur Grocery and Deli has become a popular fixture in the community. Open daily 7 days a week.

The Oxford, 319-105 Fayetteville St., Raleigh; (919) 832-6622; oxfordraleigh.com; American/Pub; $. Located in the heart of downtown Raleigh, The Oxford offers a relaxed yet upscale environment to enjoy traditional gastropub fare. The menu is a step above your average "pub grub," with creative twists on familiar favorites. A wide variety of small plates are ideal for sharing, including the fried guacamole (crispy panko- and chile-crusted avocado served with pico de gallo and chipotle ranch dressing) and Wellington Bites (grilled beef tips with Boursin cheese, mushroom, and wilted spinach wrapped in a flaky pastry, served with onion marmalade). Plenty of soups, salads, and sandwiches grace the menu as do classic items like bangers and mash or fish-and-chips. For a real treat try the Scottish salmon, pan-seared and served with goat cheese and spinach polenta cake with a white balsamic–beet jus. Happy Hour half-price appetizers every Mon thru Fri from 3 to 6 p.m.!

Peak City Grill & Bar, 126 North Salem St., Apex; (919) 303-8001; thepeakcitygrill.com; American; $$. The Peak City Grill & Bar is owned by local Apex residents Steve and Julie Adams; Chef Propst maintains the stellar reputation for fine dining by using the best products he can find and using simple techniques for execution. The Grill building, which took a year of remodeling before it opened its doors to the public, has quite a history: The building has served as a hardware store, a general store, and a feed and mill store. In fact, mules used to be sold in what is now the parking lot. The building was only sold to the Adamses by the original owners' family in 2004. The menu is certainly directed toward carnivores with burgers, steaks, and chops dominating.

Community Supported Fisheries (CSFs)

The goal of the NC fisheries is to support CFAs as a viable means to market seafood directly to the consumer through prepaid orders. Arrangements are tailor-made to the consumer's seafood preferences and the fisherman has advance orders to provide him or her with a guaranteed market for seafood and the capital to keep fishing. In the Triangle area, there are a handful of CSFs from our eastern seaboard that guarantee seasonal fresh seafood (fish or shellfish) delivered weekly to a prearranged locale. The idea for CSFs grew out of the popular approach to buying fresh produce through Community Supported Agriculture, known as CSAs.

Core Sound Seafood: Seafood shares are delivered on Thursday at multiple locations around the Triangle. There is a choice of weekly or biweekly delivery, a full share or half share. The season runs from early April to early June. To participate, call (919) 926-9599, but check the website every Thursday to see what is available (coresoundseafood .org) or e-mail questions to coresoundseafood@gmail.com.

Dock to Door: Does not require a seasonal commitment. It posts the current availability on its homepage by 5 p.m. on Thursday evening. At that time the store is open for customers who can then secure their order with a credit card. All orders must be placed in 1-pound increments. The minimum order of any item is 1 pound. All orders for Chapel Hill (Friday pickup) must be placed by 10 p.m. on Wednesday evening. All orders for Durham (Tuesday pickup) must be placed by 10 p.m. Saturday evening. Check online for the exact pickup location. To find out what the catch of the week is, check the website on Thursday evening: docktodoorseafood.com. If you have questions, e-mail info@docktodoorseafood.com.

Locals Seafoods: Join The Locals Catch by purchasing shares for pickup beginning in April. There are several pickup locations around Raleigh only. As a member of The Locals Catch, you sign up for 6 weeks of seafood, whereby you choose 6 of the 10 pickup dates during the period. Of course, you can also choose all 10 pickup dates. Members also get first choice of special add-on seafood items at an additional discount. For all the details, visit the website localsseafood.com, or call with questions, (919) 675-2722.

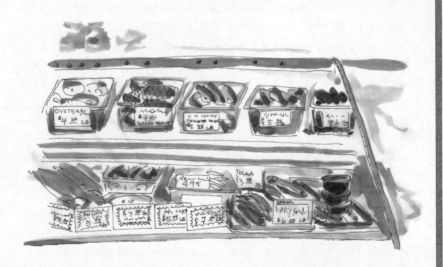

Pho Far East, 4011 Capital Blvd., Raleigh; (919) 876-8621; Vietnamese; $. Located in a small strip mall off of Capital Boulevard, Pho Far East is serving up some of the best Vietnamese food in Raleigh. The bustling restaurant fills up quickly during lunchtime hours and it's not rare to have to wait 10 or 15 minutes for a table, and for good reason. The menu consists of authentic fare, ranging from noodle and rice dishes, spring rolls, hot pots, and *banh mi*, a Vietnamese sandwich filled with pork or chicken, pickled daikon, carrot, and jalapeños served on a crusty baguette. The summer rolls are made with a soft rice paper wrapper filled with thin vermicelli noodles, mint, basil, lettuce, sliced shrimp, and pork and served with a tasty peanut sauce or fish sauce. Try the *pho* and you will not be disappointed, it is one of the best in the area. A rich and flavorful beef broth, spiced with cardamom, star anise, and cinnamon is ladled over a heaping portion of vermicelli noodles and topped with thin slices of onion, cilantro, and scallions and your choice of protein, and served with the traditional accoutrements of fresh sprouts, basil, jalapeños, and lime. Pho Far East offers friendly service and great Vietnamese fare at reasonable prices.

Pie Bird, 618 N. Person St., Raleigh; (919) 508-7612; piebird raleigh.com; Bakery/Sandwiches; $$. Sheilagh Sabol Duncan began making pies for her neighbors in the historic Oakwood neighborhood, but when she outgrew her kitchen space, it was time to find a restaurant. Her neighbor Krishna Bahl also had a love of baking, and the two now own and operate Pie Bird. Sourcing locally as much as possible, Pie Bird makes sweet and savory pies, hand pies, soups, salads, and sandwiches. All are affordably priced, and enjoyed in their modern, cheery space. Bright textiles, a large bar, and the location at the tip of the historic Oakwood neighborhood make for a mighty inviting little spot! Finish off your meal with a rich slice of honey and sea-salt pie for dessert, and a French press of their Pie Bird Nest Blend, roasted exclusively for them by Durham's Counter Culture coffee. Pie Bird is open for lunch and dinner, Tues through Sat (11 a.m. to 10 p.m.) and a full bar selection is available. They also do catering.

Players' Retreat, 105 Oberlin Rd., Raleigh; (919) 755-9589, players retreat.net; Burgers; $. Players' Retreat is a Raleigh institution, known since 1951 for its warm, jovial atmosphere and solid pub grub, and it's now also known for an incredible scotch menu. A long wooden bar and plenty of booths fill up quickly with everyone from college students to state government employees, and the walls are lined with NCSU memorabilia dating back to when the bar opened; the PR owners and patrons are generally North Carolina State University fans, and the college is only a couple of blocks away. Fantastic burgers made from Angus beef and ground on-site mean you can order your hamburger any way you want it. Aside from some of the best burgers in town, they also have a stellar chicken salad sandwich with homemade fried chips, and definitely do not deny yourself an order of Mimi's sausage dip: creamy, salty, porky

goodness served with Frito chips for scooping. A good selection of craft beer, including local beers, is available, and they were a recipient of the *Wine Spectator* Award of Excellence for 2010 for their great wine list. But you *must* check out the scotch menu—it is the largest single-malt scotch selection anywhere in North Carolina. A scotch tasting at the Players' Retreat is highly recommended. Pool tables, darts, and an excellent jukebox add to the fun, and the large outdoor patio with plenty of umbrella-covered tables is perfect for enjoying the Carolina sunshine.

Poole's Downtown Diner, 426 S. McDowell St., Raleigh; (919) 832-4477; poolesdowntowndiner.com; American/Southern; $$$. First opened as Poole's Pie Shop in 1945, Chef-Owner Ashley Christensen has turned this small space on the fringes of downtown into a hip destination for a memorable meal complemented by an enticing selection of inventive cocktails. You won't find any printed menus; instead there's a chalkboard list of the day's offerings. The menu, which changes daily, has also been known to change mid-evening. Dishes are prepared simply and eloquently with locally sourced ingredients. When North Carolina soft shell are in season, they arrive perfectly seasoned, fried crisp on the outside, tender on the inside. And for the ultimate comfort food, choose the made-to-order macaroni gratin robust with sharp cheddar, Parmesan, and gruyère. Also a huge supporter of the **Southern Foodways Alliance** (p. 17), Ashley hosts the Stir the Pot fund-raiser several times a year to raise money for their documentary program. See Chef Ashley Christensen's recipe for **Macaroni au Gratin** on p. 259.

The Raleigh Times Bar, 14 E. Hargett St., Raleigh; (919) 833-0999; raleightimesbar.com; American/Burgers/Pub; $. This place is easily the busiest place in downtown Raleigh. And for good reason—not only does it have one of the best and largest selections of rare Belgian beers around, the pub food is great (full menu served until 2 a.m.), and the space is super cozy. The 100-plus-year-old building used to house the now defunct *Raleigh Times* newspaper. And the history is kept alive in the old newspaper clippings that line the walls and the huge mural of early 1900s newspaper delivery boys. President Obama had a pint of PBR here when he was campaigning in Raleigh, and his pint glass can be seen up on the shelf behind the bar. If you're hankering after handcrafted, fresh pub food, choose the half-pound house burger (named one of the top 50 in the US by the Food Network), cooked to order. Other pub fare includes pastrami on rye, great salads, BBQ pork nachos, and most certainly, the chicken-fried pickle chips.

Remedy Diner, 137 E. Hargett St., Raleigh; (919) 835-3553; theremedydiner.com; Sandwiches/Vegetarian; $. From Sunday brunch to late-night pub grub, omnivore, vegetarian, or vegan, Remedy Diner has got you covered. Known for creative cocktails and an excellent selection of vegan and vegetarian fare, try the vegan meatball sub, or soy wings in buffalo sauce—you won't even miss the meat. Remedy Diner is committed to using fresh, local, and organic ingredients whenever possible and uses only Boar's Head meats for its deli sandwiches. The Reuben is out of this world and so is the turkey pesto, thin slices of turkey, homemade pesto, applewood-smoked bacon, avocado, lettuce, and tomato. All sandwiches are served on toasted sourdough. They offer an excellent selection of North Carolina craft beers and a small but decent wine list. The decor is eclectic—there is always art displayed from a local artist and featured in the dining room, and the restrooms sport delightful bright murals on the walls. The backyard patio is a great place for an afternoon summer beer. It's located across the street from Marbles Kids' Museum and just down the street from the Pour House, so you can have a sandwich after seeing your favorite band.

The Rockford, 320½ Glenwood Ave., Raleigh; (919) 821-9020; therockfordrestaurant.com; American/Sandwiches; $. Located on the second floor of an unassuming building, the Rockford offers an eclectic mix of reasonably priced entrees, gourmet sandwiches, and daily soup specials in a comfortable cozy atmosphere. Weekly food specials rotate to reflect what's in season while favorites such as the fish tacos and ABC (apple, bacon, cheddar) sandwich, so popular it has an almost cult-like following, remain on the menu year-round. Small plates, available only during dinner, range from pot stickers or crab cakes to a fabulous sweet potato and cheese quesadilla with hints of cinnamon, cumin, and cayenne pepper, served with sweet and spicy pepper jelly. The relaxed atmosphere and funky vibe of the bar make it a popular destination to enjoy a good beer and conversation.

Saint-Jacques French Cuisine, North Ridge Shopping Center, 6112 Falls of Neuse Rd., Raleigh; (919) 862-2770; saintjacques frenchcuisine.com; French; $$$$. In their North Raleigh strip-mall restaurant, owners Lil and Lori Lacassagne have created a cozy and elegant atmosphere in which to enjoy seasonally inspired, classic French dishes for lunch and dinner. The lunch menu offers light fare such as crepes, omelets, quiches, and salads as well as classic favorites like mussels in garlic and shallot-infused white wine broth or escargots—snails served in garlic and parsley butter, accompanied by pesto toast. A native of Provence, France, Lil takes great pride in bringing guests a truly unique dining experience through food, wine, and service. The waitstaff, most of whom are French natives, deliver gracious and attentive service and are very knowledgeable when it comes to pairing wines with the food. Main courses may be pan-seared, wild caught scallops, laid atop homemade crispy lobster and shrimp ravioli; braised veal osso buco in a tomato and fennel broth; or crispy-skin duck medallions, finished with a delicious apple cider and cranberry gastrique with hot seared duck leg confit. Desserts are equally delightful, including the fresh cherry clafoutis with Cognac and sugar-coated dark cherries, served with homemade brown sugar and whiskey ice cream. The intimate setting makes

Saint-Jacques a popular destination for a special celebratory dinner or romantic evening; be sure to make a reservation ahead of time.

Salem Street Pub, 113 North Salem St., Apex; (919) 387-9992; salemstreetpub.com; Burgers/Pub; $. Looking for a great place to grab a burger? Look no further than Salem Street Pub in the historic part of Apex. Husband and wife Jared and Jennifer Duckart have decided that typical pub fare (the burger in this case) warrants their full attention to serve the best. Favorite burgers include the pattymelt burger, Philly steak, black bean burger, spicy burger, even a peanut butter burger with bacon and cheese! I haven't quite brought myself to order this one, yet. Then you can choose the toppings you want. Their french fries and onion rings are all homemade. The atmosphere is definitely down-home friendly, and when the weather is just right, sitting outside with a chilled NC brew makes for a perfect spot to chat with friends. Trivia night is Wednesday.

Second Empire Restaurant and Tavern, 330 Hillsborough St., Raleigh; (919) 829-3663; second-empire.com; American; $$$$. Two restaurants in one, this landmark eatery, housed in the historic 1879 Dodd-Hinsdale mansion, offers both a refined atmosphere for an elegant dining experience in the formal restaurant or a more relaxed atmosphere in the downstairs tavern for a more casual meal or after-work "happy hour." The restaurant, with its 14-foot ceilings and elegant dining rooms, is the ideal location for celebratory occasions, whether it is a birthday, anniversary, or special "date night." Chef Schurr's dinner menu changes seasonally and offers guests only the freshest that is seasonally available. Start with the warm New Zealand venison tenderloin salad, decadence at its best, or the "Empire" cioppino: local Sneads Ferry clams, bay scallops, shrimp, calamari, and seasonal fish with crushed red pepper and grilled red onion in a garlic and roasted cherry tomato broth, a seafood lover's dream. For a memorable entree, look to the crispy panfried Chesapeake Bay striped bass with grilled prosciutto ham, grain mustard spaetzle, brussels sprouts, melted saffron leeks, smoked cauliflower slaw, and a dried cherry and poblano jus. Be sure to leave room for the classic Empire chocolate soufflé, baked to order, topped with powdered sugar, and served with chantilly cream or vanilla ice cream. Descend the stairs to the exposed brick tavern and consider ordering the perfectly crispy fried calamari, warm and crispy duck confit salad, or the braised, local bison short ribs for an enjoyable meal. For an unforgettable experience, book the Chef's Table where two to eight people can dine in the kitchen and enjoy a menu, along with wine pairings, specially designed just for you and your dining companions. A consistent winner of the *Wine Spectator* Award of Excellence, Second Empire's wine list does not disappoint, nor does the excellent selection of beers on tap at the tavern.

Sitti, 137 S. Wilmington St., Raleigh; (919) 239-4070; sitti-raleigh.com; Lebanese; $$. Warm colors, hardwood floors, exposed wood support beams, and imported 1930s art-deco bar, give this authentic Lebanese restaurant an old-world feel that is charmingly simple and rustic, upscale and inviting. Sitti, meaning "grand-mother" in Lebanese Arabic, pays tribute to family traditions of sharing a table with family, friends, and strangers alike, indicated by the large communal table that sits in the middle of the restaurant. The extensive menu of shareable small plates (mezze), encourages sharing, allowing each diner to sample several dishes at once. To start, try the goat cheese and orange salad (mixed greens topped with orange slices, goat cheese, walnuts, and dates, drizzled in a sweet, citrusy, lemon vinaigrette) or cheese rolls, where gruyère, feta cheese, spices, and mint are rolled into paper-thin pancakes, then fried until perfectly crispy. The Sitti tasting option—hummus, baba ghanoush, *fattoush,* chicken shawarma, *kibbe mikli* (fried dumplings with ground beef and lamb), and cheese rolls—offers a wonderful sampling of traditional mezze and is a great introduction to the bright, subtle flavors found in Middle Eastern cooking. Entrees like the okra stew with tender chunks of lamb in a tomato sauce are quite popular as is the mixed grill of kebabs, a delightful combination of flawlessly seasoned chicken, kofta (ground beef and lamb), and beef fillet served with rice and garlic whip, their version of *tzatziki* sauce. During warmer months, snag a seat on the enclosed patio out back, order a few mezze and a glass of wine, and enjoy the relaxed environment.

Snoopy's Hot Dogs & More, 1931 Wake Forest Rd., Raleigh; (919) 833-0992; 600 Hillsborough St., Raleigh; (919) 839-2176; 3600 Hillsborough St., Raleigh; (919) 755-9022; 2431 Spring Forest Rd., Unit 161, Raleigh; (919) 876-3775; 82-101 Glen Rd., Garner; (919) 779-2545; American/Hot Dogs; $. The "original" Snoopy's opened in Raleigh in 1978 in a converted gas station and has since grown to multiple locations with a large following of dedicated and loyal fans. Customers line up for hot dogs and hamburgers, served Eastern Carolina style with mustard, onion, chili, nestled inside steamed buns. An order of hot fries is a must to round out the meal. The menu has grown over the years and now includes a popular homemade chicken salad, scratch-made vegetable soup, deli sandwiches, salads, wings, subs, and desserts. Snoopy's opens daily at 10:30 a.m. and offers late-night closing hours at all downtown locations. On Tuesdays, Snoopy's famous hot dogs are only 99 cents. Service is fast and efficient, and your meal is always served with a smile!

Spize Cafe, 121 Fayetteville St., Raleigh; (919) 828-5000; spizecafe.com; Asian Fusion/Thai; $. A bright, modern spot with an unassuming storefront in downtown Raleigh, Spize Cafe serves Pan-Asian soups, salads, sandwiches, and rice plates influenced by Thai and Vietnamese cuisines. The Vietnamese *banh mi* sandwich comes with your choice of filling, but the lemongrass pork with honey mayo or the cumin chicken with sweet chile mayo are among the most popular. Sandwiched inside a fresh, crispy baguette and topped with the traditional strips of pickled carrot and daikon, jalapeño, and cilantro, this is perfect for a lunch on the go. Other gems include the Thai basil red curry with your choice of chicken, tofu, or shrimp or grilled jumbo prawns with cilantro and crispy garlic. All rice dishes are served with fragrant jasmine rice and seasonal vegetables or fresh Asian salad greens. You can indicate the level of heat, but be warned that when you ask for hot, it is Thai hot. Counter service is friendly and efficient and prices reasonable. Open 11 a.m. to 7 p.m., Mon through Sat.

The Square Rabbit, 19 E. Martin St., Raleigh; (919) 829-9223; squarerabbit.com; American/Sandwiches; $. Situated on the corner of Martin and Wilmington Streets since 1991, this quaint, counter-service-only cafe features a menu of fresh salads, soup, sandwiches, quiches, and savory entrees. The lunch menu changes daily with specials like chicken paprikash (sautéed chicken breast in a tomato-paprika-onion cream sauce on a bed of poppyseed noodles) or roasted vegetable salad with mixed greens topped with roasted vegetables and goat cheese with balsamic vinaigrette. The Take-n-Bake option is a delightful way to put a delicious and nutritious meal on the dinner table without having to slave over the stove after a long day at work. The Parmesan herb stuffed mushrooms with rice and asparagus, white-bean cassoulet, or chicken française with lemon and Parmesan over spaghetti will have the family singing your praises. Lunch specials and weekly Take-n-Bake options are posted daily on their website. The cafe is open Mon through Fri 9 a.m. to 6 p.m. and Sat 9 a.m. to 3 p.m.

State Farmer's Market Restaurant, 1240 Farmer's Dr., Raleigh; (919) 755-1550; realbiscuits.com; American; $. The State Farmer's Market restaurant offers delicious down home–style meals made with the best of the market's fare. As the website name suggests, the restaurant specializes in biscuit making. They use NC flour, buttermilk, and a "lil secret" that makes their biscuits flaky, buttery, and incredibly tasty. You can also get breakfast all day, or try one of their "meat and 3" daily specials, which come with two vegetable sides and a dessert. For a real indulgence, probably best shared, try the Granny Cone's Sampler; two eggs any style, bacon, sausage, North Carolina country ham, sausage gravy, spiced apples, three silver dollar hotcakes, home fries or grits, and toast or biscuits. There is a tractor on display outside (you can climb on it and take a picture if you like!). Inside is full of farming and "country life" decor and a mural depicting life in the state, from the Outer Banks to the North Carolina Mountains. The State Farmer's Market Restaurant is located at the North Carolina State Farmers' Market off Lake Wheeler Road (near its intersection with I-40) in Raleigh.

Sushi Blues, 301 Glenwood Ave., Raleigh; (911) 664-8061; sushibluescafe.com; Japanese/Sushi; $$. Located in the popular Glenwood South district next to **Zely & Ritz** (p. 118), Sushi Blues serves some the best sushi and Japanese cuisine in Raleigh surrounded by a blues- and jazz-themed atmosphere. The menu is big; there are approximately 300 selections to choose from, including sushi and

sashimi combinations, noodle soups and *temaki* (cone-shaped seaweed hand rolls). Traditional items include the California roll or dynamite roll, but look for the rolls named for some of the jazz greats, like the Lena Horne (mackerel, scallions, avocado, cucumber, sesame seeds, and spicy mayo) or the Santana (tuna, salmon, yellowtail, avocado, cucumber, scallions, sesame seeds, and roe). Before heading out on the town, relax in the lounge while sipping on a wide selection of martinis, cocktails, and imported and domestic beers. Sushi Blues can get very busy on weekend nights, but the great food and music and a friendly and courteous staff make it well worth the wait.

Tasca Brava, 607 Glenwood Ave., Raleigh; (919) 828-0840; tasca brava.com; Spanish/Tapas; $$$. Tucked into an old converted house, Tasca Brava is best known for authentic Spanish tapas, entrees, and wines. The atmosphere is intimate and inviting, with tiny cafe tables snugly arranged in the two small dining rooms and bay windows that offer a romantic setting for a special occasion. To start, choose from a large selection of tapas, such as Ceviche Bucanero (fresh fish and shrimp marinated in spicy citrus juices) or the *pulpo a la gallega* (thinly sliced boiled octopus and goat cheese mashed potatoes sprinkled with smoked paprika and Spanish olive oil). The *paella valenciana*, made for a minimum of two people, though it could easily feed more, arrives studded with your choice of chorizo, pork, chicken, or rabbit and an array of fresh seafood. The flavors are superbly well balanced, and it is evident that Chef-Owner Juan Sampler's passionate personality becomes an extension of his dishes. Wines are a must with dinner, and great care has been taken in the selections available. Be sure to ask for a recommendation; Juan has a great knowledge of the wines and always suggests a good choice. Nothing is rushed here, as it is usually only Juan and one other server, so plan to spend a few hours enjoying what is sure to be a delightful and memorable experience.

Tyler's Taproom, 18 Seaboard Ave., Raleigh; (919) 322-0906; 1483 Beaver Creek Commons Dr., Apex; (919) 355-1380; tylers taproom.com/restaurants; Pub; $. See write-up in the Chapel Hill chapter, p. 237.

Udupi, 590 E. Chatham St., Cary; (919) 465-0898; sriudupi.com; Indian; $. This hard-to-find Indian restaurant is known to diners throughout the Triangle for its extensive vegetarian-only menu and daily lunch buffet. Meat eaters are even seduced by the wide range of flavors, textures, and ingredients. Curries like the *palak paneer* or the vegetable korma with garden fresh vegetables cooked with spices and coconut milk are well seasoned, and the *dopai,* thin rice crepes, are a popular choice. Try the chef's special *uthappam,* an Indian-style pancake topped with tomatoes and peas, and finish with the *rasmala* for dessert (cheese balls soaked in condensed milk with rosewater and garnished with pistachio nuts).

Vinos Finos y Picadas Wine Bar, 8450 Honeycutt Rd., Ste. 110, Raleigh; (919) 747-9233; vinosfinosypicadas.com; Tapas; $$. A South American wine bar with over 350 wines to select from and servers in the know to assist you with your choice of vino! A menu of tapas is available to accompany your wine choice and features small plates meant for sharing, like meat and cheese platters, savory empanadas, and grilled crostini. While Vinos Finos is known for its wine, there is also a great selection of beer, too. Check the website for wine tastings, ladies' night, and other community events.

Vivace, 4209 Lassiter Mill Rd., #115, Raleigh; (919) 787-7747; vivaceraleigh.com; Italian; $$. Tucked into the corner of an upscale shopping mall, Vivace is one of Raleigh's best-loved contemporary Italian trattorias. With a lively bar, warm, inviting decor, and impressive umbrella-covered patio, it can be either a casual spot for dinner or a destination for a romantic evening out. Start with the *calamari fritti* with strips of red pepper, basil, and lemon peel, and served with a spicy tomato aioli; move on to the pan-seared salmon with notes of fennel and rosemary, expertly executed, offering a crispy exterior and moist center. The wood-grilled hanger steak and house-made pastas are also great choices, as are the brick-oven pizzas. The pies have a rustic, crisp crust with some unique toppings—try the braised short rib with garlic tomato puree, cipollini onions, and cherry peppers, or the four cheese with caramelized onions and portobello mushrooms. The staff is friendly, knowledgeable, and always happy to suggest a wine pairing from the exclusively Italian wine list. Don't overlook the specialty cocktails;

they are all constructed using house-made 'cellos, and the *miscela di agrume* made with orangecello, lime, soda, and pomegranate juice is especially refreshing on a warm afternoon. The restaurant also offers a gluten-free menu, a vegetarian/pescatarian menu, and an afternoon (2:30 to 5 p.m.) "intermezzo" menu. Open for lunch and dinner.

Waraji, 5910 Duraleigh Rd., Ste. 147, Raleigh; (919) 783-1883; warajirestaurant.com; Japanesse/Sushi; $$$. Located just off Glenwood Avenue, Waraji is considered by many Triangle residents as having the best—and freshest—sushi in the area and fantastic specialty rolls. On the menu are the traditional Japanese dishes such as udon, tempura, miso soup, yakitori, and seaweed salad, or more interesting items like shabushabu, a Japanese-style fondue where thinly sliced beef and vegetables are cooked in broth tableside. Waraji has an extensive specialty sake selection as well as a variety of Japanese microbrewery beers. Open for lunch and dinner daily.

Weinberg's The Delicatessen, 6016 Falls of Neuse Rd., Raleigh; (919) 621-4271; weinbergsthedeli.com; American/Deli; $$. Tucked into the corner of a North Raleigh strip mall, Weinberg's is a bright, lively, and family-friendly deli with table service and carryout, deli counter, and bakery case. Much of the menu is made in-house, including a stellar corned beef that can be ordered on its own as a sandwich, topped on a burger, or in the brunch hash platter. Several other deli-style sandwiches are available, including a hot pastrami sandwich that is moist and perfectly seasoned. All sandwiches come on your choice of nine different types of bread with a side of potato chips. Traditional whitefish or chopped liver, both rich in flavor, creamy, and delicious, are must tries as are the cabbage rolls, stuffed with ground meat and rice and served in a sweet-and-sour tomato sauce with mashed potatoes. Homemade soups are excellent, and the combination option with light and airy matzo balls and fried meat-filled dumplings called kreplach is a meal in itself. The menu also includes salads, burgers, specialty sandwiches, and several blue-plate specials. Desserts are homemade and include a variety of cookies, rugalach, filled croissants, and mini Danishes in rotating flavors. Absolutely do not forgo a piece of the cheese pie. Similar in flavor to cheesecake, except the filling is much creamier with the addition of sweetened sour cream, this is a true and honest cheese pie. Weinberg's is open seven days a week.

Wilmoore Cafe, 223 S. Wilmington St., Raleigh; (919) 424-7422; wilmoorecafe.com; American/Sandwiches; $. Located in the heart of downtown, Wilmoore Cafe offers a serene and inviting environment enhanced by exposed brick walls, hardwood floors, and cozy banquette-lined wall. They offer superb coffee and quality sandwiches and salads that draw local business professionals throughout the day. A small but satisfying breakfast menu is offered daily until

10 a.m., but it's the lunch menu that is the true gem. The lunch menu is made up of soups, salads, and sandwiches, or a combination of any two. Vegetarians will delight in the "PLT," where soy-glazed portobello mushrooms replace the requisite bacon on the classic BLT. The pork *banh mi,* a traditional Vietnamese sandwich on a toasted baguette, is a carnivore's dream, filled with house-roasted pork, pickled Asian radish, carrots, cilantro, and jalapeños with a spicy mayo. Wilmoore Cafe is open Mon through Sat.

Winston's Grille, 6401 Falls of the Neuse Rd., Raleigh; (919) 790-0700; winstonsgrille.com; American/Steak House; $$. Locally owned and operated, Winston's Grille has been a Raleigh landmark for 23 years, a testament to the loyal patrons who come back again and again. Dark wood tables and neutral colored walls lend a casual and comfortable atmosphere with an upscale vibe conducive to a fine-dining experience. The menu offers guests a solid list of appetizers, salads, sandwiches, entrees, and desserts, but it's the steaks, prime rib, fish, and baby back ribs that are the real hit. The filet mignon is wrapped in sweet applewood-smoked bacon and flame grilled to your liking, baby back ribs are house smoked until falling off the bone, salmon arrives encrusted in a crunchy coating of chopped cashews, and the aged prime rib, served only after 5 p.m., is slow roasted until fork tender. To further enjoy your meal, choose where to sit:

A beautiful outside patio, spanning three sides of the restaurant is the ultimate in alfresco dinning during the warmer months, or enjoy the sights, sounds, and smells of the kitchen and dine at one of 11 bar stools at the grill. Winston's is open for dinner nightly, lunch Mon through Fri, and brunch is offered Sun. The restaurant can get crowded, so I would recommend calling ahead for a reservation.

Zely & Ritz, 301 Glenwood Ave., Raleigh; (919) 828-0018; zelyand ritz.com; Middle Eastern/Vegetarian; $$$. In the Glenwood South district of downtown Raleigh, Chef-Owner Sarig Agasi creates globally influenced cuisine using locally sourced and organic ingredients, while his wife Nancy Agasi manages the wine program. Having a partnership with Coon Rock Farm, a sustainable family farm in Hillsborough, NC, means not only are they provided fresh seasonal meats, eggs, and produce from their own farm, they also support and purchase from 50 other farms. The atmosphere is casual upscale with colorful decor and art-lined walls, the perfect backdrop for enjoying a casual dinner date or celebrating a special occasion. For starters, try Chef Sarig's hummus and pickles, with olives, hot sauce, and pita bread, or the wonderfully fresh tuna carpaccio with baby arugula, cilantro, and tangerine. Entrees are exceptionally prepared and range from pan-seared mahimahi and local 100 percent grass-fed beef tenderloin to roasted Coon Rock Farm heritage chicken and fabulous sweet potato gnocchi with caramelized butternut squash, glazed carrots, and tatsoi, finished with local honey. Weekly specials include half-price bottles of wine on Monday and $5 martinis on Thursday. A monthly wine lunch is offered on the third Friday, and at $15, books up quickly.

Landmarks

Angus Barn, 9401 Glenwood Ave., Raleigh; (919) 781-2444; angusbarn.com; American/Steak House; $$$. The Angus Barn, affectionately referred to as "Big Red" because it is housed in a large red barn, is Raleigh's go-to destination restaurant for birthday, anniversary, graduation, and special occasion dinners. Enjoy the complimentary cheese and relish tables located throughout the restaurant before dining on in-house wet-aged beef, perfectly prepared to your liking. From a mouth-watering chateaubriand and slow-cooked fall-off-the-bone ribs to crab cakes and the *Iron Chef*–winning ostrich satay, Walter Royal has made a name for himself as one of the most respected and highly acclaimed executive chefs in the Triangle. Be sure to leave room for a piece of the sawdust pie—their version of the classic pecan pie that is truly a decadent experience. The expansive restaurant seats 550, includes a small country store, 25,000-plus-bottle wine cellar, private wine cellar dining rooms, and the famous Wild Turkey Lounge, named for the more than 600 Wild Turkey decanters found throughout the lounge. Angus Barn is owned and operated by Van Eure, daughter of original owner Thad Eure, and her commitment to customer service is unparalleled. She, along with her "Angus Barn family," believes each guest is a privilege, one to be honored. In her own words, "I may own the Barn but the customer is the true boss." For a unique dining experience make reservations at the Captain's Table, where you and three other guests will enjoy a 4-course meal nestled in the wine cellar kitchen, or get a firsthand look into the Angus Barn kitchen at the Chefs Table, a private table for two where you can enjoy the sights, sounds, and smells and get a behind-the-scenes look into the Angus Barn kitchen. Or make a reservation for the yearly Titanic dinner—a "re-creation of the last dinner aboard the ill-fated liner." The Pavilion, located in the wooded area behind the barn, is a striking lakeside location for weddings, receptions, and corporate events. Cooking classes as well as holiday and themed dinners dot the events calendar and are well worth the splurge.

Big Ed's City Market, 220 Wolfe St., Raleigh; (919) 836-9909; Breakfast/Southern; $. With walls heavily adorned with old farm equipment, pictures of politicians who have dined here, and bric-a-brac hanging from the ceilings, this Raleigh institution offers classic Southern country cooking at its best. Big Ed (yes, he's real) is known for his legendary scratch-made biscuits that are light, fluffy, and positively decadent, smeared with a generous portion of butter or jam—or both. Tables are covered with checkered table-cloths and provide the perfect backdrop for Southern breakfast

favorites like country ham served with grits and a red-eye gravy that is thick and full of finely ground seasoned sausage, or large pancakes that are light and airy with crispy edges. If you're feeling adventurous, try the brains and eggs. Yes, it is on the menu, and no, I have not tried them.

42nd Street Oyster Bar, 508 W. Jones St., Raleigh; (919) 831-2811; 42ndstoysterbar.com; Seafood; $$$. Opened in 1931 as a grocery store serving oysters, this landmark restaurant has been delighting diners for eight decades. The list of oysters is impressive and includes a selection from all over the country. The Kumamoto from Washington State offers a sweet flavor with a hint of honeydew melon finish that's love at first slurp. An extensive seafood selection is available along with fresh pastas and steaks so that there is something for everyone to enjoy. The Cioppino, the San Francisco Bay area's famous tomato-based Italian-style seafood stew, is brimming with delicious shrimp, scallops, white fish, peppers, and onions, and is a seafood lover's dream come true. For the steak lover, options include rib eye, filet, and New York strip; for a real treat add a lobster tail or snow crab legs and make it a surf and turf. A good selection of wines is available and make sure to leave room for dessert.

The Irregardless Cafe, 901 W. Morgan St., Raleigh; (919) 833-8898; irregardless.com; American/Vegetarian; $$. Irregardless was "green" before it was cool—they've been serving up traditional American cuisine with an emphasis on local farmers' produce and vegetarian meals since opening in 1975. The colorful atmosphere is comfortable and relaxed, making it the perfect backdrop for Chef-Owner Arthur Gordan's fun and creative dishes. Irregardless is known for its vegetarian and vegan choices, although there is plenty for meat lovers, too. For vegetarians and vegans, you can't

beat the Vegan Sex appetizer, a quivering tower of colorful, delicious veggies, quinoa tabouli, and mashed sweet potato. Salads are always fresh and delicious and come with your choice of dressing, but the lemon tahini is excellent and most people's favorite. Omnivores should try their amazing paella, offered Friday and Saturday nights only, so you will want to plan for this one. There are plenty of gluten-free options on the menu as well. Save room—the desserts are to die for! A favorite is the Track Side pie, a chess pie with coconut, pecans, and chocolate chips. Live music, from jazz and acoustic singer-songwriter to bluegrass, plays in the background most nights and for Sunday brunch; a dance band takes the floor Saturday night.

Mecca, 13 E. Martin St., Raleigh; (919) 832-5714; American; $. The vintage cash register at the front of the restaurant is a true testament to the longevity of this downtown restaurant that started off 80 years ago as a simple lunch counter. Opened in 1930 by Nick Dombalis, then run by his son John and wife Floye starting in the '50s, it is now operated by a third generation, Paul Dombalis.

Although father John is no longer alive, Floye is still likely to greet you with a smiling face when you walk through the door. The motto here is "He Profits Most Who Serves the Best," and classic breakfast, lunch, and dinner options attest to this. The clam chowder is creamy and chock-full of clams, and the glorified jumbo burger served on a sesame bun with lettuce, a savory sauce, sliced onion, and a kosher dill slice is well seasoned and charbroiled to perfection. Mecca is open Mon through Thurs 7:30 a.m. to midnight and Fri through Sat 7:30 a.m. to 2 a.m.

The Roast Grill, 7 S. West St., Raleigh; (919) 832-8292; roastgrill .com; American/Hot Dogs; $. A Raleigh landmark since 1940, The Roast Grill is known for one thing: hot dogs. Don't be put off by the lack of menus, limited options, and limited toppings, just follow the three simple rules to ordering: Choose a topping, drink, and degree of burn. Don't expect ketchup, kraut, mayo, fries, chips, or other thrills from the grill. Options are mustard, chili, onions, or slaw; that's it. Are you in the mood for some competitive eating? The Roast Grill was featured on *Man v. Food,* where host Adam Richman took the title for most hot dogs eaten when he ate 17 at one sitting. Since then the record has reached 24 hot dogs. Are you up for the challenge?

Shorty's Famous Hotdogs, 214 S. White St., Wake Forest; (919) 556-8026; American/Hot Dogs; $. This family-owned business has kept locals coming back since it opened in 1916. The traditional red, Jesse Jones–style hot dogs come grilled and sandwiched inside a soft steamed bun and topped with your choice of mustard, onion, relish, chili, or slaw. I am a minimalist when it comes to hot dogs and prefer just mustard and onions, but I recommend the addition of chili for a more traditional approach. Don't be surprised to see a line out the door and folks walking out with a bag full of dogs to bring home to an excited and expectant crowd.

Barbecue

Clyde Cooper's Barbeque, 109 E. Davie St., Raleigh; (919) 832-7614; clydecoopersbbq.com; $. Since 1938, Cooper's has been offering Carolina-style barbecue with Southern hospitality to loyal locals and visitors alike. Chopped or sliced pork barbecue, barbecued, fried, or chopped chicken, and hearty ribs are the staples here. Pair them with a number of traditional sides, including collard greens, corn, butter beans, or boiled potatoes and a basket of hush puppies and you know you've found a little slice of heaven. The Brunswick stew is also fantastic; studded with vegetables, shredded chicken, and simmered in a rich flavorful broth, it is comfort food at its finest. Portions are generous and prices reasonable, making it easy to understand why this tiny storefront has garnered such a loyal following. Takeout is always available, and Cooper's offers buffet and catering options for your next business meeting or special event.

Danny's Bar-B-Que, 9561 Chapel Hill Rd., Morrisville; (919) 468-3995; 311 Ashville Ave., #G, Cary; (919) 851-5541. See write-up in the Durham chapter, p. 199.

Ole Time Barbecue, 6309 Hillsborough St., Raleigh; (919) 859-2544; oletimebarbecue.com; $. For 15-plus years, this tiny yellow barbecue joint has been dishing up Southern country classics for breakfast, lunch, and dinner. Start your day with a breakfast sandwich, pancakes, or the country breakfast plate; two eggs, grits, or hash browns, and choice of meat with a fluffy buttermilk biscuit. Breakfast is served 6 to 10 a.m. Monday through Saturday. Lunch and dinner feature Eastern-style barbecue sandwiches and plates, burgers, fried and grilled chicken, ribs, and combination dinners. For a satisfying meal, order the pulled-pork combination platter. The vinegar-based pulled pork is moist and delicious and comes with two sides and hush puppies. Sides range from fried okra, collards, and coleslaw to mac-n-cheese, baked beans, and boiled potatoes. Don't leave without getting some banana pudding to go, and while you're at it, purchase a bag of their hush puppy mix or bottled barbecue sauce to relive the experience at home. Ole Time closes at 8 p.m. Mon through Thurs and 9 p.m. Fri and Sat. Closed Sun.

The Pit, 328 W. Davie St., Raleigh; (919) 890-4500; thepit-raleigh
.com; $$. This contemporary Southern restaurant located in a
renovated 1930s meatpacking warehouse in downtown Raleigh
specializes in serving authentic whole-hog pit-cooked barbecue,
served chopped or pulled. The Pit takes enormous pride in using
only free-range, locally raised pigs for their BBQ and sourcing the
freshest local produce available. To start, treat yourself to fried
green tomatoes, pumpkin skillet cornbread with maple
butter, or the amazing barbecue fries—hand-cut
fries with melted pimiento cheese, chopped 'cue,
chives, and BBQ ranch dressing. The Pit also serves
Texas-style brisket, ribs, smoked turkey, crispy
golden Southern fried chicken, and for the
vegetarian, a surprisingly delicious barbecue
tofu. Sides range from coleslaw, mac and cheese,
or collard greens to fried okra, BBQ baked beans, and cheesy
bacon grits that are truly out of this world. Your barbecue experi-
ence doesn't just stop at the food in this upscale barbecue restau-
rant—great care has been taken to add a solid North Carolina draft
beer lineup and inexpensive wines, as well an excellent selection of
small-batch bourbons that expertly enhance the smoky flavor of the
pork. Of course no Southern meal is complete without dessert, and
you won't want to leave before delving into the decadent banana
pudding: creamy vanilla pudding layered with bananas, wafers,
marshmallow fluff, and meringue. The Pit is open daily for lunch
and dinner, and the bar is a perfect gathering spot for after-work
drinks and appetizers.

Smokey's BBQ Shack, 10800 Chapel Hill Rd., Morrisville; (919) 469-1724; smokeysshack.com; $. Smokey's BBQ Shack is a gem—excellent smoked meat in great quantities at a very reasonable price, with a down-home atmosphere. You can order pulled pork, brisket, chicken (pulled and wings), and ribs. The meats are not sauced, but they provide two sauces on the table: one is a thin vinegar and red pepper sauce (in the vein of an Eastern NC–style barbecue sauce), and one is a thicker, tomato based sauce (similar to a Western NC–style barbecue sauce). No fights please! The vegetables are mostly standard fare: french fries, fried okra, and green beans, but the macaroni and cheese is always a hit, with adults and kids alike! The casual atmosphere is typical of a barbecue restaurant, where the staff is very friendly and treats regulars like family, and the "picnic" area out back with tables, lots of wooded space for kids to run, and a tiny pond really sets the scene. You can't miss the ever-present woodpile beside the restaurant, hinting at the reason Smokey's 'cue is so delicious—it's cooked right there on-site with wood. Very busy Mon through Fri from 11:30 a.m. to 2 p.m. due to the popularity of the restaurant with the nearby RTP office crowds.

Brewpubs & Microbreweries

Aviator Brewing Tap House/Aviator Brewing Smokehouse, Tap House: 600 E. Broad St., Fuquay-Varina; (919) 567-2337; Smokehouse: 525 E. Broad St., Fuquay-Varina; (919) 557-PORK

(7675); aviatorbrew.com; Brewery; $. Aviator Brewing brings you terrific, award-winning craft beer and delicious food, all in quaint downtown Fuquay-Varina, a short drive from both Raleigh and Cary. At the Tap House look for all Aviator brews on tap all the time. Make sure to try the Black Mamba Oatmeal Stout, one of the local beer lovers' favorites—creamy body and hints of chocolate and coffee make it one of the best stouts in the area. At the Smokehouse, burger buns and all the desserts are made with beer! And not only are the smoked meats fantastic, but you get your choice of two sides or one beer with your smoked meat entree. The portobello and mushroom veggie burger is even marinated in beer. The Tap House is located in the old Varina train depot—very cool. The lower left side of the building is the old Varina telegraph office and now houses a pool table. They also have Wii games for the young (or young at heart) and a large patio out back for cigar smoking. The Aviator is kid-friendly on weekend afternoons. The Smokehouse, located directly across the street from the Tap House, offers a large, casual, open space that is definitely kid-friendly. This is a definite must-visit for any beer enthusiast.

Big Boss Brewing Co., 1249 Wicker Dr., Raleigh; (919) 834-0045; Brewery. On the outskirts of Raleigh in an industrial warehouse area off Capital Boulevard is Big Boss Brewing Co. Its brews are sold at bars and stores all over the Triangle, or you can visit Horniblow's, the on-site tavern, to enjoy a pint. The taproom is open 6 days a week and offers a game room with darts, Ping-Pong, and pool, as well as picnic tables outside. The brewery currently produces five year-round brews: Angry Angel, Helle's Bells, Blanco Diablo, Bad Penny, and High Roller, and several seasonal brews. On the second Saturday of each month, the brewery offers a free tour of the facility where you will learn about Big Boss's beer-making process. Afterwards, enjoy samples of its stellar brews and purchase a T-shirt or hat to take home as a souvenir. The tours are very popular and result in long lines, but it is well worth it to see firsthand where the magic happens.

Boylan Bridge Brewpub, 201 S. Boylan Ave., Raleigh; (919) 803-8927; boylanbridge.com; Brewery/Brewpub; $. With a bright and open atmosphere and a brewery on-site, Boylan Bridge offers casual dining inside and an expansive view of the Raleigh skyline from a large patio outside. The brewery makes a variety of year-round and seasonal brews, many named using railroad terms to salute the railway tracks the brewery sits beside—Gantlet Golden Ale, Pullman Porter, Southbound Stout, and Hopped Off the Tracks IPA. The food here is typical American, with onion rings and fries, burgers, salads, and sandwiches. The brewpub is open seven days a week.

Foundation, 213 Fayetteville St., Raleigh; (919) 896-6016; founda tionnc.com; Cocktail Lounge; $$. With only an unassuming neon sign, this intimate little underground bar with sidewalk patio on Fayetteville Street offers creative cocktails, spirits, mead, and a small but solid selection of local beers in a cozy and comfortable atmosphere. Handcrafted cocktails inspired by the seasons, are expertly made by knowledgeable and passionate mixologists using only the freshest ingredients and house-made mixers. Several intriguing concoctions warrant repeat visits, including the Southern 77, a combination of moonshine, sparkling wine, simple syrup, and lime, or the Farmer Collins, a twist on the classic, using gin, market jam, and house-made soda. No food is available, making this the perfect pre- or post-dinner destination; a onetime $1 membership fee can be purchased online or at the bar.

Fox Liquor Bar, 237 S. Wilmington St., Raleigh; (919) 322-0128; ac-restaurants.com; Cocktail Lounge; $$. For a selection of unique cocktails, walk down the flight of stairs to Fox Liquor Bar for an experience you won't soon forget. A custom bar, comfy couches, and intimate lighting set the scene to enjoy the seasonally inspired cocktail menu designed by owner Ashley Christensen and New York cocktail guru Karin Stanley. The menu offers classic cocktails like the Tom Collins, Dark and Stormy, or Old Fashioned to more contemporary creations like a Wonka Fizz, made with aged rum, lemon juice, sugar, a whole egg, Fee's chocolate bitters, and soda water. Drinks are made using fresh-squeezed juices and house-made sodas and are served in the appropriate glassware with various shaped pieces of ice to enhance the overall experience. All drinks are $11 and include tax. A small but thoughtful wine and beer menu is available as is an excellent selection of cheeses, meats, and small snack items like the *boquerones,* marinated white anchovy fillets with white wine vinegar, lemon zest, and olive oil. Fox Liquor Bar is open every day from 4 p.m. to 2 a.m.

LoneRider Brewing Company, 8816 Gulf Ct., #100, Raleigh; (919) 442-8004; loneriderbeer.com; Brewery. Tucked away in a warehouse, LoneRider is a local brewery that consistently puts out some of the Triangle's best locally made "Ales for Outlaws." The brewery makes several different beers, including the Peacemaker, American Pale Ale, Sweet Josie, Brown Ale, and the popular Shotgun Betty, a refreshing Hefeweizen with notes of banana and clove. Deadeye Jack, the seasonal porter with hints of roasted chocolate, recently won the silver medal at the Great American Beer Festival. To enjoy LoneRider beers, visit the tasting room on Thursday, Friday, or Saturday where you can sip a delicious pint while enjoying a game of cornhole or pick up a growler to take home. You can also find them on tap at various bars and restaurants and in your local grocery store. If you are an avid home brewer, LoneRider also hosts an annual event called "Brew It Forward," where locals can compete to have their beer selected to be brewed by LoneRider for a limited time.

Natty Greene's, 505 W. Jones St., Raleigh; (919) 232-2477; natty greenes.com; Brewery/Brewpub; $. With vaulted ceilings, exposed brick, and an industrial warehouse feel, Natty Greene's has fast become downtown Raleigh's favorite brewpub. The three main rooms offer a War of Independence–themed dining room, large pub area with several TVs, or Game bar, featuring darts, pool table, and shuffleboard. The brewery produces 12 handcrafted beers including five year-round offerings—Guilford Golden Ale, Buckshot Amber Ale, Southern Pale Ale, Old Town Brown, and Wildflower Witbier. You can try all five by ordering the sampler, and if you find a personal favorite, you can take it home in a growler. Pub fare ranges from appetizers and salads to burgers, sandwiches, and signature "Greene Plates" like the McGee's Fish-and-Chips, Carolina catfish lightly breaded and fried, served with spicy remoulade, house-made coleslaw, and fresh-made potato chips. Start with the popular mesquite fries—a delicious pile of fries covered in homemade cheese sauce, applewood-smoked bacon, and scallions, or delve into the Jones Street Philly, grilled chicken breast, green and red peppers, mushrooms, and onions smothered in a roasted garlic aioli and topped with swiss cheese. Overall, the menu is expansive with plenty of options for everyone to enjoy.

Roth Brewing Company, 5907 Triangle Dr., Raleigh; (919) 782-2099; rothbrewing.com; Brewery. Tucked in back of an industrial park through a maze of warehouses is Roth Brewing Company. The relaxed and cozy taproom consists of a small bar with a few bar stools and a couple of couches where you can enjoy their flagship Raleigh Red, a medium-bodied amber that provides a distinct crisp, hoppy finish, or any one of their other tasty brews. Brewery tours run at 5, 7, and 9 p.m., every Thurs, Fri, and Sat by a staff that is welcoming and enthusiastic and eager to answer any questions you might have.

Specialty Stores, Markets & Producers

American Brewmaster, 3021-5 Stony Brook Dr., Raleigh; (919) 850-0095; americanbrewmaster.com. A home-brewing supply store in a strip mall near Capital Boulevard in North Raleigh, this small shop offers an excellent selection of grains, specialty malts, and yeasts on-site to all beginner or experienced home brewers. The store is well organized, and the quality of product is guaranteed by the owners. The experienced and knowledgeable employees, most of whom home-brew themselves, can and will answer all questions, regardless of what level of brewer you are. Not only are they the Triangle's go-to home-brew shop, they also have a good selection of winemaking equipment and supplies as well as a limited amount of cheesemaking supplies and information. Weekends are usually very busy; go during the week if possible.

Antonio's Gourmet Market, 8460 Honeycutt Rd., Ste. 112, Raleigh; (919) 887-6310; antoniosgourmetmarket.com. In Lafayette Village in North Raleigh, Chef Antonio Saladino offers his customers a continuous selection of gourmet prepared foods, fresh produce, meats, and fresh seafoods in a small store that appears to have everything you need. Antonio's offers a catering menu as well, plus twice-monthly cooking classes. Check out the website for details and various menus. Great things come in small packages!

Crumb, (919) 413-8134; justcrumb.com. The "Crumb-bots," as I lovingly refer to them, are Carrie Nickerson and David Menestres, two of the most sought after bakers in the Triangle. Although they do not have a brick and mortar location, the fabulous cakes that make their way out of the tiny kitchen they work from will leave you begging for more. With a passion for using local and artisan ingredients like **Escazu Chocolates** (see below) or **Big Boss Beer** (p. 128), they offer not only cakes but muffins, pies, bagels, and much more. You can place an order via their website, find their treats at local coffee shops, or look for them at the **Saturday Market** at Rebus Works (p. 36) and various special events around town.

Escazu Artisan Chocolates, 936 N. Blount St., Raleigh; (919) 832-3433; escazuchocolates.com. Located in Raleigh next to **Market Restaurant** (p. 91), Escazu Artisan Chocolates is a handcrafted "bean to bar" operation. Owner Hallot Parson and Chocolatier Daniel Centeno source only the highest quality product and sort and roast everything on-site in their small shop to create what is some of the best chocolate in the state and in the country. Chocolates are available in bar form and small confections. Personal favorites include the Good Food Awards–winning Dark Goat's Milk, Dark Chocolate with Pumpkinseed and Guajillo Chili, the Beaufort Bar with Sea Salt, and 81 percent Carenero Venezuela Dark Chocolate bar. But it doesn't end there. The small confections peeking out from behind a glass case are so artfully and beautifully decorated, they could easily be hung in a gallery. Flavors vary, but look for chocolates made with fruits, spirits, herbs, nuts, and spices. And as if chocolate in solid form weren't enough, Escazu makes the most decadent hot chocolates, even going as far as to re-create historical recipes. It is not uncommon to see several people at the hot chocolate bar, savoring their cup as if it were the nectar of the gods. You can find Escazu Chocolates at most specialty stores around the Triangle, or order online from their website. Open Tues through Sun.

Goodberry's Frozen Custard, 9850 Leesville Rd., Raleigh; (919) 847-0453; 2042 Clark Ave., Raleigh; (919) 833-9998; 2421 Spring Forest Rd., Raleigh; (919) 878-8159; 9700 Strickland Rd., Raleigh; (919) 676-8580; 2325 Davis Dr., Cary; (919) 469-3350; 1146 Kildaire Farm, Cary; (919) 467-2386; 3906 N. Roxboro St., Durham; (919) 477-2552; 1407 Garner Station Blvd., Garner; (919) 772-0205; 11736 Retail Dr., Wake Forest; (919) 554-2875; goodberrys.com. There is no doubt that Goodberry's Frozen Custards are a step above regular ice cream. The rich custards are made using fresh heavy cream, whole milk, natural cane sugar, and eggs, the eggs providing that extra creamy texture. A new batch is made every hour, ensuring you are only getting the freshest quality product. Chocolate and vanilla and a daily rotating special mean there is always a surprise in store. On any given day you may find maple almond and pistachio to mint chocolate chip or raspberry. To keep up with your favorites, a schedule of flavors can be found on their website. Hugely popular is the "Carolina Concrete," a blend of your choice of fruits, nuts, or flavorings, mixed into the vanilla, chocolate, or specialty custard of the day. It is so rich

Moravian Spice Cookies

Several specialty shops in the Triangle sell these spice and molasses wafer-thin cookies—you can even purchase them at the Raleigh/Durham International Airport in the Southern Season Gift Shop. The cookies originated in the communities of the Moravian Church, whose followers settled in North Carolina over 200 years ago to escape religious persecution in their homeland, bringing with them the recipe that bears their name. Originally handmade for the Christmas season, they are now machine-made to meet the high demand. Most often these cookies are bought and served at Christmas, especially in Winston-Salem, NC, which is home to one of the largest Moravian communities in the United States. A tin or two of these cookies are in my pantry no matter what the season.

and thick that it is actually served to you upside down. A popular place for families, the lines can get long, so be prepared to wait.

Grand Asia Market, 1253 Buck Jones Rd., Raleigh; (919) 468-2988; grandasiamarket.com. The Grand Asia Market has been selling Asian groceries since 1977, and it is well worth a visit even if many of the items sold are labeled in a language unknown to you. Give yourself enough time to roam unhurriedly along the aisles so that you can see all that the store has to offer. Check out the fresh produce and the live seafood section as well as the specialty medicinal herbs and Asian skin-care products. At the Hong Kong–style Chanelle Cake Bakery, indulge in a freshly steamed BBQ pork bun or a mini lotus cake followed by a cup of milk tea. And right inside the entrance to Grand Asian Market is the Joy Luck Club Restaurant, where you can grab a lunch all day long that includes rice with three selections from the hot bar. Watch what other patrons are eating, especially the Asians, who just might be ordering something that you don't recognize but that is absolutely delicious. Worth noting: The bakery and restaurant are cash only.

Locopops, 1908 Hillsborough St., Raleigh; ilovelocopops.com. See write-up in the Durham chapter, p. 209.

Midtown Olive Press, The Lassiter at North Hills, Raleigh; (919) 510-5510; midtownolivepress.com. Located in an upscale shopping center in Raleigh's North Hills area, Midtown Olive Press offers guests the opportunity to taste and purchase unique balsamic vinegars and fresh olive oils as well as gourmet foods, specialty items, and skin-care products. Authentic balsamic vinegars from Modena, Italy, are aged anywhere from 12 to 18 years, while traditional white balsamic vinegars come in a range of flavors like dark chocolate, honey ginger, and fig. Gourmet oils are from all over the world and include flavors like Eureka lemon, organic basil, and roasted walnut. Inventory rotates every 6 months, so check back regularly for new flavors and varietals. Wondering how to cook or bake with such an array of oil and vinegar options? Midtown Olive Press offers several tips and recipes on their website.

Raleigh Wine Shop, 126 Glenwood Ave., Raleigh; (919) 803-5473; theraleighwineshop.com. Owners Seth, Ryan, and Jeff are buddies and wine-industry veterans who take great care in selecting wines that are ethically produced, choosing only wines that pay respect to the land, the grape, and to the finished product. The rustic yet modern space  welcomes you the moment you walk in the door, and the owners are always friendly and willing to help you find your next favorite bottle. Wines are well organized and easy to find. Special wines that are really affordable are lined up at the ends of the aisles. Upstairs is a small wine bar where you can sit and have a tasting of one or more of their featured wines on tap. The WineStation offers 1-, 2-, and 4-ounce pours. For $5, purchase a WineStation card and load it up with any dollar amount. With this you can have tastings anytime you want. If you purchase $25 or more on the card, there's no $5 fee. All bottles in the wine station are 10 percent off. If beer is your drink of choice, there is also an excellent selection of craft beers available. Locally sourced food products are also sold. Delivery is available for a small fee.

Savory Spice Shop, 8470 Honeycutt Rd. (in Lafayette Village), Raleigh; (919) 900-8291; savoryspiceshop.com. Wanting to create an outlet for their mutual passion for food and cooking, Bob and Cindy Jones opened Savory Spice Shop in North Raleigh's Lafayette Village in 2011. The store carries hundreds of different spices and spice blends, all ground fresh on a weekly basis. Recipe cards are scattered throughout the store for shoppers to get ideas on how to use them, and the staff is always full of extra ideas to pass along. The energetic, fun-loving personalities of Bob, Cindy, and their staff have built a loyal and consistently growing customer base, evident by the amount of savory dishes and delicious desserts brought in by customers raving about the success they had using the recommended spices to create them. This is a must-stop shop for any chef or home cook. Regular cooking classes fill up quickly and are always informative and fun. Although their shop is part of a small national chain, Bob and Cindy have created a warm and friendly environment that is completely their own.

Sip . . . A Wine Store, 1059 Darrington Dr., Cary; (919) 467-7880; sipawinestore.com. Located in a small strip mall in Cary, Sip offers eco-friendly wines and beverages at affordable prices in a quaint and cozy environment. Owners Josh and April Schlanger are extremely friendly and knowledgeable, which makes shopping here a delight. They happily answer questions, and their recommendations never disappoint. For a real treat, join the Wine of the Month Club where each month you will receive a selection of six bottles of eco-friendly wine for $60. Tasting notes, viticulture information, and a recipe card are also included with your selection. Wine classes are offered monthly and are a great opportunity to learn, taste, and enjoy a wine from their featured producer, wine region, or grape variety. Classes include four to five glasses of wine to taste, additional educational materials, and light snacks. The store also has a great beer selection, including some rare and hard-to-find bottles.

Durham

For decades, Durham was a city that visitors drove by on their way between the capital city Raleigh and the funky college town of Chapel Hill. Its historical roots were in tobacco, and even at the end of the 20th century, the smell of curing tobacco wafted through the air when the wind was just so. But that has all changed. Today, Durham receives over 6 million visitors a year, its downtown is revitalized mainly due to repurposed tobacco warehouses renovated into condos, art studios, radio stations, small business co-ops, and restaurants, and its food scene is recognized regularly in the national press.

The downtown area of Durham has undergone a huge revitalization in the past 10 years to become a go-to spot to eat (for example at Rue Cler, Revolution, Piedmont, Toast, Dos Perros, DaisyCakes, Scratch), gallery hop (Durham Art Guild, Gallery at Vega Metals, LabourLove Gallery, Through This Lens), shop (Brightleaf Square), work out (Downtown YWCA), see movies, plays, and concerts (the Carolina Theatre, Manbites Dog Theater), study various forms of art (Durham Arts Council, Claymakers), and dance the night away at sponsored events at the Durham Armory or skateboard at Skatepark. The permanent home of the Durham Farmers' Market anchors the core of Durham's Central Park every Wednesday seasonally in the late afternoon and Saturday morning year-round. Bring your scissors to snip herbs for free at the public herb garden adjacent to the market! And if after all the walking and shopping, you have a thirst for a craft beer, head over to Fullsteam Brewery or Triangle Brewing, just two of the microbreweries that make their brews in the downtown core. My favorite is the seasonal Basil Beer made by Fullsteam.

The arts thrive in Durham as well. It is home to the new Durham Performing Arts Center (DPAC) which in its short 4-year history is now one of the top-10 in the US for box-office sales, hosting such shows as the Radio City Music Hall Rockettes Christmas Show, *Wicked,* and Willie Nelson. Each year Durham hosts the international Full Frame Documentary Film Festival at the Carolina Theatre, where locals have the chance to volunteer to exchange time worked for tickets to view some of the best documentary films produced worldwide. If you are into dance, the Chuck Davis African American Dance Ensemble makes its home here, and the internationally acclaimed annual American Dance Festival schedule brings 6 weeks of contemporary dance performances from around the world to Durham. Musician Branford Marsalis and blues singer and songwriter Nnenna Freelon are residents of Durham and frequent performers.

The famous 1988 movie *Bull Durham,* starring Kevin Costner and Susan Sarandon, was filmed in Durham, and the mechanical bull featured in the film still snorts steam each time there is a home run for the Durham Bulls Triple-A baseball team in the Durham Athletic Park. But it is Durham's food scene that has recently garnered national attention, which in turn is making the downtown and surrounding area popular with residents and visitors alike.

Ten years ago, downtown Durham was an eclectic mix of buildings, some being repurposed, others boarded up, and others just empty shells of businesses that had moved away. It was not an area that you ventured into after dark, not because it was overly dangerous but simply because there was nowhere to go; when the few businesses that inhabited downtown closed at the end of the day, everyone went home and no one was downtown. However, at that time downtown rents were affordable, buildings were available to buy, restaurant entrepreneurs with vision moved in, and a new era for downtown Durham took hold. And over time, newcomers have discovered Durham, and new residential communities have been built beyond the city core, which have also attracted new eateries.

Today, the national press lauds Durham as a foodie destination. Durham has been ranked as the "Foodiest Small Town in America" by Andrew Knowlten of *Bon Appétit* in 2008, and our chefs and restaurants have been lauded in publications such as *Bon Appétit, Food & Wine,* and the *New York Times*. Residents and visitors with social media know-how on Twitter or Facebook can follow the food trucks to sample everything from sliders to dumplings, burgers to pizzas. Durham now rivals Raleigh and the Chapel Hill/Carrboro area as a dining destination. Durham residents are great restaurant-goers, and reservations are a must, or at least patience if you have to wait in line for a table. We love and support our local chefs and their use of "farm-to-fork," locally grown ingredients. And here in the Durham section of this *Food Lovers' Guide,* you will discover independently owned restaurants with Durham-based chefs who offer local and regional menus using farm fresh ingredients whenever possible.

Getting Around

Once in Durham, getting around with your own car is probably most convenient, but the City of Durham has also worked hard to bring public transportation to the forefront as a viable option, at least in the central downtown area. The Bull City Connector is fare-free and serves key destinations in and around Durham's central corridor, including the two Duke University campuses, the historic district, Ninth Street shopping area, and the Golden Belt studios and galleries. Buses run every 15 minutes, and you can check times and routes at **bullcityconnector.org.** Along the way, you can hop on and off to eat at one of the restaurants mentioned in this book.

The **Durham Convention & Visitors Bureau** has transit maps and schedules that you can download, as well as walking maps to some of the more popular areas. Maps for the extensive bicycle trails are also available. If you are a bicycle enthusiast, Durham has several miles of paved paths, including a number of entrances to the American Tobacco Trail, a 22-plus-mile "Rails to Trails" project that covers much of the Triangle region. To find a Wi-Fi-friendly location, download the Durham Wi-Fi Locations map. All can be discovered and downloaded at **durham-nc.com/visitors/maps.**

There is also an intercity transit system between Durham, Raleigh, and Chapel Hill. Service runs primarily on weekdays with only a few Saturday routes operable. For schedules and fares, visit **triangletransit.org.**

Foodie Faves

Alivia's Durham Bistro, 900 W. Main St., Durham; (919) 682-8978; aliviasdurhambistro.com; American; $$. A neighborhood bistro serving creative and approachable food in an environment that evokes the Art Deco movement of the 1920s, enlivened by colorful Warhol-esque celebrity-themed artwork, bold colors, and geometric shapes. Soups, salads, and sandwiches make up the bulk of the menu, but creative entrees should not be overlooked. Popular choices include peppercorn-crusted rare ahi tuna, *steak-frites,* and a fabulous pasta dish consisting of cheese-filled tortellini, mushrooms, and spinach tossed in a Parmesan cream sauce and topped with blackened chicken, grated Parmesan, and fresh herbs. Large garage doors lead to a great outdoor patio that is perfect for people-watching during the summer, while cooling down with a refreshing "grown-up" slushy.

Bali Hai Mongolian Grill, 811 Ninth St., Durham; (919) 416-0200; balihainc.com; Mongolian; $. See write-up in the Raleigh chapter, p. 65.

Beyu Caffé, 335 W. Main St., Durham; (919) 683-1058; beyucaffe .com; American/Sandwiches; $. A local hot spot that runs the gamut from early morning coffeehouse to popular lunch cafe to late night lounge, offering locally sourced menus, live jazz music, cocktails, spirits, and more. Widely accepted as a downtown location to enjoy a tasty and healthy lunch, Beyu offers an array of appetizers, pizzettes, salads, and sandwiches to satisfy the soul. I am particularly fond of the Southwestern spicy chicken salad: spicy roasted chicken piled high on top of mixed greens and tossed with chipotle ranch dressing and topped with spicy roasted pecans, black beans, tomatoes, onions, cheddar cheese, and tortilla strips. Ample seating and free Wi-Fi make it an ideal location for early morning business meetings or lunches.

Blend Cafe, 807 E. Main St., Durham; (919) 294-9465; facebook .com/blendcafegoldenbelt; American/Cafe/Sandwiches; $. Blend Cafe opened in Durham at Golden Belt in spring 2012. It offers coffee by Counter Culture in addition to breakfast and lunch options. Owner Howard Udell, who operates Yogen Früz franchises in Raleigh, stocks that line of frozen yogurt at the new shop. In addition, Courtney and Camryn Smith of Sudie's Fresh Baked Goods in Durham manage the day-to-day cooking. Expect soups, sandwiches, and other grab 'n' go options. Blend is open 7 a.m. to 7 p.m. Mon through Fri and 9 a.m. to 3 p.m. Sat. Blend is located in the newly restored, green Golden Belt—one of Durham's "repurposed" textile mills designed to house artist studios, offices, apartments, and entertainment venues.

Blu Seafood and Bar, 2002 Hillsborough Rd., Durham; (919) 286-9777; bluseafoodandbar.com; Seafood; $$. Hailing from coastal Florida, Chef-Owner Tim Lyons' menu offers Gulf Rim specialties and innovative regional classics in a setting that instantly transports you to the sunny Southern shores of Key West. The restaurant itself is bright and airy, accented by bright blues and white, evoking a sense of calm and serenity. A daily assortment of oysters is served raw on the half shell, baked, or fried, and expertly crafted seafood options include yellowfin tuna tartare, organic salmon, and diver scallops and shrimp with an Asian barbecue soy sauce, butter roasted shiitakes, and bok choy. Patio seating is a haven as is the enclosed patio. Open for lunch and dinner Mon through Sat. Closed Sun.

Broad Street Cafe, 1116 Broad St., Durham; (919) 416-9707; the broadstreetcafe.com; American/Pizza; $. This friendly and relaxed neighborhood restaurant with a wood burning pizza oven and menu of salads, sandwiches, and burgers is good for the whole family. An edamame hummus appetizer, with pecorino and homemade focaccia crostini, is a delightful lunch when paired with one of the fresh salad options, and the pizzas are perfectly sized for those with a big appetite or when shared with a friend. Creative twists on pizzas include the house-smoked chicken with basil pesto and garlic compote or the Turkish pie with ground lamb, garlic, parsley, feta, tomatoes, and kalamata olives. The full bar with a great selection of draft and bottled beer and live music calendar draws crowds.

Bull Street Gourmet & Market, Hope Valley Square, 3710 Shannon Rd., Durham; (919) 237-2398; bullstreetgourmetand market.com; American/Breakfast/Cafe; $. Once an inauspicious strip mall with the US Post Office and a laundromat garnering most of the retail space, Hope Valley Square (formerly Shannon Plaza) is quickly becoming the foodies' mall of choice, especially with the recent addition of the Bull Street Gourmet and Market, a fresh retail and restaurant concept sourcing locally. In addition to great coffee, breakfast, lunch, and dinner, owner Anne Nimenn offers such pantry staples as house-cured bacon, milk, eggs, and bread, plus boutique wines and high-gravity beer and house-made dips and spreads. The atmosphere is warm and comfortable with an old-world charm that is both classic and contemporary. Popular sandwiches include a delicious hot pastrami (a twist on the classic Reuben, it is made with goat cheese, pepper relish, and seasonal slaw), and the "Mozz," a must-try with fresh mozzarella, marinated fresh tomatoes, walnut pesto drizzled in a balsamic reduction—fresh and fabulous! Salads are refreshing, especially the "Chappy," with diced green apple, shaved red onion, toasted walnuts, and feta on romaine with a lemon poppy-seed dressing, or the "Drunken," prosciutto, drunken goat cheese, and toasted pine nuts with a balsamic reduction. And most exciting are the prepared meals-to-go for when you want to serve a home-cooked meal but don't feel like cooking. There are two choices available daily and may include dishes like crab and salmon cakes on wild rice with roasted turnips and kale or stuffed poblano peppers with farro, cheese, and cilantro with a blue-cheese fondue. Foods are fresh and locally sourced, especially from the Durham area. Other eateries in this mall include **Only Burger** (see p. 175), Tutti Fruitti, **Rick's Diner** (p. 182), and **Pop's Backdoor South** (p. 180). And while the laundromat has moved away, you can still visit the post office.

Bull McCabe's Irish Pub, 427 W. Main St., Durham; (919) 682-3061; bullmccabesirishpub.com; Pub; $$. Located in downtown Durham, Bull McCabe's Irish Pub serves lunch, dinner, and a late-night menu daily. A local favorite of the downtown community this authentic Irish pub is made cozy with the addition of an authentic wooden bar, church pews for booth seating, and a unique collection of books that line the walls. Chef John Spicer's house-cured corned beef or pastrami sandwich (the delicate peppered pastrami is a personal favorite) are raved about among guests. If it's a burger you're craving, this is your spot. There is a build-your own option, but also find out-of-the-box creations like the Carpetbagger with Cajun seasoning, bacon, mushrooms, swiss cheese, and fried oysters, the briny pop of the oysters a welcome change. Traditional Irish fare like bangers and mash, with a rich, deep brown gravy begging to be mopped up with every last bite of creamy mashed potatoes, or fish-and-chips, lightly battered and fried for a crisp exterior and a moist and delicate fish center. Wednesday night is Trivia Night at Bull McCabe's, winner of the *Independent*'s 2010 and 2011 "Best Trivia in the Triangle," and when you see the crowds gathering, the glares passing from team to team, and the competitive camaraderie, you will understand why this is the trivia haven.

Cafe Meridian, 2500 Meridian Pkwy., Ste. 130, RTP, Durham; (919) 361-9333; cafemeridian.com; American; $. Locally owned and operated by Rich and Gina Kazazian, Cafe Meridian is, like the other RTP eateries mentioned in the Durham section, open for the busy professional at lunchtime only (Mon through Fri 11 a.m. to 2 p.m.; free Wi-Fi). Its widely renowned signature dishes include poached salmon with lemon and dill, grilled vegetable frittata, and spanakopita with *tzatziki*. There is also a wide range of hot specials that change daily, creative signature sandwiches, and fresh salads made every day; everything is homemade.

C&T Wok Restaurant, 130 Morrisville Square Way, Morrisville; (919) 467-8860; ctwokrestaurant.com; Chinese; $. Located in the Morrisville Square Shopping Center, this tiny restaurant serves Szechuan and Thai dishes from two different menus. The Szechuan menu is the real draw and offers traditional dishes like stir-fried pork with peppers or the lightly battered and fried Szechuan peppercorn shrimp. You'll notice that a lot of Chinese people eat here, usually a good sign that the food is authentic. Lunch specials include some Chinese-American favorites along with some more authentic choices. Check the website for the hours as C&T Wok is open for lunch, closes, and reopens for dinner. Hours vary by day of the week.

Carolina Ale House, 3911 Chapel Hill Blvd., Durham; (919) 490-2001; 7981 Skyland Ridge Pkwy., Raleigh; (919) 957-4200; 2240 Walnut St., Cary; (919) 854-9444; 4512 Falls of Neuse Rd., Raleigh; (919) 431-0001; 512 Creekside Dr., Raleigh; (919) 835-2222; 11685 Northpark Dr., Wake Forest; (919) 556-8666; carolinaalehouse.com; American/Burgers/Pub; $$. Recognized as having "One of the Best Beer Selections in the Triangle" by Metro Bravo Award 2006 and 2007, this local, family-friendly, sports-themed restaurant chain with five Triangle locations draws large crowds come game day. Watch and cheer for your favorite team on the numerous TVs surrounding the bar area while feasting on game-day favorites like burgers, ribs, and wings. The wings are expertly seasoned with a spicy dry rub made up of several flavorful herbs and spices then baked to fall-off-the-bone perfection. The ribs are perfectly tender and messy, clearly meant to be washed down with a refreshing beer, and the choices are many. A full menu is served 11 a.m. until 2 a.m. daily.

Char-Grill, 1125 W. NC Hwy. 54, Durham; (919) 489-6900; chargrillusa.com; Burgers; $. See write-up in the Raleigh chapter, p. 74.

Chosun Ok Korean Restaurant, 2105 NC Hwy. 54 East, Durham; (919) 806-1213; chosunokkorean.com; Korean; $. Come and eat where many Koreans and their families eat. There is an extensive menu of traditional Korean dishes, many spicy enough already so that you don't need to ask for extra heat. Consider the traditional dish of spicy kimchee soup with pork and tofu, or seasoned chitterlings with vegetables, and udon noodles in spicy soup, and for the vegetarian eating out, try cold buckwheat noodles with pickled vegetables in spicy chile sauce. Come to the all-you-can-eat lunch buffet, served daily between 11 a.m. and 2:30 p.m. (prices are slightly higher for the Sat and Sun lunch buffets).

Chubby's Tacos, 2806 Miami Blvd., Durham; (919) 558-6611; 748 Ninth St., Durham; (919) 286-4499; 4711 Hope Valley Rd., Durham; (919) 489-4636; 2444 Wycliff Rd., Raleigh; (919) 781-4480; 10511 Shadowlawn Dr., Raleigh; (919) 846-7044; 12513 Old Creedmoor Rd., Raleigh; (919) 846-6565; chubbystacos.com; Mexican; $. Freshly made ingredients, authentic preparations, quality ingredients, and generous portions make this locally owned and operated taqueria with multiple locations a local favorite among college students and those looking to dine on a budget. Choose from tacos, burritos, *gorditas,* and *tortas* from the a la carte menu or for a mere $2 extra, make it a meal with rice, fresh tortilla chips, and your choice of either black or refried beans.

City Beverage, 4810 Hope Valley Rd., #105, Durham; (919) 401-6500; citybeverage-durham.com; American; $$. This unique and casual restaurant with its funky atmosphere and retro decorations offers indoor dining, a late-night bar scene, and the most popular outdoor patio in SW Durham. The restaurant is divided in two: an upscale dining room and the Lava Lounge that opens nightly. Walls are painted with purple and orange dots, leis hang from the ceilings, and vintage records, retro posters, and wooden Hawaiian tiki masks line the walls top to bottom. The kitschy ambience throughout is a playful background to the eclectic menu of "pupus" (appetizers), sandwiches, burgers, and entrees. Start with a black olive hummus dip with roasted cherry tomatoes and feta cheese or the mussels with chickpeas, roasted tomato, and red peppers in a delicious saffron- and garlic-infused fish broth, just begging to be mopped up with the accompanying crostini. Sandwiches and burgers are plentiful with several stellar options but the *banh mi chay,* their version of the popular Vietnamese sandwich, with grilled tofu, pickled vegetables, and spicy chile dressing, is a vegetarian's delight. For the carnivore, the "Ridiculous Steak Sandwich," a grilled rib eye topped with lettuce, tomato, and a generous portion of crispy fried onion rings served open-faced on thick-cut country bread and topped with a Gorgonzola sauce, is both messy and "ridiculously" good. The parking lot fills up quickly, but the food and beer offerings make circling around the lot a few times looking for an empty space well worth it.

Dain's Place, 754 Ninth St., Durham; (919) 416-8800; dainsplace .com; American/Hot Dogs/Pub; $ Adam Richman, on the Travel Channel's *Man v. Food,* featured this tiny pub as one of his favorite picks. According to Adam, "Dain is the perfect bar owner" and his place offers "great beer, great tater tots, and great service." The build-your-own hot dog, burger, and chicken sandwich menu has winning options, or try the Defibrillator, featured on the show—a half-pound burger topped with chili, cheese, slaw, *and* a hot dog. Fries and tots come plain, with bacon and cheese, or the local favorite, "Tots on Fire," loaded with melted cheese, jalapeños, and sweet chile. Be warned, the place is small and during peak hours quite busy, but the food is worth the wait. Pass the time by enjoying a beer from the small but solid draft selection or from the over 50 microbrews available in a bottle.

DaisyCakes, 401 Foster St., Ste. A, Durham; (919) 389-4307; eatdaisycakes.com; American/Cafe; $. A tiny cafe nestled in a small space a block from the Durham Farmers' Market, DaisyCakes offers decadent cupcakes and homemade pastries and sweets, as well as seasonal soups, sandwiches, frittatas, and other light fare. Owners Tanya and Konrad Catolos and their staff are friendly and helpful and together have created a relaxed environment for their patrons to peruse the blackboard menu that begs you to eat dessert first! Popular lunch items range from frittatas to a turkey sandwich made with avocado, bacon, and onion jam or the half sandwich with soup or salad option. The frittata selections change daily to reflect what's in season, and there is always a meat and vegetarian option.

First known for the cupcakes they sold out of their vintage 1978 31-foot Airstream Sovereign mobile cupcake unit dubbed "Sugar," DaisyCake's tasty treats continue to fly out the door. Kids love the vanilla cupcake with vanilla buttercream, while adults are never disappointed by the red velvet cupcake with cream cheese frosting that makes you smile at first bite. Wi-Fi is readily available with multiple outlets surrounding the small dining space, making it an ideal location for a midmorning meeting.

Dame's Chicken and Waffles, 317 W. Main St., Durham; (919) 682-9235; dameschickenwaffles.com; Fried Chicken/Southern; $$. In the heart of downtown Durham, this restaurant offers a cozy atmosphere with a hip cafe vibe in which to enjoy the best chicken and waffles in town. With 10 variations on the menu, there is sure to be something for everyone. Noted as "Dame's personal favorite," the Carolina Cockerel is a trio of whole chicken wings served with a side of hot sauce, a tender blueberry waffle, and a "shmear" of peach and apricot. All dishes come with the famous shmear: Whipped sweet cream butters flavored with fresh ingredients, an ingenious accompaniment to the tender, succulent fried chicken and fluffy, buttery waffles. Try the chocolate hazelnut shmear on a classic waffle, joined by four crisp fried drumsticks and drizzled with a warm caramel-cashew sauce, or the Orange Speckled Chabo, where an orange honeycomb shmear meets a sweet potato waffle topped with a fried chicken cutlet and is drizzled with honey Dijon sauce for a quirky yet delicious combination. All meals come with homemade sides ranging from mac and cheese to collard greens or fresh fruit to round out the offering. It all may sound somewhat excessive, but you won't want to miss the experience of eating that combination of sweet and salty and soft and crunchy from the chicken and waffles served at Dame's.

Dos Perros, 200 North Mangum St., Ste. 101, Durham; (919) 956-2750; dosperrosrestaurant.com; Mexican; $$. Conveniently located downtown, Dos Perros serves authentic Mexican cuisine in a casual, yet refined environment. Food is thoughtfully prepared using traditional Mexican spices and flavors, and whatever your mood, you're going to find something to fall in love with. Dishes range from a marinated cactus salad to braised chicken enchiladas with mole to Yucatan-style Poulet Rouge chicken with pickled onions, black bean *refritos,* fried plantains, and a habañero salsa that offers just the right amount of heat without overpowering the dish. An equally impressive beverage menu, including a variety of reasonably priced wines and plenty of margarita flavors, rounds out the dining experience. Dos Perros offers a full bar, private dining room, and late-night "Tacos After 10." Beer and wine events are hosted monthly.

Elmo's Diner, 776 Ninth St., Durham; (919) 416-3823; 200 N. Greensboro St., Carrboro; (919) 929-2909; elmosdiner.com;

American/Breakfast; $. A favorite among locals for their all-day breakfasts, Elmo's Diner is truly the local go-to destination for friendly service and home-cooked meals. Food Network's *$40 a Day* host Rachael Ray proclaims that Elmo's is an "awesome pick. Everything here looks great! Try some eggs in their infinite variety." Omelets can be customized to your liking, pancakes come in several flavors such as chocolate chip or pecan, and the waffle batter is made from scratch and cooked to a fluffy golden brown. Classic comfort foods include shepherd's pie, chicken and dumplings, and the ultimate home-style turkey entree: freshly roasted turkey breast served open-faced on toast with a side of mashed potatoes, both smothered in turkey gravy. Weekend brunch can get quite busy, so be patient, it is worth it.

Fairview Restaurant, 3001 Cameron Blvd., Durham; (919) 493-6699; washingtondukeinn.com; American; $$$$. Located in the affluent Washington Duke Inn & Golf Club, the Fairview Restaurant is most noted for its seasonally inspired upscale American specialties. The lavish setting of this formal dining room and outdoor terrace offers stunning views of the award-winning golf course and sets the bar high for fine-dining experiences. Fairview's award-winning wine list offers a diverse selection of vintages, and Executive Chef Jason Cunningham's seasonally changing menu is designed to impress. First course options range from Low Country fried quail with hoop cheddar grits, crispy collard greens, and grain mustard gravy to a sautéed Fairview lump crab cake with spiced spaghetti squash, smoked bacon, and roasted pepper relish. Entrees are even more luxurious with options like grilled chile-rubbed Niman Ranch pork tenderloin with sweet potato spaetzle, oyster mushrooms, mustard greens, and rosemary sorghum jus or basil pesto–crusted wild striped bass with Elodie Farms goat cheese polenta and tomato-caper sauce (recipe on p. 277). Dessert selections are plentiful, and sweet brie cheesecake with an oatmeal crumble crust and honey roasted pears is a real treat. Also open for lunch, the Fairview is a prime location for a business or special event luncheon.

The Federal, 914 W. Main St., Durham; (919) 680-8611; American/Burgers/Pub; $. This popular pub in Durham's Brightleaf District draws a diverse crowd that is a cross section of the local population. There is a large selection of craft beers on tap, a full bar, and daily food specials. Don't judge The Federal by its dark, dive-like feel—the creative food making its way out of the kitchen is a step well above that of normal bar food. "The Fed," as it is called by locals, draws crowds at lunch and dinner. Try the veggie sliders (lentil and leek burgers with guacamole, fresh salsa, romaine, and curry aioli), or the Fed burger au poivre, regularly noted as being one of the best in town. Burgers and sandwiches come with your choice of fries or salad, but this is no time to count calories, go for the fries. The fresh-cut fries are twice cooked, then tossed with a crisp, fragrant, garlic

SWEET POTATOES

Native Americans were growing sweet potatoes when Columbus came to our shores in 1492, and since that time, they have been a staple in traditional Southern cuisine. The popularity of the sweet potato is rising rapidly as more and more folks are discovering the sweet potato fry, which is the trendy new addition to many restaurant menus. North Carolina is the number-one producer in the United States, accounting for nearly 50 percent of the US supply, and according to the United States Department of Agriculture, North Carolina harvested nearly 50,000 acres of sweet potatoes in 2010. The nutritional properties of a sweet potato make them a natural choice for inclusion in our diet. Sweet potatoes have four times the recommended daily intake for beta carotene. They are a good source of vitamin C and magnesium. Also, sweet potatoes are made of complex carbohydrates (think energy) and are high in antioxidants and low in calories. If you want to know more about the fabulous sweet potato, visit ncsweetpotatoes.com for a lot more information and a great recipe collection.

and parsley blend that is so good they quickly disappear off your plate. There's no telling what creative dishes the chef will put on the nightly special, but don't be surprised to find delicacies like chicken pâté, braised pork belly, lamb lollipops, or duck confit. The restaurant fills up quickly, especially on weekends, but the food is well worth the wait.

Fishmongers Restaurant and Oyster Bar, 806 W. Main St., Durham; (919) 682-0128; fishmongers .net; Seafood; $$. A Durham favorite since 1983, Fishmongers is *the* place for fresh oysters, peel and eat shrimp, clams, crab legs, and fried seafood platters. Brown paper–covered picnic tables allow you to get messy, and the windows that run the length of the restaurant are ideal for people-watching while slurping down tasty bivalves. According to the *New York Times,* "you can't go wrong with the cleanly fried fish-and-chips." Add to that a repertoire of barbecue and certified Angus beef dishes and fish dishes available grilled, steamed, blackened, or broiled, and there is truly something for every palate. Come Friday afternoon to the upstairs oyster bar from 2 to 6 p.m. for steamed or raw oyster specials.

Foster's Market, 2694 Durham-Chapel Hill Blvd., Durham; (919) 489-3944; 750 Martin Luther King Jr. Blvd., Chapel Hill; (919) 967-3663; fostersmarket.com; American/Breakfast; $. Foster's Market is a combination cafe, gourmet food market, and coffee bar, open seven days a week, focusing on made-from-scratch soups, wraps, casseroles, salads, and more. Brunch at Foster's Market is a Saturday or Sunday morning tradition for many Durhamites who have to vie for a table, bench, or lawn chair after lining up to place their order. Boasting a sunny location, it's refreshing to sit outside on the covered patio even when there is a definite chill in the air. Breakfast or brunch can be a simple pumpkin scone (large enough to share) and cafe latte or for heartier fare choose the breakfast burrito or the salmon bagel; even a simple BLT is mm-mm good. Daily specials are offered for lunch and dinner. And for dual-career-track couples with families, sign up for the popular family dinners—a week of heat-and-eat entrees you take home with you. If you have time to cook, consider *The Foster's Market Cookbook* by owner Sara Foster, wherein you will find a collection of her best recipes including the perfect caffeine high, the Chocolate Whopper. And, from the gourmet marketplace shelves, pick up a jar or two of the seven-pepper jelly—deliciously sweet and spicy hot and especially good with cream cheese and crackers or used as a glaze over pork tenderloin.

Geer Street Garden, 644 Foster St., Durham; (919) 688-2900; geerstreetgarden.com; American/Fried Chicken/Southern; $$. In what was once a gas station, Chef-Owner Andy Magowan has created a place that offers great food in a setting that is distinctly Durham. With a bar, large sheltered patio, and a garage door opening toward the street, the place is historic and modern, cozy and open. The exposed brick walls, visible under the translucent layers of original paint, are adorned with quirky art and randomly sized mirrors. The food is elevated pub grub, with an emphasis on local and seasonally prepared ingredients. Great for sharing are the salami and cheese board or "The Pile," french fries topped with fried chicken, jalapeños, bacon, melted cheddar cheese, with gravy and two sauces. Sauces come in 10 flavors, the wasabi, garlic aioli, and "sriracha-naise," a blend of sriracha hot sauce and mayonnaise, are popular choices. The fried chicken plate with potato salad is testament to Andy's commitment to using seasonal ingredients. The perfectly crispy, tender, and juicy chicken may arrive accompanied by fresh local corn in the summer or braised collard greens in the fall and winter. The draft beer selection is solid, and the creative house cocktails like the Durhamite (made with vodka, black tea, and lemonade) or the Corn'n'oil (blackstrap rum, Falernum, and lime juice) are expertly prepared by friendly bartenders. The small space fills up quickly and can get a bit loud, but the smiling faces and the cacophony of laughing voices are signs that clearly a good time is being had by all.

Gregoria's Kitchen, 2818 Chapel Hill Rd., Durham; (919) 797-2747; gregoriaskitchen.com; Cuban; $$. Dining at Gregoria's Kitchen is reminiscent of dining in a comfortable home: warm-colored walls and dark-wood furniture that make you remember your nana's dining room. Although, your nana probably didn't make a great mojito, which on a Tuesday evening is part of the $5 mix—both mojitos and appetizers are $5 each—which no doubt accounts for the full house on that day. For starters, try the *relleno de platano maduro*—stuffed sweet plantains with Cuban-style ground beef or the *mejillons*—mussels and chorizo in a roasted tomato and white wine broth. If you have room left for an entree, consider *lechon asado*—roasted pork marinated in herbs and spices, served with grilled vegetables—or the *ropa vieja*—shredded skirt steak braised with roasted tomatoes, garlic, and herbs. Then share dessert with your dinner mates by indulging in the flourless chocolate torte. Area theater patrons can take advantage of the "Early Theater Dinner" menu for about $20, available from 5:30 to 6:30 p.m.

G2B Gastro Pub, 3211 Shannon Rd., Durham; (919) 251-9451; g2b-restaurant.com; American/Farm to Table/Pub; $$. Tucked away in the back of an office building, G2B, meaning Gastro Pub and Beer House, is well worth seeking out for upscale renditions of classic bar foods. The contemporary atmosphere, modern decor, and playful addition of a "games lounge" are the perfect backdrop for the sophisticated culinary creations of Chef de Cuisine Carrie Schleiffer and Pastry Chef Deric McGuffey. The menu, found on a tablet computer, boasts a delectable assortment of well-executed entrees, house-made charcuterie, bar snacks, salads, wood-fired pizzas, burgers, and steaks. The bar snacks menu offers warm marinated olives, grilled prosciutto-wrapped figs, crispy pork belly, and melt in your mouth goat cheese croquettes; excellent accompaniments to the expertly crafted cocktails and stellar wine and draft and bottled beer selections. Start with a house-made platter of charcuterie or cheeses, which can be ordered on their own or as a combination, in various sizes to suit your group, or the roasted beet salad, accentuated by the addition of goat cheese and candied walnuts. The burgers are seasoned well and cooked to your specification, but for a truly decadent indulgence, ask for the *foie* burger: fresh ground meat stuffed with *foie,* grilled to medium rare, and topped with garlic aioli, creamy cheese, and arugula. Although not on the menu, ask and you will be rewarded . . . but shhh, that's our little secret. For entrees, a daily fish offering may include pan-seared bass, arctic char, or other seasonal varieties, while the hickory-grilled hanger steak with brandy cream sauce, beef and lamb shepherd's pie, or house-made gnocchi with puttanesca or tarragon cream sauce, are sure to satisfy many an appetite. Don't leave without a sample of Pastry Chef Deric's masterful dessert creations, especially the chocolate tasting: a triple chocolate masterpiece made up of bittersweet chocolate *pot de crème,* chocolate-chicory sorbet with sea salt, and chocolate espresso pâté.

Guglhupf, 2706 Durham-Chapel Hill Blvd., Durham; (919) 401-2600; guglhupf.com; Bakery/Cafe/German; $$. Featured in *Cooking Light* and on the Food Network, this popular restaurant is known for local and seasonally inspired German and European cuisine. Opened originally in 1998 as a bakery and patisserie by Claudia Kemmet, it has expanded to include a highly popular cafe next door that offers multilevel dining options and a coveted biergarten. Breakfast offers omelets with house-made country sausage, fluffy scrambled eggs, house-made granola, and muesli to start your day while sandwiches, grilled paninis, salads, and small plates grace the lunch menu. Bring a dining companion to share the *Wurstplatte*—a charcuterie platter with a selection of artisanal meats and house-made sausages  accompanied by gruyère cheese, hard-boiled eggs, house-made pickles, and mustard for a true European dining experience. Chef David Alworth brings creative classics to the dinner menu. Start with the sauté of chanterelle mushrooms, served over herb spaetzle, topped with a poached egg and shaved grana before moving on to the Wiener schnitzel, pan-seared to perfection and served with seasonal vegetables. Don't leave before making a stop in the bakery to bring home an assortment of baked goodies, like fresh bread, fruit tarts, pastries, and the famous bretzel roll. Guglhupf is open Tues through Sun. See Guglhupf's recipe for **Zwiebelkuchen** on p. 269.

Kabob & Curry House, 2016 Guess Rd., Durham; (919) 286-3303; Indian; $. Here is another strip-mall eatery whose exterior belies what tasty delights await inside. Don't be fooled by the drab exterior: the food and the prices are great. The owner is the chef and will make your order however you would like it. The meals are made from scratch so be patient as you wait for your order; it may help to call ahead. The lamb is always a good choice as is the chicken tikka masala and the *paneers*—always my favorite—are excellent. Open for lunch and dinner seven days a week, 11 a.m. to 9 p.m., no alcohol; delivery available.

King's Sandwich Shop, 701 Foster St., Durham; (919) 682-0071; kingssandwichshop.com; American/Burgers/Hot Dogs; $. Located diagonally across the street from **Geer Street Garden** (p. 161), this tiny hot dog stand serves up great burgers, barbecue, and milk shakes with some modern-day additions like a spicy black bean burger and veggie dog. There is no indoor seating available; orders are placed through a small window and enjoyed at one of the few communal picnic benches off to the side or back in the comfort of home. Although there is usually a line of people, and service can sometimes be slow, the simple but delicious food has kept people coming back for over 6 decades.

La Superior, 22842 North Roxboro Rd., Durham; (919) 220-9884; Taqueria; $. The large cafeteria at the back of this medium-sized Latin American grocery store offers delicious selections from a taqueria, *panaderia/tortilleria,* and juice bar. The taqueria's tacos are filled with generous portions of chicken, steak, and pork as well as chorizo and *lengua* (beef tongue). Top everything off with fresh cilantro, onions, salsa, pickled onion, and jalapeño from the salsa bar. The menu also includes quesadillas, *gorditas, sopes, tamales,* and other Mexican fare. Stop by the juice bar for a refreshing *agua fresca* in flavors like mango and tamarind or order an *elote*—an ear of corn slathered with *crema,* then sprinkled with cheese, lime juice, and chile powder. After your meal, visit the *panaderia* counter for a bag of Mexican pastries to go.

La Vaquita, 2700 Chapel Hill Rd., Durham; (919) 402-0209; lavaquitanc.com; Taqueria; $. Except for the giant cow (a Durham landmark and an instant stand-out) on the roof, this small taco stand doesn't look like much, however the authentic Mexican specialties coming out of the small window are nationally acclaimed for being fresh and flavorful. "The *barbacoa* is so good at Taquería La Vaquita—so juicy and dark and perfectly seasoned—that it might almost be some long-cooked *daube* at a reputable bistro in

Provence," writes *Gourmet* magazine. Tacos, *sopes, tortas,* quesadillas, and other specialties can be made with carnitas, *al pastor,* or *lengua* (Veracruz-style braised beef tongue), and although you can stick to simpler options like steak or chicken, I don't suggest this. Their slow-roasted meats are full of flavor and the reason there is often a line. Tacos are served on fresh homemade corn tortillas with cilantro, lime, and slivers of radishes, and I would suggest ordering a variety to fully enjoy the experience. Beverage options range from tamarind *agua fresca* and sweet *horchata* to refreshing Mexican sodas. Service is quick and efficient, and most customers will call an order in ahead of time and take their bag of tacos to go.

Loaf, 111 W. Parish St., Durham; (919) 797-1254; Bakery/Sandwiches; $. Located on a small side street in the heart of downtown, this tiny takeout-only bakery produces excellent baked goods, pastries, and fresh, rustic brick-oven breads. Once only available at the Durham Farmers' Market, Ron and Jaime Graff's cookies, croissants, scones, cinnamon rolls, and more are now offered at their store. The daily bread selection spans four to six different varieties that include personal favorites like polenta bread, olive loaf, and a hearty multigrain. For a grab-and-go breakfast, try the country ham and cheddar scone and a cup of Counter Culture coffee or treat yourself to the twice-baked almond croissant, made with almond cream, brandy syrup, sliced almonds, and dusted with confectioner's sugar, it's been said to make people cry! For lunch they offer a variety of light vegetarian and hearty meat sandwiches and several sweet and savory scones and croissants. In addition to the offerings baked on-site, they also carry local cheeses from **Reliable Cheese Co.** (p. 210) and sausages from **Farmhand Foods** (p. 44). Loaf is open 5 days a week (Tues through Sat, 7 a.m. to 6 p.m.).

Los Comales, 2103 N. Roxboro Rd., Durham; (919) 220-1614; loscomalesncdurham.com; Taqueria; $. Known by most Durhamites as one of the best places for authentic Mexican cuisine, this casual taqueria is a popular spot for dining in or taking food to go. The menu, located on a board behind the counter, is in Spanish, so it helps to know some, but if you ask, they do keep an English paper menu behind the counter. The tortillas for the tacos are made to order and are empty canvases for beautifully prepared fillings like *al pastor* (roasted pork), carnitas (braised pork), or *barbacoa* (slow-roasted beef). All are highly seasoned and flavorful and arrive in heaps on the hot fresh tortillas. Stop at the salsa bar for any number of toppings from fresh cilantro, salsa, cucumbers, or hot peppers and limes. The rest of the menu is well worth perusing and several plated options are available for a more substantial meal nicely washed down with any one of their tasty *horchatas* or *agua frescas*. For entertainment value, large TVs hang from the walls showing Spanish soap operas or the latest soccer game.

L'Uva Enoteca, American Tobacco Campus, 406 Blackwell St., Ste. 105, Durham; (919) 688-8181; luvaenoteca.com; Italian; $$. Located on the popular American Tobacco campus, L'Uva's (by Jim Anile of **Revolution,** p. 181) inviting and refined atmosphere makes a leisurely lunch or date night out a special experience. The menu is simple and highlights Italian cuisine at its purest. Seasonal ingredients are prepared with care so they are the star of the show. The menu rotates regularly, and on any given occasion you might find roasted pork loin with Gorgonzola gnocchi or roasted pumpkin ravioli or super-tender beef short ribs served in a rich sauce cut with a bright citrusy gremolata. The daily lunch special is worth a visit alone where for $10 you can choose two items: half a sandwich, soup, salad, or gelato. If you're lucky enough to arrive on a day the porchetta sandwich is on the lunch menu, don't pass it up—it is succulent, juicy, and really just perfect. The restaurant is fairly small and they don't take reservations, so expect a bit of a wait on weekend evenings or before catching a show at the Durham Performing Arts Center, located a short walk away.

Mad Hatter Bakeshop and Cafe, 1802 W. Main St., Durham; (919) 286-1987; madhatterbakeshop.com; Bakery/Cafe; $. Located in the Bull City Market shopping center adjacent to Whole Foods and across the street from Duke University's East Campus, Mad Hatter Bakeshop and Cafe offers a cozy coffee shop ambience. Free Wi-Fi means there are students from Duke and busy professionals in the cafe working at all hours of the day. Glass cases display an excellent selection of tasty sweet treats including scones, cupcakes, croissants, cakes, and cookies, while the breakfast and lunch menus showcase a full offering to satisfy all your appetites. Counter Culture Coffee, one of North Carolina's best, is served with free refills, making Mad Hatter a perfect spot for an afternoon pick-me-up. Breakfast is served all day along with a variety of sandwiches and salads. Try the cashew apple chicken salad for a fresh twist on an old favorite. The Rancheros breakfast basket—two eggs any style, black beans, Monterey Jack cheese, lime cilantro sour cream, pico de gallo, and salsa verde—is a filling and nutritious start (or finish!) to your day.

Mami Nora's, 302 Davidson Ave., Durham; (919) 220-9028; maminoras.com; Peruvian; $. The only Peruvian-style rotisserie in Durham, this unassuming, hard-to-find restaurant is worth seeking out. The rotisserie chicken, roasted in an oven imported from Peru, is so tender and juicy, it falls right off the bone. Order a quarter, half, or whole chicken and pair it with traditional South American sides like fried green or sweet plantains, yucca fries, or black beans. Round out your meal with a refreshing *chi cha morada* (house-made purple corn and pineapple drink with hints of cinnamon and clove).

Nana's Restaurant, 2514 University Dr., Durham; (919) 493-8545; nanasdurham.com; American/Farm to Table/Southern; $$$. Chef-Owner Scott Howell, "a man of formidable talent" (*Food & Wine*), serves Southern regional cuisine with strong Italian and

French influences at one of Durham's best-known restaurants. The dark red and yellow hues, dramatic chandeliers, and whimsical paintings provide a warm and cozy feel to the dining room, while the Lounge's dark wood and stainless steel bar offers a pleasant and sophisticated environment to enjoy a glass of wine or cocktail before heading to your table for dinner. To start, choose from a large selection of small plates, such as the yellowfin tuna carpaccio or Nana's truffled chicken liver pâté with toasted crostini, grain mustard, kumquat chutney, and house-pickled green beans. Entree options include cast-iron-roasted chicken or duck and a savory pork schnitzel made with local pork and served alongside a warm five-onion potato salad and savory cabbage in crème fraîche finished with brown butter sage sauce. Seafood is delicately and expertly prepared, and the pan-roasted halibut, served over wilted spinach with roasted fingerling potatoes, is moist and delicious. If you have trouble deciding on one of the tempting entrees, Nana's offers a tasting menu that at $50 and 5 courses is a steal. Whatever you decide to eat, make sure to save room for one of the decadent desserts or an after-dinner drink in the lounge. Scott and his team of attentive and knowledgeable waiters will make any special occasion memorable; Nana's is also a popular location for private parties.

Nanataco, 2512 University Dr., Durham; (919) 489-8226; Mexican; $. Opened last year by Scott Howell of **Nana's** (p. 170), this colorful taqueria has fast become a local favorite for fresh Mexican fare. Inside, the soft buttercup-yellow walls are cheerful, while an outside patio offers a comfortable setting to enjoy a beautiful

Carolina day. The menu is an assortment of burritos, quesadillas, tacos, and *tortas* all worth the indulgence. Your choice of corn or flour tortilla can be filled with meats that range from chile-rubbed pork to house-made chorizo or "dirty meats," like braised hog jowl, house-smoked duck, or crispy pork belly. Add a side of black beans or pinto beans and rice to round out the meal and don't overlook the sizable condiment bar with its assortment of salsas, limes, cucumber-onion salad, cilantro, house-pickled jalapeños, and jicama slaw. Lunch draws a crowd and there is often a line out the door, but a large chalkboard menu makes it easy to know ahead what you plan to order. However, I would stick to the lunch special: two tacos with rice and beans for $6.50; it is one of the best deals in town. Service is quick and efficient, so even if you arrive and there is a line, it moves fairly quickly.

Neo-China, 4015 University Dr., Durham; (919) 489-2828; Chinese; $. At Neo China lunch is probably the best deal in town: eggroll or soup, choice of rice, and an entree. I always ask for rice on the side, wistfully thinking that my savory portion will be larger. The menu is not extensive, but then I always come back and order the same thing: Marco Polo Spicy Chicken with sautéed jumbo onions, asparagus, cauliflower, yellow squash, red bell pepper, and mushrooms in a hot and spicy brown sauce served over chunks of battered chicken breast. The food here is well above average for an American Chinese restaurant. It is not gourmet Chinese, but the ingredients are fresh and the quality is good. The vegetables are bright and crispy and not drowning in sauce.

Ninth Street Bakery, 136 E. Chapel Hill St., Durham; (919) 286-0303; ninthstbakery.com; Bakery/Breakfast/Cafe/Sandwiches; $. The aroma of freshly baked bread instantly hits you upon entering this wholesale bakery, coffee shop, and take-out lunch counter. The menu offers salads, soups, chili, and sandwiches served on house-baked bread made with organic, unbleached flour and whole grains. Although Ninth Street bread is available at many area specialty stores, nothing beats taking home a fresh-out-of-the-oven, still-warm loaf of sourdough, baguette, or cinnamon raisin bread from the bakery itself. Super-tasty pastries, plus cookies, brownies, muffins, scones, croissants, Danishes, and cinnamon buns are a welcoming treat to any business meeting or taken home and enjoyed as a late-night snack. The Ninth Street Bakery is open Mon through Fri from 7 a.m. to 4 p.m. and Sat from 8 a.m. to 3 p.m. Closed Sun.

Nosh, 2812 Erwin Rd., Ste. 101, Durham; (919) 383-4747; nosh food.com; Bistro/Breakfast; $. Cheerful service and good food in an atmosphere where everyone feels part of a community is what Wendy and Piper were looking to achieve when they opened this quaint colorful bistro. Diners can enjoy a delicious array of breakfast, lunch, and dinner fare at a scattering of tables inside or outdoors under shady umbrellas. Breakfast biscuits are scratch-made in house and come in an infinite number of variations. For a hearty breakfast, order the Maggie's Scramble—three eggs with caramelized onions, peppers, portobello mushrooms, and Asiago cheese, wrapped into a warm tortilla and topped with a roasted red pepper sauce. On the lighter side, muffins, bagels, yogurt, and smoothies will be sure to please and satisfy. The lunch and dinner menu offers a wide range of sandwiches, salads, burgers, and pizzas. Sandwiches and burgers come with your choice of veggie coleslaw, pasta salad, potato salad, or a delicious couscous salad flavored with mildly spiced curry and slivered almonds. Their version of chicken salad made with green goddess dressing and piled high between sun-dried tomato bread or a vegetarian hot sandwich like the Gonzalo (hummus, sautéed peppers, caramelized onions, and shaved Parmesan) are some of my personal favorites. With free Wi-Fi, the environment is ideal for students and business lunches.

Old Havana Sandwich Shop, 310 E. Main St., Durham; (919) 667-9525; oldhavanaeats.com; Cuban/Sandwiches; $. Pop into Old Havana for lunch or dinner and you are sure to be greeted by the smiling face of owner Robert Copa, outfitted in his signature straw hat and jovially talking to his customers. The slow-roasted pork is the source of the mouthwatering smell as you enter the shop and the magic behind great selections of authentic, traditional Cuban sandwiches and plates. Classics include the Havana sandwich featuring layers of pork, Boar's Head ham and cheese, pickle, mustard, and delicious mojo sauce, or the simpler Santiago with only pork, mustard, and mojo sauce. For a more complex meal, the sampler platter with a generous serving of pork, tender rice, slow-cooked black beans, and a half order of *maduros* (oven-roasted sweet plantains) is a solid choice. Get your day off to a delightful start with a cafe Cubano with Cuban toast or a basket of pork *croquetas* and sweet, oven-roasted *maduros*. They use only local, pasture-raised, heirloom pork to ensure high quality, and they also offer vegetarian options.

Only Burger, 3710 Shannon Rd., Ste. 118, Durham; (919) 724-1622; onlyburger.com; Burgers; $. Although Only Burger got its start as a food truck, the popularity of the burgers eventually resulted in this vibrant and bustling brick-and-mortar location. The truck is still making rounds throughout the Triangle, and steady lines at both the restaurant and mobile locations continue to gain notoriety. The menu is simple and concise: Burgers come as singles or doubles, topped with lettuce, onion, tomato, ketchup, and mustard, then layered between a crisply toasted buttered hamburger bun. Noteworthy specials include the pimiento cheeseburger with a fried green tomato and fried egg or the lamb sliders with *tzatziki* sauce and feta cheese. French fries are fresh-cut daily, fried crisp, and seasoned perfectly; this is no time for calorie-counting, friends, just go for it. Specials and truck location are updated daily on Facebook and Twitter (@onlyburger).

Palace International, 1104-A Broad St., Durham; (919) 416-4922; thepalaceinternational.com; African; $. The Palace International, owned and operated by Kenyan natives Caren and Maurice Ochola, is downtown Durham's destination for authentic African cuisine. Traditional dishes include oxtails, goat curry, and African three-bean soup as well as beverages like Nairobian punch and a delicious chai latte: Kenyan tea cooked with masala and cream. The Kilimanjaro beef ribs, braised in a honey-kissed barbecue sauce, are tender and flavorful, as is a pan-seared whole tilapia and *maharagwe ya nazi,* red pinto beans cooked in coconut milk and well-seasoned with ginger and cayenne. Serving Durham foodies for over 20 years, the Palace International has a lively and vibrant atmosphere, reasonably priced food, and quick, friendly service, making it an excellent choice for lunch or dinner. Enjoy live jazz at brunch every Sun from 11 a.m. to 4 p.m.

Papa Mojo's Roadhouse, 5410-Y Hwy. 55 (Greenwood Commons Shopping Center), Durham; (919) 361-2222; papamojosroadhouse .com; Cajun/Creole; $$. Authentic Cajun/Creole specialties abound in this funky vibrant spot that features a colorful decor reminiscent of New Orleans and live music that completes the scene. Classic Cajun and Creole dishes like red beans and rice, jambalaya, gumbo, and crawfish étouffée, as well as seasonal specials like crawfish boils and authentic New Orleans BBQ shrimp (see recipe on p. 271) are always satisfying. Don't miss the Friday special when seafood gumbo makes its appearance. Rich and spicy, it's chock-full of catfish, shrimp, crab, and crawfish, and it's absolutely delicious. Po' boys, with choice fillings like andouille sausage, steak, or catfish, are a popular choice and make for a quick and easy lunch while heaping baskets of shrimp, oysters, or crawfish come fried to perfection every time. A Bayou Brunch is served on Sunday from 11 a.m. to 3 p.m., and the warm powdered sugar–dusted beignets, perfectly crispy on the outside and chewy on the inside, make you feel like you've bitten into a little slice of heaven. There is live music at least three nights a week, so check the website for the bands playing.

Parizade, 2200 W. Main St., Ste. B-100, Durham; (919) 286-9712; parizadedurham.com; American/International; $$$. Vibrant whimsical art on the ceiling and walls, bold hues, and soft mellow lighting make walking into Parizade feel like you've entered a magical fantasy world that you never want to leave. Indulge in the fine Mediterranean-inspired cuisine coming from the kitchen and you may never want to. The menu, made up of small plates, seafood, meats, and pastas, is carefully crafted to include local and often organic ingredients for a seasonal approach to your dining experience. Entrees include fennel and mustard seed–crusted pork chops, fettucine Bolognese with a beef and pork sauce, and an extravagant Spanish paella with plenty of garlic sausage, chicken, clams, shrimp, and calamari. All food is prepared in a vast open kitchen that runs the length of the restaurant, which makes dining indoors an exciting experience. For a romantic evening, ask to be seated in the outside courtyard where dining under twinkling lights next to a 12-foot waterfall takes eating alfresco to a new level.

Pho 9N9, 2945 Miami Blvd., Ste. 102, Durham; (919) 544-4496; pho9n9.net; Vietnamese; $. Pho 9N9 is a bustling Vietnamese restaurant located in a strip mall in the middle of Research Triangle Park. Although the place quickly fills up with RTP professionals during lunch, quick and friendly service means you can be in and out in a reasonable amount of time. The *pho* here is very good as are a variety of noodle and rice dishes, and *banh mi,* a Vietnamese sandwich filled with pork or chicken, pickled daikon, carrot, and jalapeños served on a crusty baguette. The prices are inexpensive, and the venue is perfect for sharing a variety of dishes with friends. Unlike many other RTP restaurants that close over the weekend, Pho 9N9 is open all weekend long.

Piedmont, 401 Foster St., Durham; (919) 683-1213; piedmont restaurant.com; Farm to Table; $$. Inspired by fresh local produce and artisanal products, Executive Chef Marco Shaw's creative force in the kitchen is evident on a constantly changing, seasonally focused menu. Leather banquettes, exposed brick, and high ceilings lend an inviting environment with just a little bit of a cool factor in which to enjoy a thoughtfully crafted meal. For a first course, the charcuterie platter: House-made pork terrine, lamb liver pâté, and smoked guanciale, served with ginger-apple mustard, pickled vegetables, and toast is a nice option for sharing. Entree options may include house-made pasta like pappardelle, topped with a hearty and rich braised grass-fed beef Bolognese or a grilled pork leg with sweet potatoes and black lentils. Desserts are as seasonal as the rest of the menu, and the butternut squash bread pudding with lemongrass curd, an homage to winter flavors, is a warm and pleasing end to dinner on a cool crisp evening in winter. Whatever the season, Chef Shaw is sure to delight guests with dishes using fresh, local ingredients.

Piper's in the Park, 2945 S. Miami Blvd., RTP, Durham; (919) 572-9767; pipersinthepark.com; American/Breakfast/Sandwiches; $. Owners Piper Lunsford and Wendy Woods (also of **Nosh,** p. 173) are affectionately known in this area as "the Girls," who for the past 10 years have built a reputation for quality and service at a reasonable price. Like many eateries in the Research Triangle Park, the Girls keep lunchtime hours and foster an active catering service for local businesses. I don't work in "the Park," as RTP is referred to, but when I do have occasion to be nearby, I head to Piper's to indulge myself in Papa Sweeney's Pimiento Cheese—Southern-style pimiento cheese, portobello mushroom, and roasted peppers on Texas three–seed bread. There is a great selection of standard lunch foods; sandwiches, wraps, soups, and stews.

Pop's, 605 W. Main St., Durham; (919) 956-7677; pops-durham .com; Italian/Pizza; $$. This popular restaurant located in down-town's West Village features an open kitchen and a wood-fired oven perfect for the northern Italian cuisine they are known for. Appetizers are a must, especially a dish of warm olives or almonds, crispy calamari, or the popular "Big Bowl of Mussels," served in a white wine broth, flavored with toasted garlic, chile flakes, and roasted tomatoes. The menu ranges from classic to seasonal dishes like a rich lasagna Bolognese, spicy gnocchi with pepper-braised pork, or lobster stuffed shells. Pizzas are made in the wood-fired oven, and creative toppings like Granny Smith apple, ricotta cheese, and white truffle cream or salty egg and prosciutto with roasted garlic and kalamata olives have garnered a loyal local following. If a traditional pie is more to your liking, the pepperoni and sausage is a solid choice. Save room for dessert so you can enjoy the house-made gelato, sorbetto, or the decadent tiramisu. Pop's is open for lunch Mon through Fri and dinner 7 nights a week.

Pop's Backdoor South, 3710 Shannon Rd., Durham; (919) 956-7437; popsbackdoorsouth.com; Pizza; $$. This casual, family-friendly interpretation of the original Pop's Backdoor offers pizzas, calzones, pastas, sandwiches, and salads and some die-hard classics like the crispy calamari and famed mussels. The menu offers excellent build-your-own pizza or calzone options with a wide variety of fresh toppings, but it's the Veggie Lovers' pizza I come for. Loaded with artichokes, onions, green pepper, mushrooms, green olives, and paired perfectly with tangy goat cheese, it is hard to resist. For a real treat, try the Polpette calzone. Dough is stuffed with house-made meatballs, spinach, roasted garlic, and Parmesan cheese, baked to a perfect golden brown, and served with marinara.

Lunch and dinner options include dine-in, takeout, and delivery 7 days a week.

Revolution, 107 W. Main St., Durham; (919) 956-9999; revolution restaurant.com; American; $$$$. The boutique setting of this sleek, modern restaurant in the heart of downtown is a temple to the contemporary global cuisine found on the menu. Executive Chef and Proprietor Jim Anile's innovative menu highlights his creativity and talent in the kitchen, bringing diners a meal that is not only perfectly executed but beautiful to look at. The menu consists of a raw bar, small plates, and big plates. Raw bar options range from octopus salad bathed in a tangy citrus vinaigrette to oysters on the half shell or venison carpaccio in which shaved fennel and Dijon mustard are the perfect accompaniments to the sweet, thinly sliced meat. Small plates such as the lemongrass mussels, or the cinnamon- and coriander-infused pumpkin soup with salt-cured *foie gras* are a delicious start to the evening, especially when paired with a glass of wine from the extensive wine list. Big-plate options are varied and well balanced with everything from stuffed mountain trout or crispy duck to a deliciously tender Dijon-encrusted lamb loin. For an extra special experience choose a 3-, 5-, or 7-course tasting menu with optional wine pairings for a meal that will leave you in awe of the talents in the kitchen. With an eclectic menu that changes seasonally and food that is consistently excellent, Chef Anile will continue to delight foodies for a long time to come. See Chef Jim Anile's recipe for **English Sweet Pea Salad with Warm Bacon Vinaigrette** on p. 263.

Rick's Diner, 4015 University Dr., Durham; (919) 419-0907; ricks diner.com; American/Breakfast/Sandwiches; $. Rick's Diner has been serving traditional American fare in a comfortable and cozy environment to a loyal following of locals for over 10 years. The breakfast menu, available all day, features eggs in many variations, pancakes, waffles, and biscuit sandwiches. A variety of salads, sandwiches, and entree options is available for lunch, including a generous slice of their "secret recipe" meat loaf that arrives slathered with delicious gravy. Dinner specials are popular here and rotate weekly. The popular Sunday brunch may have you waiting for a table, but it is well worth the time.

Rue Cler, 401 E. Chapel Hill St., Durham; (919) 682-8844; ruecler-durham.com; French; $$. A Parisian-style restaurant and bakery, Rue Cler offers classic bistro cuisine combined with fresh ingredients and French wines for lunch, dinner, and brunch. The restaurant is upscale with a hip urban vibe while the bakery side is more casual and cozy, perfect for enjoying an afternoon coffee and sharing a basket of beignets with a friend. Lunch fare ranges from salads to sandwiches, entrees, and crepes. The entrees here are solid, including a fabulous coq au vin or *moules frites,* steamed in a white wine broth with a hint of lemon and cooked to perfection.

The crepes are wonderfully delicate and come in several delicious variations, but the duck confit with spinach and roasted potatoes is unbelievable. The dinner menu offers a few a la carte options, but it is the prix-fixe menu that will have you raving to your friends. The menu changes daily but may include beluga lentil soup, herb spaetzle gratinée, or a tender pan-roasted pork chop with roasted asparagus and red potatoes with a caper brown sauce. *Food & Wine* praises the hot, powdered-sugar-covered beignets sold by the dozen, so be sure to bring a bag home with you.

Saigon Grill, 2929 N. Roxboro St., Durham; (919) 220-5979; Vietnamese; $. This unassuming Vietnamese restaurant in North Durham offers inexpensive food in a very friendly environment. It's a favorite among devotees of Asian food, for their *pho,* vermicelli, and rice dishes, which come with your choice of pork, beef, chicken, or shrimp and all come topped with cooked scallions, fried onions, peanuts, and pickled carrots and daikon. The *pho* here is exceptional: rich flavorful broth, perfectly cooked noodles, and the usual meat options including tendon and tripe for the more adventurous. Saigon Grill is a comfortable place for friendly service and great Vietnamese fare.

Saladelia Cafe, 4201 University Dr., Ste. 100, Durham; (919) 489-5776; saladelia.com; Middle Eastern; $. Nestled in a strip mall off University Drive, Saladelia has been delighting foodies for over 20 years with its Mediterranean fare. Vegetarian friendly, Saladelia offers a combination of Lebanese and Greek cuisine with all the

NC State Grape:
Scuppernong Grape, a Muscadine Variety

In 2001, the North Carolina General Assembly named the Scuppernong grape as the official state fruit. (The same session also declared the strawberry and blueberry state berries.) The Scuppernong is a variety of the Muscadine grape and is said to be the first grape ever actively cultivated in the United States. In North Carolina, grapevines bearing this variety were found back in the 1500s along the eastern shore in our Outer Banks region, where they still grow wild. There is a small window of time to enjoy Muscadine grapes, from mid-August to late September. September is when the grapes hit their peak harvest season and when they show up at farmers' markets, roadside stands, grocery stores, and pick-your-own fields. The grapes thrive in hot, humid weather, making them well suited for production in North Carolina.

traditional dishes on the menu and by far the best baklava—either pistachio or walnut—in the tri-city area. If you're stymied at the huge variety of fresh-from-scratch food items in the display case as you stand in line to place your order, consider one of the "Mixanmatchous Platters": Vegetarian Sampler (your choice of three vegetarian signature sides), the Specialty Sampler (one specialty entree and two vegetarian signature sides), or the Gyro Sampler (either chicken souvlaki or vegetable plus two vegetarian signature sides). By the time you reach the register, you will have decided. And if you haven't, then your best choice is the Tuna Melt. Owners,

These sweet Muscadines are a bronze-green color and have very thick, bitter outside hulls, while the inside is sweet and juicy. To eat a scuppernong, first hold the grape stem-side up and squeeze the grape. The juicy inside will squirt into your mouth. Be careful to spit out the seeds and don't chew the skin, as it is bitter. Scuppernong grapes are extraordinarily high in antioxidants and are said to be great for your cardiovascular health. Store the grapes in a covered shallow container in the refrigerator and wash them just before use. The Scuppernongs should keep for a week if they are healthy when harvested. The Muscadine grape variety continues to grow wild in North Carolina and, of course, is highly cultivated for wines as well. For more information visit the North Carolina Wine & Grape Council Facebook page or the North Carolina Muscadine Grape Association, ncmuscadine.org/vap.html.

Robert and Fida Ghanem have several locations in the Durham/ Chapel Hill area so check the website for one near you.

Scratch Seasonal Artisan Baking, 111 Orange St., Durham; (919) 789-9431; piefantasy.com; Breakfast/Cafe/Farm to Table/ Southern; $. Before pie-meister Phoebe Lawless opened her restaurant Scratch in downtown Durham, she was a conspicuous presence every Saturday at the Durham Farmers' Market because of the long lines that queued for anything that she baked—empanadas, doughnuts, pies. Now faithful Scratch patrons can choose to eat breakfast

or lunch made from locally sourced ingredients Tues to Fri, 7:30 a.m. to 4 p.m. and Sat and Sun, 9 a.m. to 3 p.m. Savory dishes are good and wholesome but splurge a little and try pie for breakfast or lunch. My favorite is the Shaker lemon pie: total pucker-up lemon flavor.

If you want to try your own hand at pie-baking, sign up for Phoebe's "Pie 101," a great evening for $60 that includes sipping wine while watching her make four kinds of pies, which you get to taste (and you're sent home with the recipes as well as samples of each). And yes, Phoebe is still present at the farmers' market on Saturday morning.

Sitar Indian Cuisine, 3630 Durham-Chapel Hill Blvd., Durham; (919) 490-1326; sitar-indiancuisine.com; Indian; $$. Decorated simply but elegantly with deep red and white linens on the tables, this cozy Indian restaurant offers northern and southern Indian specialties, a full bar, and private dining space. Order from the a la carte menu and enjoy items like *paneer makhani* (homemade cheese in a delicate sauce), *chana masala* (chickpeas with curry sauce), or a the lamb *dhansak* (tender cubes of lamb cooked with yellow lentils and an array of flavorful spices). The popular buffet, available for lunch seven days a week and dinner Friday and Saturday, offers a great selection of meat and vegetarian dishes including traditional chicken or lamb tikka masala, tandoori chicken, and *saag paneer*—spinach cooked with chickpeas (or mushrooms). On the weekend,

Sitar sometimes has live sitar music during dinner, creating a lovely atmosphere in which to enjoy your meal.

604 at West Village, 604 Fernway Ave., Durham; (919) 680-6333; 604westmorgan.com; Italian; $$. Although slightly hidden within a renovated tobacco warehouse that is now home to the chic West Village Apartments, 604 is worth seeking out. Traditional central and southern Italian cuisine is presented in a casually elegant atmosphere accentuated by dark wood, warm colors, and low lighting. The menu is a thoughtful collection of antipasti, gourmet pizzas, and pastas, while the entrees are rustic and comforting, a clear indication the chef is thoughtful of what he puts on the plate. The Dijon-crusted rack of lamb with Cabernet wine reduction and pan-roasted bone-in veal chop with an earthy wild mushroom jus are both excellent dinner choices. For less sophisticated dining, step next door to the cozy pizzeria where the atmosphere is more casual but the food equally outstanding.

Six Plates Wine Bar, 2812 Erwin Rd., Ste. 104, Durham; (919) 321-0203; sixplates.com; Small Plates/Wine Bar; $$. Matthew Beason, a Durham native and former co-owner of **Pop's** (p. 179) and **Rue Cler** (p. 182) opened Six Plates Wine Bar in order to combine his love of good food and passion for wine in a welcoming environment. Exposed ductwork, leather couches, red plush chairs, and dramatic chandeliers create an upscale vibe that is both chic and inviting, while a small, seasonally focused menu with paired wine selections change often to offer guests variety. You might find a rich, flavorful beef osso buco spring roll paired with a Merum Monastrell Jumilla, a Spanish wine with notes of rich plum and prune and a slight hint of coffee, or a clean crisp Ostatu Rioja Blanco, perfect for seafood like the smoked mushroom–stuffed skate wing. The small plates encourage sharing, allowing friends to gather together and try and sample several dishes at one time. Start with the olive plate or truffle *frites* for a little nibble or share a plate of lamby joes or local beef sliders with serrano bacon, barbecue sauce, and smoked Gouda. Weekly wine specials include $12 select bottles of wine on Monday and 4 for $4 Tuesday, when Matthew chooses four terrific wines for $4 a glass. To round out a solid wine selection, Six Plates Wine Bar also has a good bottled beer selection and a few draft choices. See Chef John Eisensmith's recipe for **Mussels with Cranberry–White Balsamic Gastrique** on p. 273.

Straw Valley Cafe, 5420 Durham-Chapel Hill Blvd., Durham; (919) 403-2233; strawvalleycafe.com; Cafe/Sandwiches; $. Tucked away in between a major highway, a storage facility, and a strip mall, Straw Valley is a quiet, quirky oasis of calm in the city, literally! The large and spacious outdoor patio is surrounded by trees and greenery with an open courtyard scattered with couches, chairs, and tables tucked into each room or alcove. The result provides privacy and comfort, good for relaxing with friends at night or working undisturbed during the day. Art is on display and the modern-style furniture gives it a cool, funky feel. The menu is small and includes a daily sandwich, light fare, and excellent desserts. Coffee and coffee drinks, wine, and a small but tasty selection of beer are available.

Super Taqueria, 2842 N. Roxboro St., Durham; (919) 220-9884; Taqueria; $. It helps if you speak Spanish at this taqueria. However, the English menu is well photographed so your fingers can quickly point to what you want. The regular menu hangs from the ceiling on a painted wooden board. As you peruse the menu, you'll see about six meat choices which you can then top up from the extensive salsa bar, reputed to be the best one in Durham. Portions are plentiful and the taquitos are decidedly overstuffed with chorizo, *al pastor, cabez,* and *lengua.* While the taqueria appears to operate like a fast-food joint, you can actually watch the chef make your lunch or dinner in the kitchen behind the cash register. Additional items are added on the weekend, like soup specials and ceviche. A big-screen television is tuned to Univision.

Thai Cafe, 2501 University Dr., Durham; (919) 493-9794; thai cafenc.com; Thai; $$. This bright, casual restaurant offers authentic Thai recipes that include the balance of the four basic tastes found in all Thai food: salty, sweet, sour, and bitter—plus hot. There is a variety of solid stir-fries, curry, and rice dishes, and although the pad thai is a an excellent choice, it is the BBQ chicken that has me coming back as often as possible. Marinated overnight in a house special BBQ sauce, the chicken is then char-grilled to fall off the bone perfection and served with a tasty shrimp fried rice and sweet and sour sauce for dipping. Most dishes are not overly spicy, but you can spice anything up by asking for the trio of Thai spices, including crushed chiles, to take your meal up a notch. The beef salad is a great option for those who like their food on the spicier side. Strips of grilled steak are mixed with cucumbers, tomatoes, red onions, then tossed with fresh lime juice, fish sauce, and crushed Thai chiles and served over a bed of crisp romaine lettuce that provides just the right cooling effect. Thai Cafe is a reliable choice for good Thai food that is reasonably priced.

Toast, 345 W. Main St., Durham; (919) 683-2185; toast-fivepoints .com; Farm to Table/Sandwiches; $. This quaint *paninoteca* (pronounced pa-nee-no-TEK-a), meaning an authentic Italian sandwich shop, takes local, fresh, seasonal ingredients and carefully transforms them into delicious panini, tramezzini, bruschetta, and crostini. Note: Always look to the specials board for Chef Billy Cotter's latest market creation. You never know, you may find yourself biting into a warm toasty panini filled with grilled asparagus, a farm-fresh fried egg, and decadent truffle cheese and think you've found heaven. For a light lunch, order the chicken-liver crostini topped with crispy pancetta and pickled fennel, or the warm goat cheese crostini drizzled with local honey and a twist of fresh cracked pepper, and round out the meal by adding a seasonal soup. Billy's devoted local following knows he puts only the freshest ingredients into his dishes, and if the crostini is topped with something pickled, he is sure to have pickled it himself. Billy and his wife Kelly run Toast as a duo, and it is Kelly who runs the front of the house, taking orders at the counter, with a smile always at the ready. They have a long restaurant background, well seasoned with many years at Durham's former landmark Magnolia Grill (now closed).

Tobacco Road, 2850 S. Mangum St., Ste. 100, Durham; (919) 937-9909; tobaccoroadsportscafe.com; Burgers/Pub; $. Tobacco Road Sports Cafe is a sports-themed restaurant featuring a menu of fresh, local favorites, an abundance of TVs, and unmatched views of the Durham Bulls Athletic Park from the patio, located directly next to the iconic bull in left field. The menu consists of soups, salads, sandwiches, and burgers with enough variety to suit all tastes, and there is a solid draft beer selection. Appetizers like chicken wings and the heaping portion of nachos are great to share with friends on game day while entree dishes like black-eyed bean cakes or shrimp and grits make a nice meal before catching a show at the Durham Performing Arts Center located next door. Mock stadium seating, with a wall of television screens that can be viewed by customers relaxing in recliners at the base, makes this bar an ideal location for sports enthusiasts to cheer for their team from any seat in the house.

Tonali, 3642 Shannon Rd., Ste. 1, Durham; (919) 489-8000; tonalirestaurant.com; Mexican; $. This hidden jewel offers a colorful, cozy, and casual atmosphere in which to enjoy authentic Mexican fare. Head Chef Andre Macias takes great care and skill in creating exceptional dishes including scratch-made tortillas for a wide variety of flavorful tacos. The frequently changing menu showcases ingredients that are in season and organic whenever possible. According to *Food & Wine,* Tonali's "expertly executed Mexican staples (fish tacos, shrimp fajitas, corn salads) and modest prices ensure a packed house on most nights." Although hard to find, this is one restaurant worth seeking out. (Hint: It's next door to the Shannon Road US Post Office!)

Twisted Noodles, 4201 University Dr., Durham; (919) 489-9888; twistednoodles.com; Thai; $. Located in the same nondescript strip mall as **Saladelia** (p. 183), Twisted Noodles offers a wide variety of authentic Thai dishes in a small and cozy environment. Plenty of rice and noodle dishes and delicious curries served by a friendly and efficient waitstaff make this casual restaurant a local favorite. The *tom yum* chile oil soup is a perfectly balanced mix of sweet and sour with a slight hint of spice, while the green papaya salad is light and refreshing. The house special volcano chicken, a half chicken marinated in yellow curry–spiced honey dramatically served on a hot sizzling plate steals the show. If you're in the mood for some heat, try the green curry, a spicy coconut broth chock-full of vegetables and your choice of meat or tofu. Vegetarians delight here, as all menu items can be made using tofu, the fried rice with eggs, tomatoes, onions, and scallions being a local favorite. Twisted Noodles can get busy on the weekend, which often results in slower service, so plan accordingly.

Tyler's Taproom, 324 Blackwell St., Ste. 400, Durham; tylerstap room.com/restaurants/durham; Pub; $. See write-up in the Chapel Hill chapter, p. 237.

Vin Rouge, 2010 Hillsborough Rd., Durham; (919) 416-0406; ghgrestaurants.com; French; $$$. Vin Rouge is an elegant and cozy cottage-like bistro that offers intimate indoor seating and a beautiful back courtyard to enjoy classical French fare for dinner and brunch. Executive Chef Matthew Kelly has built a reputation for being at the forefront of local chefs for his talent and dedication to the art of cooking. The tiny kitchen is in view of all those dining in the main dining room, so you can watch as Matt and his staff prepare classics like steak tartare, French onion soup, bouillabaisse, or roast chicken with Lyonnaise potatoes. There are five versions of *moules frites,* a sweetbread du jour, and all charcuterie is made in-house. The luxurious *fruits de mer* are offered as a *petit* or *grand plateau,* and the tower arrives brimming with succulent oysters, clams, shrimp, lobster, and crab legs—perfect for sharing with a group while enjoying a fine glass of French wine. Be sure to save room for dessert—the crème brûlée is divine. Though Sunday brunch is wildly popular and the restaurant fills up quickly, it is well worth the wait.

Vit Goal Tofu Restaurant, 2107 Allendown Dr., Durham; (919) 361-9100; Korean; $. Vit Goal is Durham's first Korean restaurant specializing in tofu soup, which arrives at your table bubbling away in oven-heated stoneware bowls. The soup menu variations include seafood, beef, mushroom, or oyster soup with clam, beef, pork, or vegetable dumplings. The rest of the menu includes more familiar Korean dishes such as BBQ ribs, seasoned beef, and a mung-bean pancake laden with seafood and vegetables. For a real feast, try the Korean casserole, which serves up kimchee, noodles, and at least three kinds of sausage in a paella-sized platter; order one dish for two people! For starters, as is a Korean custom, pickled vegetable dishes are placed on your table. Iced jasmine tea is served to everyone and refilled frequently. Lunch and dinner are served daily.

Watts Grocery, 1116 Broad St., Durham; (919) 416-5040; watts grocery.com; American/Farm to Table/Southern; $$. Chef-Owner Amy Tornquist's commitment to sustainable agriculture is evident on her Southern-inspired menu of dishes prepared using local and seasonal ingredients. Amy's reputation for the best of Southern cuisine is also evident by the line outside prior to opening on a Saturday morning. The warmly decorated former store also features art by her husband, Jeremy Kerman. The menu is distinctly Southern: a grits bowl with a choice of toppings on the side; fried chicken on a biscuit with sausage gravy; the "Pickles Sandwich" with green-tomato pickles, bread and butter pickles, and pimiento cheese; or a fried leg of rabbit with white beans, winter-squash mole, roasted sweet potato, and golden raisin gremolata. And if it's an after-movie snack at the bar, you don't want to miss the farmer's cheese hush puppies with a spicy basil mayonnaise. Finger lickin' good!

West 94th St. Pub, 4711 Hope Valley Rd., Ste. 6C, Durham; (919) 403-0025; west94stpub.com; Burgers/Pub; $$. This cozy neighborhood pub whose slogan appropriately states "where everyone knows your face" is the beloved gathering place to a daily fold of regulars who are quick to make newcomers feel welcome. Owned by Sarah Bonner and her daughter Kerrie Bonner-Bryant, the Pub has served up food and drinks to SW Durham's crowd of loyal followers for over 16 years. The Pub keeps patrons happy with numerous daily food and drink specials, including a $6 lunch menu, Monday to Friday from 11:30 a.m. to 2:30 p.m. With free Wi-Fi available, you are likely to find regulars settled in at the cozy bar tables working through lunch. For a hearty lunch, go for the Pub smokehouse burger. Topped with BBQ sauce, bacon, and cheddar cheese, it is juicy and full of flavor. For a lighter lunch, try the Pub shrimp salad: mixed greens and vegetables topped with grilled marinated jumbo shrimp. The full menu is available for dinner in addition to some notable platters. The NC BBQ Pork Platter's aroma packs a powerful punch, leaving you leaning over your neighbor's shoulder to get a look at what has started your stomach grumbling, while to your other side, the fish-and-chips have you longing for your own. Join the crowds for trivia or karaoke and you will be surrounded by rollicking fun, or gather a team together and participate in the Susan G. Komen for the Cure or St. Baldrick's charity events held yearly. Located in the Woodcroft Shopping Center, The Pub (as it is referred to) offers a comfortable homey inside, a covered patio, and ample parking.

Worth It Cafe, 2945 S. Miami Blvd., Ste. 122, Durham; (919) 381-6493; heyyoureworthit.com; American/Farm to Table; $. Chef Chuck Hayworth and his soul mate Aileen Scott Hayworth co-own this lunchtime-only cafe that is touted to be the first restaurant in the Research Triangle Park (RTP) to offer farm-to-table food sourced from area farms. Chef Chuck serves scratch-made soups, salads, and an assortment of sandwiches ranging from Cuban (shaved Cuban pork and all-natural ham with provolone cheese hot pressed on Cuban bread and, of course, served with pickles and a house-made dijonnaise dressing) to buffalo shrimp or catfish po' boys (breaded shrimp or catfish tossed in Carolina bayou hot sauce, served with lettuce, tomato, and a smoky remoulade dressing). Each entree is served with a choice of NC sweet potato fries, house-made root chips, or a pasta salad. Situated in a nondescript mall in the heart of the RTP, the Worth It Cafe offers lunch daily, Mon to Fri, from 11:30 a.m. to 2 p.m. However, a huge plus is the curbside meals-to-go that you can order ahead of time and pick up between 4:30 and 7 p.m—ideal for busy parents who want ready-made wholesome meals for their kids after a long day at work.

Landmarks

Four Square, 2701 Chapel Hill Rd., Durham; (919) 401-9877; foursquarerestaurant.com; American/Farm to Table/Southern; $$$$. Housed in the historic 1908 Bartlett Mangum House, a beautiful

R.I.P. Magnolia Grill

Magnolia Grill was one of "America's Best 50 Restaurants," and its Chef-Owners Ben and Karen Barker were well-known for flavor and flair. The James Beard Foundation named Ben "Best Chef in the Southeast" and Karen the nation's most "Outstanding Pastry Chef." Sadly, they closed the doors to their beloved restaurant on May 31, 2012. For over 30 years Ben and Karen delighted their customers with superb creations based on local and seasonally available ingredients and set a standard in the industry for impeccable execution. Although Magnolia Grill is no longer, it will linger in the minds of many for a long time to come. Magnolia Grill is worthy of a mention in this book for the institution it became. Good luck, Ben and Karen. I wish you the best in your future endeavors.

Victorian mansion with a wraparound porch, Four Square brings international fare with upscale sophistication to a new level. *Bon Appétit* calls Four Square "exciting" and remarks, "the plates going back to the kitchen were licked clean." Owned and operated by Executive Chef Shane Ingram and his wife, former pastry chef Elizabeth Woodhouse, the philosophy behind the food here is about taking what is seasonal and locally available and letting those ingredients speak for themselves on a regularly changing menu. Start with the grilled pheasant sausage, roasted marrow bone, or decadent lobster ravioli with creamed cabbage collards and truffle drizzle. Move on to country ham–stuffed North Carolina flounder, habañero-spiced grouper, or the exotic grilled antelope with chestnut-rice porridge, fall squash, and mustard–brown sugar barbecue sauce that is both tangy and sweet and a perfect accompaniment to the rich meat. A refined wine list and impeccable service round out a memorable dining experience, but don't leave without succumbing to the call of dessert. Go for the divine: The chocolate turtle torte with Maldon salted pecans, vanilla-bourbon gel, and sour cream Chantilly. See Sous Chef Kyle Wilkerson's recipe for **Kyle's Collard Cook-Off–Winning Collards** on p. 257.

Wimpy's Grill, 617 Hicks St., Durham; (919) 286-4380; wimpys grillnc.com; American/Burgers; $. A Durham landmark "known for big breakfasts and even bigger burgers." According to the Travel Channel's *Man v. Food,* the "meat magic" from this take-out joint is often enjoyed curbside, "because it's just too good to wait till you get home." The menu is simple: hot dogs, hamburgers, cheeseburgers, BBQ, fries, and the like, but the flavors are anything but simple. Meat for the burgers is ground fresh daily, and the classic Carolina burger with scratch-made chili, slaw, onions, and mustard gives you need to pause after the first bite to thank the heavens for its delicious simplicity.

Backyard BBQ Pit, 5122 Hwy. 55, Durham; (919) 544-9911; sweetribs.com; $. The Travel Channel's *Man v. Food* hails the open pit–smoked chicken and other Southern classics, but "it's the succulent pulled-pork barbecue that really makes this family-run restaurant a hungry man's haven." Backyard BBQ serves traditional Eastern-style BBQ that is cooked slowly over oak and hickory woods for a subtle but distinct smoke flavor. Ribs, beef brisket, fried fish, and smoked BBQ chicken are among the other staples on the menu, as well as a variety of side dishes such as collard greens, mac and cheese, fried okra, and Brunswick stew. There are also several home-made desserts, the honey bun being the best seller.

Bullock's BBQ, 3330 Quebec Dr., Durham; (919) 383-6202; bullocks bbq.com; $. Since the 1950s, this iconic Durham landmark has been serving legendary vinegar-based whole hog, Eastern-style BBQ and traditional Southern sides to generations of loyal customers. *Southern Living* says "at Bullock's, the lines form early for chopped or sliced pork . . . great hush puppies too." Chef-Owner Tommy Bullock's "Wall of Fame" showcases photographs of the many celebrities who have dined here, providing ample evidence of its popularity. As the website states, "Bullock's is where good friends meet to enjoy delicious food!" It is also popular for take-out BBQ.

Danny's Bar-B-Que, 2945 S. Miami Blvd., Ste. 118, Durham; (919) 806-1965; dannysbarbque.com; $. The meat at Danny's is cooked over hickory wood; sauces are original as are the side dishes. Chopped pork, pork loin, St. Louis–style ribs, turkey breast, beef brisket, and chicken are sold by the sandwich, plate, or packed to take home. The homemade sides such as baked beans and creamy coleslaw are made fresh daily, and you'll want to leave room for the homemade desserts, the banana pudding being a local favorite. Dine-in and takeout are available at all locations.

The Original Q-Shack, 2510 University Dr., Durham; (919) 402-4227; theqshackoriginal.com; $. Meats at this Lakewood area BBQ joint are smoked using both hickory wood and mesquite wood. Particularly great are the beef brisket, smoked chicken, St. Louis–style pork ribs, and of course, the signature hand-pulled pork, all of which are available by the pound or bowl, or as a platter or sandwich. The desserts "expertly prepared by two serious pastry chefs take this barbecue restaurant to another level," says *Southern Living.* Perfect for game day, Q-Shack offers three different tailgate specials as well as a "Hurry Home Pack," with enough to feed a family of four.

Brewpubs & Microbreweries

Bull City Burger and Brewery, 107 E. Parrish St., Ste. 105, Durham; (919) 680-2333; bullcityburgerandbrewery.com; Brewery/Brewpub. Locally sourced ingredients define this highly focused restaurant and brewery. Burgers and beer at their purest are the objective of the owner, Seth Gross. Most everything is made from scratch: sauerkraut, pickles, house-cured bacon, and natural-casing hot dogs. North Carolina grass-fed beef is ground fresh daily for the burgers, and the buns they are served on are baked in-house. Build your own burger or dog or feast on one of the specialties like the pimiento cheese burger topped with pickled vegetables. To complement your burger, enjoy a handcrafted ale or lager made in the tanks you see from behind a glass wall; this is as fresh as it comes! Beer is available by the pint, pitcher, and sampler in the restaurant, as well as to take home in growlers and kegs.

Fullsteam Brewery, 726 Rigsbee Ave., Durham; (919) 682-2337; fullsteam.ag; Brewery. Fullsteam Brewery is Durham's second craft-beer brewery and is devoted to a "plow to pint" philosophy of celebrating local and seasonal ingredients and supporting North Carolina farmers. The on-site Tavern opens nightly, where staples like the Rocket Science IPA the Fullsteam Southern Lager or Carver Sweet Potato made with North Carolina sweet potatoes flow freely to a loyal crowd of locals while a rotating lineup of food trucks is on hand for a quick bite to eat. The Tavern also features special one-time releases, occasional music, and many one-of-a-kind events. Brewery tours take place the first Sun of every month.

Bottle Shops

Triangle area residents love their beer, and the growing number of breweries can attest to that. To add to our brewery scene, a number of new and long-standing bottle shops offer an excellent selection of regular and specialty beers from across the nation and around the world. These are the places to look for hard-to-find vintages, single small-batch releases, and specialty beers not available anywhere else. The owners and staff of these establishments are extremely knowledgeable and can readily offer suggestions and answer questions. Most offer special tastings each week, where a representative from a particular brewery will be on-site to answer questions, provide samples, and often give away their brewery memorabilia. Aside from just weekly tastings, several bottle shops have tasting taps in the store where patrons can purchase small samples of beer or full pints to enjoy as you peruse the offerings. If you love beer, or are interested in learning more about it, then find the closest bottle shop and head on over.

The Beer Dispensary, *103-A E. Chatham St., Apex; (919) 267-6040; thebeerdispensary.com.* Offers about 550 beers, from the local NC brewery Natty Green's selections to Haandbryggeriet Dark Force, a double extreme imperial wheat stout from Norway; weekly tastings, Thurs 4 to 7 p.m.

Bottle Revolution, *4025 Lake Boone Trail, Raleigh; (919) 885-4677; bottlerevolution.com.* Offers about 1,000 beer choices and four on tap; weekly tastings Thurs 4:30 to 7 p.m. If you are a jogger, join the Bottle Revolution Run Club Wed night at 6:15 p.m. After the run, sample the evening's choice beer on tap.

The Bottle Shop at Tyler's Taproom, *18 Seaboard Ave., Ste. 150, Raleigh; (919) 322-0908.* Offers about 350 beers and adding taps soon. There are frequent specials on six-packs.

Carrboro Beverage Co., *120A E. Main St., Carrboro; (919) 942-3116; carrborobeverage.com.* Offers 350 beer choices and four taps; weekly tastings Thurs 7 to 9 p.m.

Peace Street Market, *804 W. Peace St., Raleigh; (919) 834-7070.* Offers about 200 different craft beers. The shop also has a great selection of wine, and sells tobacco as well.

Sam's Quik Shop, *1605 Erwin Rd., Durham; (919) 286-4110; samsquikshop.com.* Offers at least 1,000 beer choices and 6 taps; weekly tastings Fri 4 to 7 p.m. Located on Erwin Road in the old Blue Light Restaurant, Sam's offers perhaps the best beer selection in the Triangle. Sam's has a great selection of European beers. Glassware and cigars are also sold.

Tasty Beverage Co., *327 W. Davie St., Ste. 106, Raleigh; (919) 828-2789; tastybeverageco.com.* Offers 1,200 beers and 6 taps; weekly tastings Thurs 5:30 to 7:30 p.m.

T.J.'s Beverage and Tobacco, *306 E. Main St., Carrboro; (919) 968-5000; tjsbeverageandtobacco.com.* Offers over 750 beers; weekly tastings Fri 6 to 9 p.m. Also sells cigars, pipes, and rolling tobacco. You may want to consider joining their beer club for $95 a year for the first chance to taste hard-to-find beers.

Triangle Brewing Company, 918 Pearl St., Durham; (919) 683-2337; trianglebrewery.com; Brewery. Durham's oldest operating brewery, dedicated to producing well-balanced, full-flavored, yet highly drinkable Belgian- and American-style ales, offers its product in keg, growler, and cans at several local retailers and supermarkets. Making craft beers in authentic styles has garnered the operation a strong local reputation, and their popular Belgian-style Golden Ale can be found at most local pubs and restaurants. Stop by on Saturday for a free tour and samples and be sure to attend their annual Black Friday Cask Festival.

Whiskey, 347 W. Main St., Durham; (919) 682-6191; whiskey durham.com; Cocktail Lounge. Nary is the brown liquor not found in this private bar and club. In the sophisticated atmosphere where dark wood dominates and leather chairs beckon, Whiskey offers over 200 whiskeys, bourbons, scotches, NC beers, a distinct wine list, and a creative cocktail menu. No food is served, but it is available from several neighborhood restaurants including Toast, located next door. Entrance requires membership and can be purchased on-site. Live music often—typically jazz.

Bull City Homebrew, 1906 NC Hwy. 54, Ste. 200-B, Durham; (919) 682-0300; brewmasterstore.com. Bull City Homebrew offers a good selection of supplies and equipment and is a great resource for home brewers and winemakers in the Durham area. Nate, the owner, is almost always in the store and is very friendly and knowledgeable about home brewing and always happy to answer any questions and offer suggestions and home brewing tips. The store can be a little difficult to find, but is located across the street from Chick-Fil-A on Highway 54. Turn in where you see the sign for Design Hammer, and go straight back—they are on the right side toward the back of the parking lot.

Compare Foods Supermarkets, 2000 Avondale Dr., Durham; (919) 220-9638; comparesupermarkets.com. Compare is a small chain of supermarkets that originally started in Queens, NY. Today it has several stores in the northeast with North Carolina being its southernmost location. It would be fair to say that Compare caters to an international food shopper with a special emphasis on the Caribbean and Central and South American communities. When you go for the first time, allow for extra time to browse the aisles, including the fresh produce and meat sections. Choose smoked ham hocks or a shoulder of goat, fresh beef hearts or tongue, chicken feet, mangoes, plantains, fresh tortillas (corn or flour), Mexican *calabacita,* and all kinds of chiles, dried and fresh. Food is fresh and prices comparable to most other supermarkets.

Halgo European Deli and Grocery, 4520 S. Alston Ave., Durham; (919) 321-2014; halgo-durham.com. Focused on European specialty items, this off-the-beaten-path deli/grocery is a must for anyone seeking authentic goods from Eastern European origins. Choose from packaged pierogies that come with 10 different fillings, house-made herring salads, and European meats, cheeses, and breads. Sandwiches are available to go, and the hot kielbasa with sauerkraut piled high comes on a fresh bun slathered with spicy mustard. Call ahead and arrive to a plate of hot pierogies with sautéed onions and plenty of butter. Halgo is open Tues through Sat.

Hope Valley Bottle Shop, 4711 Hope Valley Rd., Durham; (919) 403-5200; hvbottleshop.com. Hope Valley Bottle Shop opened in August of 2008, with the goal of being a community-driven neighborhood store for fine wines and craft beers. Owner and operator Drew Lazarus, who is also an accredited somme-

lier, brings a restaurant-level hospitality to this retail outlet. A balanced selection of small, family-run estates as well as carefully chosen larger production brand-name wines is what you'll find, with all major wine regions being represented. Drew was the sommelier at the Washington Duke Inn & Golf Club and general manager of

Nana's Restaurant, and he selects wines for his store much as he put together wine lists at those great eateries—looking for a great quality/value ratio, varietal typicity of the grapes used, and a wide scope of flavors and styles. Forming personal relationships with customers and making personalized recommendations are what Hope Valley Bottle Shop is all about. Not to be missed is the moderate (but growing) assortment of craft-brewed domestic microbrews and "premium imports."

King's Red & White, 305 E. Club Blvd., Durham; (919) 220-2192. Family owned and operated, King's has been providing quality meats and local fresh produce to area residents since 1956. The family atmosphere and high level of customer service are unparalleled. It's where cashiers chat with you at the register, inquiring about your family, probably by name, and the butcher will cut the meat the way you want it. Whether you are planning for a party or just cooking a nightly meal for the family, King's has what you're looking for. In addition to the best cuts of meat and farm-fresh produce, you will find a great selection of homemade pimiento cheese, chicken salad, sausages, and old-style hoop cheese as well as hard-to-find pickling items and old-fashioned candies reminiscent of the "good old days." One experience at King's and you will never want to shop anywhere else.

La Superior, 22842 N. Roxboro Rd., Durham; (919) 220-9884. This medium-size Latin American grocery in North Durham offers a full butcher shop, cheese shop, fresh produce, and all the staples to make a traditional Mexican meal. What sets this grocery store apart from others is the large cafeteria tucked into the back of the store where you will find a taqueria, *panaderia/tortilleria,* and juice bar. Tacos from the taqueria are delicious and come with generous portions of fillings that range from chicken, steak, and pork to chorizo and *lengua* (beef tongue). Top them off at the salsa bar with fresh cilantro, onions, salsa, and pickled onion and jalapeño. The menu also has quesadillas, *gorditas, sopes, tamales,* and other Mexican fare. Stop by the juice bar for a refreshing *agua fresca* in flavors like mango and tamarind or order an *elote,* an ear of corn slathered with *crema,* then sprinkled with cheese, lime juice, and chile powder. This popular Mexican street food is not to be missed. After your meal, satisfy your sweet tooth with a trip to the *panaderia* counter for a bag of Mexican pastries to go.

Li Ming's Global Market, 3400 Westgate Dr., Durham. By the sound of the name, you might think that Li Ming's Global Market is just an Asian specialty grocery store. Wrong. It offers Asian, of course, but also ingredients for different cuisines such as Indian, Mediterranean, Hispanic, and Middle Eastern—plus items that you would see in an everyday American grocery chain. The fresh vegetable selection is excellent (ask a grocery clerk if you don't recognize a particular item); the variety of fish, live and otherwise, is growing. And before you leave, stop in the small food court for lunch (lunch for one is ample for two people).

Local Yogurt, 2501 University Dr., #8, Durham; (919) 489-5900; 2816 Erwin Rd., Durham; (919) 382-7400; localyogurt.com. A bright and cheerful environment awaits you at this independently owned frozen yogurt shop. The naturally frozen yogurt is always available in four fabulous flavors with an enticing selection of fruit, cereal, candy, and other toppings, all sourced from local farms and vendors. Flavor offerings rotate, but look for a wide range. From plain or chocolate to ginger lemonade sorbet to blueberry or peanut butter, there is something for everyone to enjoy. All yogurt served contains no artificial flavors, colors, or preservatives. It's *the* place to enjoy your favorite frozen treat—delicious, all-natural, low-calorie, and low-fat, with lots of fresh and fun toppings to put on top.

Locopops, 2604B Hillsborough Rd., Durham; (919) 286-3500; 231 S. Elliott Rd., Chapel Hill; 1908 Hillsborough St., Raleigh; ilovelocopops.com. Fêted by *Food & Wine* for their "wildly popular" Mexican popsicles (*paletas*), Locopops has fast become a local favorite. Owner Summer Bicknell uses only the freshest ingredients and offers both traditional flavors, such as mango-chile or the popular Mexican chocolate with hints of cinnamon, nutmeg, and clove, and quirky ones, like honeydew-lavender and chocolate rosemary. Locopops can be found in three convenient locations and are also sold in several area specialty stores and restaurants. Check the website for other locations.

Parker and Otis, 112 S. Duke St., Durham; (919) 683-3200; parkerandotis.com. Located in the beautiful historic Brightleaf

Square, this restaurant, coffee shop, gift shop, and wine, candy, and gourmet food market is open seven days a week for breakfast, lunch, and weekend brunch. Gourmet sandwiches are made on bread from **Rue Cler** (p. 182), while prepared salads are made fresh daily with an emphasis on local ingredients. *Bon Appétit* featured the recipe for their famous pimiento cheese dip, saying "this spread makes one heck of a sandwich." For a satisfying lunch try the shrimp BLT, with Havarti and bacon on toasted sourdough or white-bean spread, avocado, red onion, sprouts, and tomato on sunflower bread. The litany of cookbooks and cookware will delight the aspiring home cook, while the assortment of gift items from toys and games, wine, haute chocolates, and vintage candies that evoke memories of childhood, appeals to many.

Reliable Cheese Company, 405-A E. Chapel Hill St., Durham; (919) 680-3939; reliablecheese.com. This tiny shop conveniently located in downtown Durham specializes in cheese, cured meats, and charcuterie with a small but solid selection of beer, wine, condiments, and baked goods. Owner Patrick Coleff is very knowledgeable and encourages his customers to taste as many cheeses and meats as they would like, while explaining what flavors to expect and what foods or wines to pair with each. The selection of meats is impressive and includes items like Italian speck, *pâté de campagne,* or Vesuvio, a spicy salami with chunks of provolone. The artisan cheese selection rotates depending on the season and includes an assortment from across North Carolina as well as international varieties. Popular cheeses include the Roncal, a buttery and nutty cheese similar to Manchego, and the Brillat-Savarin, made using a triple-cream process that gives it a luxurious and buttery quality. To retain the quality and natural flavor of the cheeses, Coleff only cuts to order. Made-to-order sandwiches are available hot or cold and a must try is the pressed country ham panini. The distinct flavor of Johnson County ham, paired with the sweetness of fig jam and pungency of blue cheese, is a delightful, balanced combination of salty, sweet, and tart. For a real lesson in cheese, take one of the cheese classes offered and learn everything from Cheese 101 to entertaining with cheese. Classes run Sun from 4:00 to 5:30 p.m.; a schedule is available on the website.

Wine Authorities, 2501 University Dr., Durham; (919) 489-2884; wineauthorities.com. Noted for its friendly and knowledgeable staff and unpretentious atmosphere, Wine Authorities has a great selection of wines, weekly Saturday afternoon wine tastings, and the Enomatic—a wine-dispensing machine that allows customers to automatically pour tastes, half glasses, or full glasses of eight different wines by scanning a prepaid card. Purchases come with a printout about the wine (history, tasting notes, and food-pairing suggestions) that can be recorded online, making it easy for you to remember which ones you loved and would like to buy again. In addition to wine, you can find a selection of local beer and artisanal products like meats and cheeses for entertaining.

Chapel Hill

Founded in 1752, Orange County is made up of Chapel Hill, Carrboro, and Hillsborough, which, for the purpose of this book, are included together. Although Chapel Hill is most distinctly defined as being the home of the University of North Carolina, Carrboro as the "Paris of the Piedmont," and Hillsborough as the county seat, all have made their mark as historic towns and places to enjoy award-winning food. This section focuses on the culinary offerings of Orange County, from restaurants to cocktail lounges, from gourmet food markets to food-related events.

Chapel Hill, affectionately known as the "Southern Part of Heaven," and named a Distinctive Destination by the National Trust for Historic Preservation® in 2011, has fast become a popular dining destination for the many award-winning restaurants that have made their home here. In 2009, *Bon Appétit's* Andrew Knowlton bestowed on the city (as well as Durham) the title "America's Foodiest Small Town," and rightfully so. A pioneer of the Triangle food frontier with landmark restaurants like Crook's Corner and Mama Dips placing Southern fare on the map, AAA Four Diamond restaurants like Il Palio and Carolina Crossroads offering up the best in fine dining, and in 2011 James Beard Foundation naming Lantern's Chef-Owner Andrea Reusing Best Chef Southeast, it's no wonder.

Residents of Chapel Hill, Chapel Hillians as they are known, are as passionate about their food as they are about their basketball—who cooks it, where it came from, and who grew it. This is evident in the popularity of the Chapel Hill Farmers' Market and neighboring Carrboro Market, the growing number of food tours, and the praised and reputed cooking classes at **A Southern Season** (p. 253). Weekly visits to the farmers' markets by both restaurant chefs and home cooks show us the connection each has with the land our food is grown on. People want the freshest, tastiest food possible, both at home and when dining out, and having a relationship with the area farmers has made this possible for all.

Whether seeking out an upscale, casual, or laid-back dining experience to enjoy ethnic, vegetarian, or good ole Southern home cooking, there is something for everyone to experience and enjoy, something memories will be made from.

Carrboro made its debut in 1882, not as a city, but as a train depot for the university. Incorporated in 1911, this once sleepy textile mill town has made its mark as a burgeoning community for foodies, farmers, and artists. Main Street and Weaver Street, Carrboro's two main roads, are dotted with restaurants, bars, and coffee shops, but the main hub is Weaver Street Market, the area's popular co-op known for locally raised meats and produce and as a place to grab a quick bite to eat off the salad bar or hot buffet. Much more than a grocery store, the picnic tables scattered across its lawn have become a gathering place for friends and family to share a meal, listen to music or on some occasions be entertained by hula hoopers. Walk or bike (as Carrboro has plenty of walkways and bike paths) a short distance and find Neal's Deli, famed for their house-made corned beef and pastrami sandwiches or stop into Cliff's Meat Market, a Carrboro institution for over thirty-five years, known as the best butchery in town.

The year-round Carrboro Farmers' Market, the oldest in the area, is a draw not only for the local community, but also attracts chefs and foodies from all over the Triangle for fresh meats, cheeses, fruits, produce, and more. Weekly canning classes, cooking demonstrations, and seasonal tastings further the experience, continuing to build the relationship between farm, food, and table, a concept that continues to grow with each passing season.

Follow the crumbs down the road to the quaint and cozy town of Hillsborough and delight in the award-winning, seasonally inspired Italian cuisine of Aaron Vandermark at his restaurant **Panciuto** (p. 232), or enjoy the fresh-smoked flavors of pulled pork washed down with a cocktail from the **Hillsborough BBQ Company** (p. 245).

Sidle up to the bar at the Wooden Nickel Public House, Hillsborough's most popular (well, only) watering hole, and immerse yourself in the lively conversation surrounding you. Known for their great selection of draft and bottled beer, strong drinks, and locally focused menu, it's easy to see why the masses flock here. A seasonal farmers' market is open April through October and offers fresh local meats, produce, and handmade craft items. If you happen to be a pig lover and BBQ enthusiast, the yearly Hillsborough Hog Day is not to be missed. The festival activities revolve around BBQ teams competing for who has the best BBQ, and once you've sampled the succulent meat, you'll understand why this food event is so popular. From upscale cuisine and artisan chocolates to barbecue and pub grub, Hillsborough has a tiny sampling of everything for the food lover.

Getting Around

Compared to Raleigh or Durham, Chapel Hill/Carrboro is probably the easiest city to get around in on foot or bicycle. Chapel Hill and Carrboro are small enough to make walking a major mode of transportation. The Chapel Hill transit system is a fare-free system. Travelers can obtain schedules and city maps for the transit system, walking, and bicycling from **townofchapelhill.org/transit,** or you can ask for information at (919) 969-4900. Intercity buses also run between Chapel Hill and Hillsborough, which is the Orange County seat. There is also **Downtown Bicycle Rickshaw,** whose vehicles run exclusively on human energy or biofuels. The fleet includes pedicabs with service in downtown Chapel Hill and Carrboro, plus limos, vans, and buses. Call (919) 957-8294 or visit **greenway rides.com.**

Foodie Faves

ACME Food & Beverage Co., 110 E. Main St., Carrboro; (919) 929-2263; acmecarrboro.com; Southern; $$. Opened by Chef-Owner Kevin Callaghan in 1998, Acme Food & Beverage Co. is one of the oldest and most beloved restaurants in Carrboro, and open for dinner only seven nights a week, plus a hugely popular brunch on Sunday. Southern born and raised, Kevin's menu reflects his heritage, and he is, like so many other restaurateurs in this book, totally supportive of buying his produce from local sources. The dinner menu speaks Southern: fried green tomatoes (see recipe on p. 267) or smoked local pork belly as "small" plates or for regular dinner-size servings, try a long-standing local favorite, pecan-crusted fried chicken with mushroom gravy, garlic mashed potatoes, and Southern butter beans, which has been on their menu since they opened. Dinner is served from 5:30 p.m.; Sunday Brunch 10 a.m. to 2 p.m.

Bin 54, Glen Lennox Shopping Center, 1201-M Raleigh Rd., Chapel Hill; (919) 969-1155; bin54restaurant.com; Steak House; $$$$. Diners are welcomed by rich red hues, romantic lighting, and beautiful hardwood floors when they set foot into this upscale steak house. The appetizers can easily be made into a meal when a few are ordered and shared. The caramelized sea scallops, *foie gras* mousse with balsamic jam, or tender lobster gnocchi with truffle brown butter are all excellent choices. Top-quality meats and seafood are prepared simply: seasoned only with sea salt and fresh ground pepper, slow grilled over a wood fire to your liking, and finished with brown butter and choice of sauce on the side. Side dishes such as the truffled four-cheese macaroni, *haricots verts* with brown butter and almonds, or the popular rosemary, Parmesan, and garlic french fries must be ordered a la carte, but the portions are generous and easily enough for two. End your meal on a sweet note with a pear crisp with rum raisin and vanilla ice cream or banana pudding with bourbon pecan cookies. The staff is attentive, friendly, and more than happy to suggest a wine pairing from their outstanding selection.

Breadman's, 324 W. Rosemary St., Chapel Hill; (919) 967-7110; breadmans.com; American/Breakfast; $. Since 1974, Breadman's has been Chapel Hill's go-to restaurant for all-day breakfast served in large portions at reasonable prices. If breakfast food is not what you're in the mood for, their lunch and dinner menus also offer a great selection of homemade soups, salads, sandwiches, as well as barbecue and home-style dishes like meat loaf, grilled chicken, or rib eye steak; all served with corn bread or biscuit and choice of two sides. Because this is a popular eatery for a weekend brunch, the wait can often be long; friendly staff move fast to accommodate you as quickly as possible. Open daily 7 a.m. to 9 p.m. and to 10 p.m. Fri.

Elaine's on Franklin, 454 W. Franklin St., Chapel Hill; (919) 960-2770; elainesonfranklin.com; American; $$$. Since 1999, Chef-Owner Brett Jennings has delighted diners with his regional American cuisine. The colorful atmosphere, highlighted by sky-lights and intimate window seating, makes this small, upscale restaurant warm and inviting, perfect for a special occasion dinner. By utilizing the finest local ingredients and preparing everything in house, Elaine's offers diners a unique culinary experience that reflects the best of what NC farmers produce. The menu changes fre-quently, so every visit results in a surprise to the palate. Appetizer options may include seared Vietnamese barbecued quail or ven-ison sausage patties with corn pancakes, roasted corn relish, and Vermont maple syrup. Entree selections may include grilled house-smoked pork tenderloin with shrimp 'n grits, country ham, onion confit, and redeye gravy, or grilled wild sturgeon with roasted garlic spaetzle, lar-dons, savoy cabbage, and Pommery mustard sauce. Save room for one of Brett's homemade desserts and indulge in a warm apple crisp with walnut streusel topping and ginger ice cream or warm chocolate cake with pistachio ice cream and chocolate sauce. A nightly 3-course early menu is available for theatergoers, and the extensive wine selection is recognized annually with *Wine Spectator*'s Award of Excellence.

Elmo's Diner, 200 N. Greensboro St., Carrboro; (919) 929-2909; elmosdiner.com; American/Breakfast; $. See write-up in the Durham chapter, p. 156.

Foster's Market, 750 Martin Luther King Jr. Blvd., Chapel Hill; (919) 967-3663; fostersmarket.com; American/Breakfast; $. See write-up in the Durham chapter, p. 160.

411 West, 411 W. Franklin St., Chapel Hill; (919) 967-2782; 411west.com; Italian; $$. A lively and energetic Italian cafe located in the heart of downtown Chapel Hill, 411 West's menu is inspired by the flavors of Italy and the Mediterranean. Featuring house-made pastas, seafood, steaks, and wood-fired pizzas, it is best known for its pasta dishes. Try the spaghetti marinara—the sauce is made in-house and is simple, fresh, and delicious, or indulge in hazelnut pesto angel-hair, made with sautéed arugula, asparagus, mushrooms, grape tomatoes, yellow squash, hazelnut pesto, and goat cheese. Pizza lovers will be delighted by the made-to-order, wood-fired thin crust pizzettes. Weekly specials and seasonal risottos may bring pan-roasted NC flounder with lemon and butter or risotto with shiitake mushrooms, carrots, golden beets, Parmesan, arugula, and butternut squash folded into creamy Arborio rice. All desserts are made on the premises including the decadent Millionaire Pie—peanut butter mousse pie on graham cracker crust, glazed with chocolate and served with whipped cream and chocolate sauce. The food is expertly prepared, the wine list extensive and affordable, and the staff friendly and knowledgeable.

Glasshalfull, 106 S. Greensboro St., Carrboro; (919) 967-9784; glasshalfullcarrboro.com; American/Tapas/Wine Bar; $$. Glasshalfull is a contemporary restaurant with a modern-day wine bar and retail wine store, all tucked into a renovated warehouse in downtown Carrboro. The restaurant is open for lunch and dinner, and the menu is built to pair perfectly with the large and impressive selection of wines. A small-plates menu incorporating meats, cheeses, pâtés, and other light fare is well thought out, with the idea in mind that friends will gather together over a glass of wine and share plates of food. Larger entree options include fish, seafood, and meat along with a good selection of vegetarian dishes. If you like what you are drinking off the wine list, be sure to pick up a bottle at the store to enjoy at home.

Gourmet Kingdom, 301 E. Main St., Carrboro; (919) 932-7222; thegourmetkingdom.com; Chinese; $$. Named one of the 50 best Chinese restaurants in the United States by CNN and considered by many a true hidden gem, this relaxed and unpretentious eatery specializes in delicious Szechuan food worthy of the mention. With more than 150 dishes on the menu, Gourmet Kingdom has something for everyone to enjoy. There are tables and booths throughout, or if dining with a large group, opt for the private room with large circular tables equipped with a lazy Susan for a family-style meal.

Notable menu items, ones that have stood the test of time and regulars rave about, include the Szechuan spicy dried beef and Tian Jin dumplings, filled with a flavorful pork mixture. For a decadent treat, feast on the crispy whole fish in black bean sauce or the green onion–fried tea-smoked duck. And if you are in the mood for some heat, order the sautéed green chile peppers: jalapeños simmered in a sweet soy-ginger sauce that pack a nice punch to the palate. The best way to enjoy a meal here is to bring the whole family or a number of friends and order several dishes to share. Gourmet Kingdom is open for lunch daily except Tues, and dinner nightly. The $5.25 lunch special is a real deal, with choice of appetizer, like the eight-piece order of dumplings, paired with an entree such as the chicken in garlic sauce—you will not leave hungry.

Il Palio, 1505 E. Franklin St., Chapel Hill; (919) 918-2545; ilpalio .com; Farm to Table/Italian; $$$. Nestled in the elegant Siena Hotel, Il Palio offers world-class dining in an intimate and elegant setting with contemporary European flourishes. The Italian-inspired cuisine, expertly prepared by Executive Chef Adam Rose and his Chef de Cuisine Isaiah Allen, showcases the diversity of North Carolina's local farmers, artisan producers, and their commitment to using what is seasonally available. The carefully crafted menus offer a wide selection of appetizers, antipasto, and entree options. To start, treat yourself to the grappa-cured salmon or the marinated beet salad—chèvre, arugula, blood orange supremes, tarragon, and fried chickpeas drizzled with aged red wine vinegar. They're known for house-made pastas—shrimp scampi and butternut squash ravioli in balsamic brown butter vinaigrette with amaretti cookie powder, shiitake mushrooms, and chives (see recipe on p. 287) will not disappoint. The selection of wines is impressive, and the knowledgeable sommelier will happily suggest pairings to complement each course. Entree options range from pan-seared scallops and balsamic-glazed duck breast to an impressive 28-day aged porterhouse served alongside a truffled twice-baked potato and creamed spinach. For dessert, the cheesecake and tiramisu are excellent choices. Since it is part of the Siena Hotel, Il Palio is also open for breakfast and lunch.

Jujube, 1201 Raleigh Rd., Chapel Hill; (919) 960-0555; jujube restaurant.com; Asian Fusion; $$. Located in the unassuming Glen Lennox strip mall next to **Bin 54** (p. 216), Jujube boasts lively atmosphere surrounded by minimalist decor, accented by large photos depicting Asian street scenes, making it a welcoming destination to enjoy Chef-Owner Charlie Deal's Asian fusion–inspired creations. The menu offers a great selection of small plates and entrees using only the freshest ingredients, presented in an intimate dining environment. To start, share the panfried pork and cabbage dumplings, tuna tartare or crispy calamari with pickled chiles, roasted ginger aioli, and scallion oil while seated at the quaint tables surrounding the main dining room. For a little more action, opt to dine in front of the open kitchen bar and watch as the chef prepares main dishes like lemongrass-grilled hanger steak with cucumber salad and spicy peanut sauce (see recipe on p. 289) or the "Angry Seafood"—shrimp, squid, crawfish, and mussels with Sichuan black bean sauce. Several vegetarian options are available, including a citrus curry with soy protein, winter squash, and Asian greens, that are sure to please. The extensive beer and wine list will enhance your dining experience, while the specialty cocktails, made

from an impressive selection of spirits, are a draw all their own. The lunch menu offers a Vietnamese *banh mi* sandwich—choice of protein on toasted **Guglhupf** (p. 164) baguette with pickled carrot and daikon, herbs, cucumber, sweet chile mayo, jalapeños, and a side of Asian slaw.

Kitchen, 764 Martin Luther King Jr. Blvd., Chapel Hill; (919) 537-8167; kitchenchapelhill.com; French; $$. Located in a nondescript strip mall near downtown Chapel Hill, Kitchen is a small and cozy bistro serving French-inspired contemporary fare. To owners Dick and Sue Barrows, it is about serving delicious food using the freshest ingredients, simple preparations, and providing friendly and efficient service, all of which they have achieved. To start, enjoy a glass of wine along with an appetizer of slow-braised Berkshire pork belly or house-smoked trout with cucumber, beet, and horseradish. Mussels come in four different variations including the traditional Provençal and a Thai version made with red curry coconut milk and lemongrass that had me begging for more bread to sop up the remaining broth. Simple, classic entrees are executed with precision, like the flatiron steak with shallot jus cooked just right and tender braised lamb shank or the duck confit with caramelized onions and fingerling potatoes. Leave room for a dessert, either the dark chocolate almond torte or the lemon ricotta cheesecake—the use of ricotta lends the cheesecake a light, airy quality that is a lovely ending to a meal here. The kitchen is open for lunch Tues through Sat and dinner Tues through Sun.

Lantern, 423 W. Franklin St., Chapel Hill; (919) 969-8846; lantern restaurant.com; Asian Fusion; $$$$. Located in downtown Chapel Hill, Lantern offers guests Asian-inspired American fare in a refined yet cozy atmosphere. The chic upstairs bar is the ideal location in which to enjoy the impressive cocktail menu while sampling from the list of mouthwatering appetizers. Try the Hibiscus Petal (hibiscus-infused vodka and fresh lime juice) paired with the local pasture-raised pork and chive dumplings or salt-and-pepper shrimp with fried jalapeños, cilantro, and sea salt and you are in for a palate-pleasing experience. If you are in a playful mood, order the make-your-own-sushi bento box for a twist on the traditional. For dinner, the James Beard Award–winning Chef-Owner Andrea Reusing offers farm-fresh, seasonally inspired dishes. Popular is the whole North Carolina flounder or lemongrass-grilled Chapel Hill Creamery pork chop with a fried farm egg, peanuts, and spicy green papaya salad served with steamed jasmine rice and chile-lime sauce. Her most renowned dish, a tea-and-spice-smoked chicken, has even been featured in *Food & Wine*. While cocktails are certainly a standout here, so are the thoughtfully chosen wine list and a friendly and knowledgeable staff, always willing to offer pairing suggestions. Be sure to save room for the hot chocolate cake with malted chestnut ice cream or the roasted banana ice cream with caramel, soft cream, and North Carolina peanut brittle dessert.

La Residence, 202 W. Rosemary St., Chapel Hill; (919) 967-2506; laresidencedining.com; French; $$$. Nestled in a 1940s home in downtown Chapel Hill, La Res, as it is lovingly known, serves French-inspired American fare in an intimate setting. The small menu changes with the seasons, highlighting the freshest ingredients available. Look for a delightfully refreshing basil-infused gazpacho in warmer months or a warming butternut squash soup with *shimeji* mushrooms, pork and apple ravioli, and a hint of white truffle in the cooler months. Order the "Petite Lettuce Salad" and it is likely to arrive with house-made raisins, beets, cherry tomatoes, and crushed nuts on one occasion or baby beets, pickled red onion, watermelon radish, buttered pecans, and goat cheese on another. Seafood selections may be flounder, salmon, or speckled sea trout, while sides for the Black Angus beef tenderloin rotate between fresh asparagus and carrots to potato gratin and collard greens. Clearly evident is the passion for quality and a commitment to supporting local farmers and offering diners only seasonally available ingredients. From the casual cafe menu available in the bar and expansive garden patio to the fine-dining menu in the cozy intimate dining rooms, "La Res" is a Chapel Hill dining destination.

Lime & Basil, 200 W. Franklin St., Chapel Hill; (919) 967-5055; limeandbasil.com; Vietnamese; $$. This cheerful and welcoming environment, enhanced by lime-green walls, is popular for its excellent selection of Vietnamese fare, and best known for its *pho,* a traditional noodle soup made with a rich beef broth, ladled over rice noodles, meat, sprouts, basil, and lime. Also on the menu are a good selection of vermicelli, rice dishes, and a fine list of house specialties like the Lime and Basil's fried rice, a delightful blend of chicken, roast pork, Chinese sausage, shrimp, peas, carrots, onions, and eggs tossed with rice. Worth noting is that vegetarian substitutions are available for most dishes. The *banh mi,* a traditional baguette sandwich, comes in five variations including a vegetarian version with stir-fried "soy" beef and sautéed onions. All come topped with a homemade mayo spread, freshly pickled carrots, daikon, cucumbers, jalapeños, and cilantro. Quick service, inexpensive prices, and a friendly staff make this a Chapel Hill favorite.

Margaret's Cantina, 1129 Weaver Dairy Rd., Chapel Hill; (919) 942-4745; margaretscantina.com; Mexican; $$. Located in the Timberlyne Shopping Center, Margaret's Cantina provides fresh, healthy Southwestern fare in a warm and welcoming setting. Chef-Owner Margaret Lundy creates her cuisine using fresh, local, and seasonal ingredients, including many vegetarian options. The guacamole and sweet potato chips with a chile mayo are a perfect beginning to a meal, especially when paired with a made-to-order margarita made with fresh-squeezed limes. The *sopas* are excellent here, especially her popular "feel-better" chicken chowder and traditional posole—pork and hominy soup with red chile in a light flavorful broth, garnished with shredded lettuce, onion, radish, a wedge of fresh lime, and crisp corn tortilla strips. Tacos, burritos, quesadillas, and enchiladas come with your choice of protein (including tempeh) and are all excellent choices, but if you haven't tried Lundy's famous rotisserie chicken, stop right now. The fresh, juicy rotisserie-roasted chicken is perfectly seasoned, finished on the grill, and served with a wide selection of sauces and sides. Sides range from Southwestern grits or Spanish brown rice to well-seasoned black beans or garlic-sautéed greens. It is a delightful, satisfying meal. Lunch served weekdays and dinner Mon through Sat.

Mediterranean Deli, 410 W. Franklin St., Chapel Hill; (919) 967-2666; mediterraneandeli.com; Bakery/Deli/Middle Eastern; $. This bustling and lively deli and bakery in the heart of Chapel Hill offers authentic cuisines from the Middle East and the Mediterranean at reasonable prices. The pristine deli case showcases a beautiful array of freshly prepared vegetarian and meat dishes including hummus, stuffed grape leaves, Mediterranean grilled tuna, lamb shank, and several mixed salads. A Middle Eastern specialties menu offers stuffed pitas and gyros with your choice of meat or vegetable and served in freshly baked pita bread topped with lettuce, tomato, peppers, onions, and *tzatziki* sauce. The shawarma—chicken or beef marinated with olive oil, cardamom, garlic, and Lebanese spices—arrives with tabouli and hummus as a platter or served with onions and tahini sauce on a pita. The *fatayer,* which resembles an Italian calzone, is fresh baked, boat-shaped dough topped with various combinations of meats and veggies. For a unique experience try the Turkish *soujouck fatayer*—aged, spicy Turkish sausage with freshly oven-baked eggs. The complimentary feta cheese, olive, and condiment bar adds to the overall experience as does a refreshing drink of pomegranate juice mixed with fresh grapefruit juice, or an authentic Turkish coffee. Be sure to take some baklava home.

Merlion Restaurant, 410 Market St., Ste. 320, Chapel Hill; (919) 933-1188; merlionfood.com; Asian Fusion/Chinese; $$. A spacious restaurant nestled in Chapel Hill's bustling Southern Village, Merlion is the hot spot for authentic Singaporean specialties. The interior is warm and inviting, and the staff is friendly and helpful. The Asian flavors found on the menu reflect the diverse population of Singapore and the country itself, combining Indian, Malaysian, Thai, and Chinese cuisines. Crowd-pleasers include Hainanese chicken rice (the "unofficial national dish of Singapore"), Hokkien noodles with shrimp and calamari seasoned with chile sambal and lemon, and *char siew* and dumpling noodle soup, a beautiful presentation of Chinese honey-roasted pork fanned over noodles with dumplings and baby bok choy. The Peking duck feast is well worth the wait (it requires 30 minutes to prepare) and a delightful sight when it arrives—hand-carved wafer-thin crispy skin and duck meat served with rice pancakes, green onions, and plum sauce. A traditional soup of tofu and salted mustard leaves is an optional side, but you must ask for it. This is a highly popular dish and because of the length of time it takes to prepare it, you must make a reservation for it on the weekends. Save room for dessert and you will be rewarded. Try the lavish sago pudding, a Merlion signature dessert of soft tapioca pearls drizzled with coconut cream sauce and palm sugar syrup or *mochi* ice cream—mango or green tea–flavored ice cream balls wrapped in *mochi,* a sweet, short-grained glutinous rice. Merlion is open Tues through Sun for lunch and dinner.

Merritt's Store & Grill, 1009 S. Columbia St., Chapel Hill; (919) 942-4897; merrittsstoreandgrill.com; American/Sandwiches/ Southern; $. Merritt's has been a much-loved and respected landmark in Chapel Hill since opening in 1929. The rustic building and down-home Southern atmosphere are warm and inviting, giving you a sense of "coming home to mom's house." A big sign hanging over the aisle reading, "Simply the Best Food in Town," competes with the fact that Merritt's is also touted as being "Home of the World Famous BLT." Merritt's also has hot dogs, barbecue, sausage, eggs, and hamburgers—but the fried bologna and egg sandwich washed down with a Coke from a real glass bottle really hits the spot. Whether you are simply stopping in this corner store grill to grab a cup of fresh brewed coffee, pantry items, or hot off the grill comfort food, it is a true experience in Southern hospitality.

Milltown, 907 E. Main St., Carrboro; (919) 968-2460; diningand
drinking.com; Burgers/European/German/Pub; $. Milltown offers a
relaxed pub environment with a hipster vibe in which to enjoy a
wide selection of beers from around the globe. There are 18 beers
on tap and more than 150 available by the bottle. Yes, they are
serious about beer. So serious in fact, the food here is largely made
up of items that either pair well with what they have to offer or are
made with it. The menu is mostly European influenced, made up
of sandwiches, meat-centric entrees, and hearty pub fare. The list
is heavy on Belgian-style beers, so look for the traditional Dubbel,
Lambic, or Tripels to pair with *moules frites* for a satisfying meal.
The curry fries are worth the splurge, as are the burgers, slow-
cooked, fall off the bone ribs, and fish tacos. Dine inside if you
choose, but if the weather is nice, the large outdoor patio is where
all the action is. Open 7 days a week.

Neal's Deli, 100 E. Main St., Carrboro; (919) 967-2185; nealsdeli
.com; American/Deli; $. Matt and Sheila Neal opened Neal's Deli in
April 2008 and in a short period of time have garnered a loyal following along with excellent reviews in the national press. Matt grew
up in Carrboro—his father, Bill Neal, started **Crook's Corner** (p.
241) in 1982—and Sheila used to be the manager at the **Carrboro
Farmers' Market** (p. 37), where she built close relationships with
the local farmers; the deli now sources most of its ingredients from
them. The Neals make their own pastrami using antibiotic and hor-
mone free brisket and cure it for a week before it's ready for serving.
The house-cured pastrami or corned beef on rye with mustard is an

absolute must for any traditional deli-goer. But you will also be won over with a breakfast biscuit stuffed with egg and sausage or a house-made porchetta sandwich with spinach and pickled peppers. Neal's Deli is only open for breakfast and lunch (7:30 a.m. to 4 p.m.) and is closed on Sunday.

One, 100 Meadowmont Village Circle, Chapel Hill; (919) 537-8207; one-restaurant.com; American/Farm to Table; $$. One's atmosphere is "one" to be reckoned with. Whether you choose to dine in the modern-looking restaurant or the separate, more relaxed bar area, Executive Chef Sean McCarthy is delivering a seasonally changing menu that showcases his talent and creativity. Try smoked onion and parsnip bisque or smoked cherry cola–marinated flank steak with spring-onion gravy to start before moving on to expertly prepared meat, chicken, and fish entrees, all prepared in an exposed kitchen, allowing diners to watch as their food is prepared. Don't skip the wine pairings; they have an extensive wine menu and an enthusiastic staff willing to offer expert suggestions. Desserts are a must so save room. Pastry Chef Deric McGuffey (also pastry chef for **G2B Gastro Pub** [p. 163]) is an absolute genius, and his creations, works of art. I am a sucker for just about anything he comes up with, but the recent chocolate-banana, five spice ganache with smoked pistachio, puffed rice, peanut butter ice cream, chocolate gel, banana brûlée, and dark chocolate mousse could easily have brought tears to my eyes. The restaurant is open for lunch, and the convenient location makes it an ideal spot for business meetings.

Panciuto, 110 S. Churton St., Hillsborough; (919) 732-6261; panciuto.com; Farm to Table/Italian; $$$. Pronounced "pan-choo-toe," this Hillsborough restaurant's menu is decidedly Southern influenced Italian using the finest local meats and produce from area farmers. Chef-Owner Aaron Vandemark offers a small-plate menu on Wednesday and Thursday that encourages guests to sample or share a variety of dishes on the menu. If you are ordering wine with your meal, know that the wines come from small family-owned and operated wineries throughout Italy. Vandemark was nominated as a semifinalist for the 2011 Best Chef: Southeast by the James Beard Foundation and by *Food & Wine* magazine for "The People's Best New Chef 2011," a clear indication that he is one of the most outstanding chefs in the area.

Queen of Sheba, 1129 Weaver Dairy Rd., Chapel Hill; (919) 932-4986; queenofshebachapelhill.com; Ethiopian; $$$. Queen of Sheba is a quaint, warm space tucked away in Timberline shopping center. You will immediately know you are in for a treat when you are seated in front of a circular woven basket. This traditional basket is actually a stand for the platter of delicious food to come. Ethiopian food is traditionally shared and eaten by scooping it up in a spongy, crepe-like flat bread called *injera*. The food is served on top of the *injera,* which soaks up the delicious sauces—finger food at its finest! Ethiopian food is all about the *watt* (stew) and its wonderful spices, such as *berbere,* an Ethiopian blend containing garlic, red pepper, cardamom, coriander, fenugreek, and several other spices. If eating with your hands presents an issue for you, they thoughtfully provide utensils. Give it a try with your fingers, though—it is fun! The *yemitten shiro watt,* a vegetarian's delight, consists of pea flour simmered in a mild sauce of onion, herbs, and spices along with a touch of garlic and fresh ginger. For the meat lover, try the *kay watt;* tender cubes of beef, first panfried with black pepper and olive oil then braised in the aforementioned *berbere*-spiced sauce. Because of the intimate size of the space and the traditional experience, it is best for couples or parties no larger than six people.

Saffron, 3140 Environ Way, Chapel Hill; (919) 240-7490; dine atsaffron.com; Indian; $$$. The lavish setting, accented by soft lighting, red and gold tapestries, colorful banquettes, and mirrored walls, instantly makes you feel as though you have been transported to the exotic Taj Mahal. A domed pavilion acts as the restaurant's centerpiece and adds to the excitement and anticipation of the meal about to unfold. Executive Chef Durga Prasad's extensive menu is a blend of northern and southern Indian specialties. Start with Rajasthani *kurkuri bhindi,* spicy crisp-fried okra with lentil-battered onion rings, or if you are dining with a group, the tandoori vegetable *khazana,* a sampler platter with many of the best items from the appetizer menu, including the *aloo tikki chana chaat,* a blend of chickpeas, onions, tomatoes, yogurt, with two chutneys over a spicy potato patty. Be sure to order plenty of crispy-chewy naan, the traditional clay oven–baked bread to accompany it. If you've stopped in just to enjoy the surroundings while sampling any one of their creative cocktails, you are in for a treat. The cocktail menu is just as exotic and lovely as the atmosphere and food menu, and you are sure to find something you love. However, if you plan to stay for dinner, entrees include plenty of meat, seafood, and vegetarian options. Lamb lovers will love their version of vindaloo and korma, and if you are a fan of goat's meat, you will not be disappointed in the Hyderabadi *buna gosht* goat meat marinated in ginger, garlic, bay leaves, cumin, and clove in a peppery onion sauce. The staff is attentive and knowledgeable, and the bar offers a solid selection of beers, wines, and enticing specialty cocktails.

Sandwich, 407 W. Franklin St., Chapel Hill; (919) 929-2114; sandwich.biz; American/Sandwiches; $$. Sandwich, you guessed it, specializes in the art of unique combinations placed between two slices of bread. Try the Outrageous BLT, their take on the classic BLT with the addition of roasted jalapeños, avocado, and garlic mayo, or the Middle Eastern–inspired *keema naan*—chickpeas, curried eggplant, basmati rice, coriander, chicken, and raita inside naan (Indian flatbread). In addition to their more offbeat selections, look for plenty of classic burgers, salads, and, you guessed it, sandwiches. A solid selection of local draft beers is available as well as wine by the glass. For a refreshing change, try the Moroccan-style iced tea, green tea infused with mint and fresh sage. Inside, Chef-Owner

Hitch Ebitri has created a relaxed atmosphere that is open and airy, while the outside patio facing Franklin Street is perfect for people-watching. For a real treat, stop in Thursday, Friday, and Saturday evenings and delve into Hitch's rotisserie chicken—moist, tender, and juicy and served with your choice of side, it is easily some of the best around.

Squids Restaurant and Oyster Bar, 1201 Fordham Blvd., Chapel Hill; (919) 942-8757; squidsrestaurant.com; Seafood; $$. The warm, inviting interior of this popular restaurant is known as the venue for the area's best fresh seafood and contemporary oyster bar. For 26 years, Squids has served top-notch wood-grilled fillets, fresh Maine lobster, lightly breaded and fried seafood, and the rotating specials that are a hit to all who dine here. Standouts include the seafood chowder—creamy New England style, with seafood, potatoes, carrots, and smoked bacon—or Chef Andy Wilson's famous horseradish-crusted tilapia, which first appeared as a special, but fast became a local favorite worthy of a permanent place on the menu. Creative weekly specials may find pan-seared NC flounder with lime and basil slaw and fragrant green curry rice or grilled scallops with roasted asparagus, new potatoes, and cremini mushrooms drizzled in lemon vinaigrette. A daily oyster happy hour is a lively affair, as people clamor to devour fresh-shucked oysters and engage in animated conversation with the folks around them. When the weather is just right, try dining on the beautiful patio.

Talullas, 456 W. Franklin St., Chapel Hill; (919) 933-1177; talullas .com; Middle Eastern; $$$. Talullas is the Triangle's most established Turkish restaurant, specializing in traditional 15th- and 16th-century Ottoman cuisine that draws its influence from Africa, the Middle East, and the Mediterranean. The interior whisks you away to a different time and place with the lush textures and colors of hand-woven carpets, as the aromas of fresh-baked breads and spices waft from the kitchen, tempting you to partake in the many delicacies of the extensive menu—multiple lamb and whole grilled fish options, organic salads, and a slew of vegetarian options. Hot and cold mezzes are meant to be shared such as the *patlıcan ezmesi*—smoked eggplant puree with yogurt and tahini topped with chopped walnuts—or *manti*—steamed dumplings stuffed with ground lamb and beef and served in a yogurt and garlic sauce. If you are a fan of pizza, you will love the Turkish twist on this classic. Combinations include fresh seasonal vegetables topped with tomatoes, olives, and cheese or feta, *kasar,* and mozzarella with air-cured spicy beef sausage, topped with an egg. The seasonal wine list complements the fare. Late evening events might bring Middle Eastern belly-dancing performances, Cuban salsa bands, or electronic DJs from Chicago and Miami.

Tyler's Taproom, 102 E. Main St., Carrboro; (919) 929-6881; tylerstaproom.com/restaurants; Pub; $$. This is your everyday local pub, favored by UNC-Chapel Hill students and professors as well as Chapel Hill/Carrboro dwellers of all ages. The Carrboro location has 38 beers on draft, and on pint night—Tuesday in Carrboro—you get to keep your glass. Traditional pub food flavored with seasonal interest includes burgers, salads, fish tacos, and a daily luncheon special. Try the Southern-style fried green pickles or an order of fries that are consistently touted as the best in the Triangle! Carrboro's location is the original Tyler's Taproom, which also owns the Carrboro Beverage Co. next door, selling beer, wine, cider, and mead to take home. Durham, Apex, and Raleigh each have a Tyler's Taproom. Carrboro hours are 11 a.m. to 2 a.m.

Vimala's Curryblossom Cafe, 431 W. Franklin St., Chapel Hill; (919) 929-3833; curryblossom.com; Indian; $–$$. "When Vimala Cooks, Everybody Eats," reads the sign on the door, a reminder that owner Vimala Rajendran has been bringing the community together to share lovingly prepared healthy, locally grown meals for a remarkably long time. After 18 years of offering donation-based community dinners out of her home, the community she nourished came together to help feed her dream. They pledged $80,000 in five days to help her open her hugely popular restaurant in The Courtyard on West Franklin Street in early 2011. Vimala's husband, son, and daughter join her in running the restaurant along with a talented crew, and all are paid a living wage. Vimala's strong belief in social justice and sustainability is seen in everything she does. She feeds

CACKALACKY

If you're looking for a new staple for your pantry shelf, try North Carolina's very own, award-winning Cacalacky Spice Sauce. (Cackalacky is pronounced "kak-uh-lak-ee.") Just over 10 years ago, Page Skelton set out to make bland food taste better and developed a zesty sweet-potato-based hot sauce that he bottled himself. After giving away dozens of bottles to family and friends, he patented the product, and it is now reaching shelves in natural and grocery stores in over 22 states. And, I would imagine that sales will continue to grow after Cackalacky received a glowing review in the February 2012 *Bon Appétit*'s Savor of the South issue. Look for great "Zestipes" at cackalacky.com, like this one for a party dip that is guaranteed to please any crowd. In a serving bowl, simply stir together ¾ cup Cackalacky Spice Sauce with a 16-ounce container of sour cream. Serve with your favorite chips and/or vegetables.

everyone who walks through the door, regardless of the ability to pay. There's a jar on the counter for donations for those who want to contribute. She has close ties to local producers—almost everything they serve is crafted using local and seasonal ingredients. Enter the bustling little cafe and you immediately smell the delicious aroma of spices wafting out of the small kitchen. Check out the chalkboard for daily specials, and order at the counter. *Chole, chaat,* tandoori chicken, samosas, *dosa*—all are basic Indian dishes, you would think, but not at Vimala's. Here you feel the love and pride that have been put into every dish, with incredible results. Just watch as people flock to this sweet little cafe; they feel it too. Vimala's also has loads of gluten-free and vegan options, as well as beer and wine. Don't miss a chance for some hands-on experience with Vimala's cooking classes, you are sure to walk away from the experience proud and humbled.

Weathervane, University Mall, 201 S. Estes Dr., Chapel Hill; (919) 929-9466; southernseason.com/cafe2.asp; American/Southern; $$. The Weathervane features a seasonal menu and highlights local ingredients, and its contemporary American fare is consistently excellent. On fair-weather days it is thoroughly enjoyable if you sit outside on the patio. Brunch on Saturday and Sunday runs 11 a.m. to 3 p.m., one of the latest-served brunch venues in the Triangle. At brunch, start with the pimiento cheese fritters served with a piquant pepper jelly, then move on to the Cackalacky, fried green toma- toes with cheddar cheese scrambled eggs, country ham topped with Cackalacky choron sauce, with your choice of grits (my choice always), hash-brown casserole, or fresh fruit.

Wooden Nickel Pub, 105 N. Churton St., Hillsborough; (919) 643-2223; thewnp.com; American/Burgers/Pub; $. A hidden gem in the heart of downtown Hillsborough, the Wooden Nickel Pub offers upscale pub grub in a cozy, laid-back atmosphere. The menu offers an excellent selection of sandwiches, snacks, and other pub fare, and a chalkboard lists daily specials. The Reuben is made with house-cooked corned beef and is a great choice, as are the chicken wings, available in six flavors, or the "Monster BLT": applewood-smoked bacon, lettuce, mayo, and tomatoes on grilled sourdough bread. For a delicious twist, sub the tomatoes for their perfectly fried green tomatoes. The small space fills up quickly with locals, but with their above-average bar food and a top-notch beer selection, I suggest just bellying up to the bar to chat with whoever is there.

Landmarks

Carolina Crossroads, 211 Pittsboro St., Chapel Hill; (919) 918-2777; carolinainn.com; American/Farm to Table/Southern; $$$. Nestled in the Carolina Inn, the Carolina Crossroads harmoniously joins traditional Southern cuisine with a contemporary touch. The refined atmosphere, superior cuisine, attentive service, and wine list are unparalleled as well-documented by the many awards they have won, including the AAA Four Diamond Award, *Wine Spectator* Award of Excellence, and *Forbes* Four-Star Service Award. Chef Jimmy Reale takes the modest pimiento cheese sandwich and adds a fried green tomato and arugula for a new interpretation of a classic. Find your senses elevated with dishes like sweet tea–brined NC chicken or the Southern seafood cioppino—sauteed NC trout, clams, scallops, Benton's country ham, braised collard greens, and fingerling potatoes in a bright lobster tomato broth. Chef Reale has built relationships with local farmers and is committed to sourcing locally to provide diners an unforgettable experience. See Chef Jimmy Reale's recipe for **Brinkley Farms Long Island Cheese Pumpkin Soup** on p. 261.

Crook's Corner, 610 W. Franklin St., Chapel, Hill; (919) 929-7643; crookscorner.com; American/Farm to Table/Southern; $$. A large pink fiberglass pig stands atop the roof, beckoning passersby to come in to this quirky but welcoming diner that has graced Chapel Hill since 1982. Originally opened by Bill Neal and Gene Hamer, with Bill Smith taking over the kitchen in 1992, their seasonal Southern menu has long made headlines, most recently receiving the American Classics Award from the James Beard Foundation. The beloved and nationally acclaimed shrimp and grits, a staple on the menu from the beginning, remains a local favorite as are the hoppin' john, jalapeño hush puppies, and green tobacco chicken. But really, it all comes down to not only the seasonally inspired "down-home" cooking with Southern flair, it's the entire ambience of the place. It's playful, comfortable, and just ridiculously charming—what's not to love? Conclude your meal by delving into the Mt. Airy chocolate soufflé cake or end on a cocktail note with the famous frozen mint julep. For seasonal treats, don't miss the persimmon pudding or the epic honeysuckle sorbet, made from hand-picked flowers and available for only a few weeks each spring. See Chef Bill Smith's recipe for **Eastern North Carolina Corned Ham** on p. 281.

The Farm House Restaurant, 6004 Millhouse Rd., Chapel Hill; (919) 929-5727; farmhousesteakhouse.com; American/Southern/ Steak House; $$$. Located just outside of Chapel Hill in a rustic building set back in the woods, The Farm House Restaurant has served old-fashioned cooking with plenty of Southern charm since 1969. Wood beams, stone fireplace, and kerosene lamps on each table add to the charm, giving it an intimate and relaxed atmosphere. The menu options are simple: Steak, chicken, and shrimp, but they are expertly prepared and brought to the table by friendly and knowledgeable staff. Steaks are the stars here, and although only three cuts are available, they are cooked to precision on the original open charcoal grill and arrive still sizzling on hot cast-iron skillets. The Farm House features a full bar in addition to beer and wine and offers multiple banquet rooms for parties of all sizes.

Mama Dips, 408 W. Rosemary St., Chapel Hill; (919) 942-5837; mamadips.com; American/Fried Chicken/Southern; $. For 35 years, this legendary establishment has been serving ultimate Southern comfort food with a little added soul. Mildred Council (Mama Dip) cooks in a way that reminds you of days gone by, when families

PERSIMMONS

It wasn't that long ago that I discovered the persimmon: A bright orange tree-borne fruit that is grown in North Carolina and harvested in the late fall, usually in the weeks leading up to Thanksgiving. Persimmon fruit is delicious to eat just as is, as you would an apple, avoiding the seeds. It can be used in baked goods such as breads, cookies, and puddings, and apparently is delicious as a sorbet, although I have not tried it this way. The persimmon should be left to ripen until the fruit is fully colored and can be eaten while still firm; some people prefer to peel the fruit before eating as the peel is rather tart. Persimmon pudding is a traditional Southern dish with a custard consistency usually served around Thanksgiving and Christmas. If you want a recipe for persimmon pudding, check out *Seasoned in the South: Recipes from Crook's Corner* by Chef Bill Neal, previously chef at **Crook's Corner** (p. 241) in Chapel Hill.

would sit at the table for a meal together dining on what had been grown in the backyard. At Mama Dips, transport yourself back to these nostalgic times with traditional Southern staples such as fried chicken, Brunswick stew, chicken and dumplings, fried okra, and stewed collards. Don't fill to the point where you don't have room for dessert . . . oh, those heavenly desserts; the sweet potato pie, banana pudding, or her famous pecan pie are all little gifts from a Southern fairy somewhere, and washed down with a cold glass of sweet tea, they are a sublime experience. Purchase her two cookbooks, cornbread mixes, and sauces on your way out the door and bring a little slice of the South home with you.

Sunrise Biscuit Kitchen, 1305 E. Franklin St., Chapel Hill; (919) 933-1324; American/Breakfast/Southern; $. This tiny brick building with drive-through service only, draws travelers from all over, begging to bite into their extra-large, buttery biscuits with fluffy interiors. You can choose from bacon and egg, sausage, pork chop, country ham, and the outstanding fried chicken biscuit. The white meat chicken emerges from the hot oil with a thin, crispy, well-seasoned crust and succulent, juicy meat. Place that chicken inside the fluffy, rich buttermilk biscuit and wash it down with an icy glass of sweet tea, and you can understand why this tiny landmark has a loyal following. The Sunrise Biscuit Kitchen is open for breakfast and lunch daily.

Sutton's Drug Store, 159 E. Franklin St., Chapel Hill; (919) 942-5161; American/Burgers; $. Since 1923, Sutton's Drug Store has occupied their storefront in the heart of downtown Chapel Hill. Popular among UNC students (the university is located across the street) for cheap eats, and returning alumni for a trip down memory lane, Sutton's is a convenience store, drugstore, and grill in one. The menu offers simple fare, namely burgers, hot dogs, fries, and sandwiches, with a few other things thrown in here and there. Dine at the old-fashioned counter or in one of the booths and look around you. Sutton's has become known for the pictures that surround you, they are a testament to the loyalty people feel to the place. Have your picture taken while you are there and become part of Sutton's Drug Store history.

 **Barbecue**

Allen & Son, 6203 Millhouse Rd., Chapel Hill (corner of Hwy. 86 and Millhouse Rd.); (919) 942-7576; $. Allen & Son is the place to go for authentic Eastern NC–style barbecue (see p. 17 for North Carolina barbecue information) cooked the old-fashioned way—over wood. There's only one reason to go to Allen & Son—to get some of the best barbecue you've ever put in your mouth, moist, tender, and delicious with just a hint of tang from the vinegar-based sauce, characteristic of Eastern-style "cue." They only serve chopped barbecue, and you'll love it that way. Of course, you may also want to try the Brunswick stew served with coleslaw and hush puppies. Grab some pigskin treats for your pup on the way out! Casual dining with typical barbecue restaurant decor: wood tables, checked tablecloths, and cinderblock walls.

Hillsborough BBQ Company, 236 S. Nash St., Hillsborough; (919) 732-4647; hillsboroughbbq.com; $$. Located a fleeting distance from downtown, this warm and casual restaurant is churning out succulent BBQ to an ever growing group of BBQ enthusiasts. Determined to continue tradition, owners Joel Bohlin, Matt Fox, and Tommy Stann pit-cook their meats the old-fashioned way using a mixture of oak and hickory wood in the smokehouse behind the restaurant. Slow cooked for 8 to 10 hours, the BBQ is served as a combination of chopped and pulled meat, lightly sauced and extremely tender. If ordering the BBQ plate, try their version of creamy mac and cheese made with roasted garlic, caramelized onions, and muenster cheese or the collard greens cooked for 14 hours in chicken stock and pork skins. Seasonal sides change monthly, and when in season, the local tomato, cucumber, and roasted corn salad is a must. If pork is not to your fancy, consider the smoked chicken, turkey, or the NC catfish bites served with a zesty remoulade sauce. Of course no BBQ meal is complete without a beverage to wash it down, and the cocktail menu is well worth a perusal over the more popular beer pairing. The Bees Knee's is a refreshing combination of gin shaken with local honey and lavender while the bourbon drinker will rejoice in the Johnston's Mule Bourbon mixed with brown sugar–clove syrup and topped with Blenheim's ginger ale. Whatever your fancy, Hillsborough BBQ is a well worth seeking out for expertly executed food and drink.

The Pig, 630 Weaver Dairy Rd., Chapel Hill; (919) 942-1133; thepig restaurant.com; $. Whole-hog BBQ, beef brisket, fried chicken, and pork ribs are all the traditional standards you expect to see on a

BBQ joint menu, but what about BBQ tempeh, shiitake mushroom po' boy, country fried tofu, or "Sweet PLT," a sweet potato "bacon," lettuce, and tomato sandwich? It is these last items that set The Pig apart and salute owner Sam Suchoff's vegan and vegetarian past. He uses only hormone-free and pasture-raised pigs and chickens, and takes his years of experience working at restaurants like **Lantern** (p. 224) and **Neal's Deli** (p. 230) to create eclectic offerings that are sure to please any palate. The menu is written on two large blackboards, one displaying the regular menu, the other for the daily specials. The whole-hog BBQ, beef brisket, and BBQ tempeh plate arrive overflowing with hush puppies, or "pups," as they are listed on the menu, while a long list of sides (including fried green tomatoes, mac and cheese, or "sprouts-n-shrooms") is available. Don't miss the cola-braised pork belly sandwich, or the ribs—dry rubbed and smoked and served with a sweet and tangy sauce on the side, they are some of the best around. Specials change almost daily and don't be surprised to find wide-ranging dishes like grilled kidneys and hearts on cheese grits or tongue and cheek *ragù* served over mashed potatoes. House-made charcuterie is just one other example of Sam's talent. Look for staples like house-cured pastrami, homemade hot dogs, smoked sausage and bologna, or specials like curry lamb wurst, andouille, jowl bacon, and *boudin blanc,* a Louisiana-style sausage made with pork, rice, and onions. Specials change often and the best way to find out ahead of time what will be posted on the board: follow The Pig on Facebook.

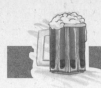

Carolina Brewery, 460 W. Franklin St., Chapel Hill; (919) 942-1800; 120 Lowes Dr., Ste. 100, Pittsboro; (919) 545-2330; carolina brewery.com; Brewery/Brewpub; $$. Founded in 1995, this locally owned brewery and restaurant is the oldest brewery in the Triangle area. The flagship IPA, Copperline Amber Ale, and Blue Sky Golden Ale and a rotating list of seasonal brews are available year-round on tap in the breweries or local bars and restaurants or by the growler to enjoy at home. The casual, family-friendly restaurant is well suited for lunch or dinner and the large, comfortable bar is ideal for game-day watching with a group of friends. Don't miss the burger made with locally raised beef, BBQ plate, fish-and-chips, or beer-battered onion rings. If pizza is what you are craving, they make their dough in-house using spent grains from the brewery. The Pittsboro location has a large, welcoming side and back patio with a small stage for live music and special events.

Mystery Brewing, 437 Dimmocks Mill Rd., Ste. 41, Hillsborough; (919) 697-8379; mysterybrewing.com; Brewery. Mystery Brewing Company, a small brewery located in historic Hillsborough, offers seasonally inspired brews made with fresh, high-quality ingredients. You won't find your typical flagship beer, but instead creative concoctions like the Evangeline, Saison (a bold, yet delicate rye saison with a soft, floral hop aroma over a spicy dry body with notes of pineapple and pear) or the Langhorne Rye Wit, a Belgian-style beer using rye instead of wheat, and a spice blend of blood orange, rose hips, and hibiscus flowers instead of coriander. Owner Erik Myers focuses on unique small-batch seasonal brews, so be sure to enjoy them while you can, because most of the beers are only around for 3 to 6 months. For a little blast from the past, try the Caswell: Historic North Carolina Beer, built from recipes found in historical documents while researching his book, *North Carolina Craft Beer and Breweries*. This dry beer contains molasses, ginger, wheat, rice, and North Carolina–grown barley. Also look for small, one-off batches and collaborations with chefs and other artisan producers from around North Carolina. They do not currently have an on-site taproom, but you can find Mystery Brewing's beers at several local bars and restaurants.

Top of the Hill Restaurant and Brewery, 100 E. Franklin St., Chapel Hill; (919) 929-8676; topofthehillrestaurant.com; Brewpub; $$. The premier location (it's located at the epicenter of Franklin Street at the corner of Franklin and Columbia) of this brewpub offers not only great food and beer but one the most sought-after views of Franklin Street in Chapel Hill, especially after a victorious game day or holiday event like Halloween. The menu features delicious appetizers such as lizard chips (sliced dill pickle and jalapeño chips fried in a homemade beer batter) and plenty of salad and sand-wich options. Entrees include specialties like Cajun-grilled salmon, French Quarter jambalaya, and slow-roasted pork mac and cheese (Carolina pork shoulder with tomatoes, scallions, Parmesan herb bread crumbs, and creamy cheddar macaroni). On tap, look for tasty brews like the Ram's Head IPA, Big Bertha Brown Ale, or the Old Well White, a smooth-tasting wheat beer spiced with orange peel and coriander. Whether you choose to dine in the restaurant, patio, or back bar, the menu and beer selection offer something for everyone.

Specialty Stores, Markets & Producers

Blue Sky Oil and Vinegar, 400 S. Elliott Rd., Chapel Hill; (919) 933-9916; blueskyoilandvinegar.com. This tiny shop offers customers fresh extra-virgin olive oils (EVOO) and balsamic vinegars, imported from artisan and small-batch producers worldwide, in a warm and engaging atmosphere. Owner Glenda Keenan is always happy to give guests a tour of the shop, offer tasting samples, and share her knowledge of which oils and vinegars to pair up and how to incorporate them into your cooking. Several recipes are available both in the store and online. Look for pearl (Israeli) couscous with dried cherries made with harissa EVOO and cranberry pear white balsamic or wild mushroom and sage stuffing using garlic-infused EVOO and wild mushroom and sage EVOO. Glenda even offers a recipe for a Perfect Manhattan with the addition of a dash of black cherry aged balsamic vinegar for a new and exciting twist. Traditional and white balsamic vinegars come in a range of flavors including an almost drinkable 18-year aged balsamic, plus fig, tangerine, and truffle-infused versions. Extra-virgin olive oils range in flavor from chipotle and *herbes de Provence* to basil or Tuscan herb. You can buy small sample sizes to try new flavors at home or larger bottles of your favorites. In addition to an impressive line of oils and vinegars, Blue Sky now carries 16 different kinds of salts from around the world. Look for small-plate tastings every month where they present a menu using the oils and vinegars or demonstrate how to use artisan salts.

The Chocolate Door, 516 W. Franklin St., Chapel Hill; (919) 240-7290; thechocolatedoor.com. The Chocolate Door is a family-run business headed by Meghan Rosensweet who oversees all the production of the chocolate confectionery in the store. It's a small shop with just one showcase of goodies and nowhere to sit, unless you count the bench for the bus stop outside the store. There are about 25 permanent flavors of chocolate with seasonal specialties. Meghan uses Swiss chocolate that she imports to her store and

there are some interesting flavors to savor. For instance, one of her most popular flavors is "chocolate bacon." But you might also want to try the coconut-curry truffle or the spiced Mayan with a hint of cinnamon and nutmeg. There are nutty varieties and caramel chocolates as well. The Chocolate Door also makes cakes to order.

Kitchenworks, Inc., 201 S. Estes Dr., Chapel Hill; (919) 967-9388; kitchenworksinc .com. This is the go-to kitchen store in the Triangle. It has a good selection of kitchen gadgets, tableware, knives, and accessories. Go for the unique and the eclectic, the essential and the whimsical. Don't be fooled by the size of the shop: Items are packed in as far as the eye can see, corner to corner and ceiling to floor. The staff is knowledgeable and really do know where to find each item. I have bought Christmas presents here for years, including linen tea cloths stamped with brightly colored Christmas designs that I use to wrap an awkward-shaped gift.

Locopops, 231 S. Elliott Rd., Chapel Hill; ilovelocopops.com. See write-up in the Durham chapter, p. 209.

A Southern Season, University Mall, 201 S. Estes Dr., Chapel Hill; (919) 929-7133; (877) 929-7133; southernseason.com. The *New York Times* food critic Craig Claiborne labeled A Southern Season "wall to wall and floor to ceiling, a visual and gustatory delight." With 60,000 square feet, this landmark market is a destination in and of itself. Visit when you have time to linger so you can wistfully browse the "Wall of Chocolate," check out the huge wine selection, find the perfect snack, sauce, or ingredient in the grocery department, and in the House & Home department, find gadgets and other housewares that you never realized you would covet. Many "Southern" products are sold including grits, Tar Heel chocolates, pralines, peanuts, and pecans. Two of my favorite gifts that I purchase for family each year are the Carolina cheddar cheese straws and the Carolina Cupboard pecan pralines. In the wine department on Friday evening, join the Fridays Uncorked wine tasting from 5 to 8 p.m. Tickets can be purchased in advance online. A Southern Season has a tempting online store where most of its signature goodies are sold.

Sugarland, 140 E. Franklin St., Chapel Hill; (919) 929-2100; sugar landchapelhill.com. An oasis for the sweet tooth, Sugarland is a locally owned dessert cafe on historic Franklin Street. Desserts such as cupcakes, cannoli, éclairs, and layered mousse cakes are made from scratch using organic flour, eggs, and dairy products. But it's the gelato that truly hits home with this writer: Daily specials of this traditional northern Italian–style gelato have a base of fresh local whole milk and pure sugarcane. For something adults-only, try frozen martinis, for instance the Italian Sunset—a taste of Portofino with blood orange gelato and a kick of Campari. If you're craving a richer, more decadent drink, then the Chocolate or Mochatini, with a base of white chocolate gelato and Godiva liqueur, is meant for you. As well, Sugarland has an extensive wine and beer list all chosen to accompany the great desserts.

Weaver Street Market, 101 E. Weaver St., Carrboro; (919) 929-0010; weaverstreetmarket.coop. The Weaver Street Market is a food co-op that began in 1988. You can shop there without being a member, but if you do invest, you are supporting a community initiative that returns its profits for the good of the community and its members. In 2011, the co-op gave back over $100,000 to reinvest in local schools, businesses, and nonprofits. The grocery store is a de facto town square for community gatherings, and food sold is sourced locally and products are based on fair-trade principles. There is a daily fresh bread schedule (available online). From May to October, come on by for the Jazz & More Brunch on the lawn from 11 a.m. to 1 p.m. on Sunday. A fully refundable "ownership" costs $75 for one adult, $135 for two adults, and $175 for three or four adults.

Recipes

Whipped North Carolina Sweet Potatoes

Executive Chef Jay Pierce at Lucky 32 says, "These whipped sweet potatoes are divine. Simply roasting the whole potatoes instead of peeling and boiling them concentrates the natural sweetness of the tubers and is the backbone of this dish." He goes on to say, "The earthiness of the sweet potatoes is accentuated by the sorghum molasses and counterbalanced by the sour cream."

Serves 4

- **2 pounds sweet potatoes (washed, roasted, and peeled per below)**
- **1 stick butter**
- **⅓ cup sour cream**
- **2 teaspoons sorghum syrup or molasses**
- **Salt to taste**

Roast the sweet potatoes until tender in a 350°F oven for about 45 minutes or until soft to the touch. You could also wrap the sweet potatoes in plastic wrap, poke a hole in each, and microwave for 5–8 minutes. Peel them, weigh them, and then heat through. When heated through, combine all ingredients in a stand mixer with a paddle attachment or mash with potato masher by hand until well combined and smooth.

Author Note: Sweet potatoes are versatile, and can be served sweet or savory. For this recipe, consider adding cinnamon, nutmeg, or white pepper to complement your entree.

Courtesy of Executive Chef Jay Pierce of Lucky 32 Southern Kitchen (p. 89)

Kyle's Collard Cook-Off— Winning Collards

Kyle Wilkerson, Sous Chef of Four Square restaurant and Executive Chef of Edible Piedmont *magazine* has this to say about his popular collard greens recipe: *"These are just old timey good eatin' collards like grandma use to make. When it comes to comfort food like cabbage collards, it's best to keep the ingre-dients simple to truly appreciate the flavor of these tasty greens. I always make my greens a couple days ahead of when I actually need them to allow the greens to marinate in the pot likker."*

Makes 6–8 servings

1 pound smoked hog jowl, finely diced

2 sweet onions, thinly sliced

1 large sweet potato, peeled and medium diced

1 quart chicken stock

1 quart beef stock

4 teaspoons grainy mustard

Hot sauce, to taste

Freshly ground black pepper, to taste

2 teaspoons Worcestershire sauce

¼ cup apple cider vinegar

2 large bunches cabbage collards, cleaned, stemmed, and wide julienned

In a large heavy-bottom pot, on medium heat, render out the jowl until almost crispy. (Note: This should be done in a dry pot, but you can use 2 tablespoons canola oil if you prefer).

Add the onions and caramelize until well browned, about 8–10 minutes. Next throw in the potatoes and cook about 4–5 minutes. Add the remaining ingredients to the pot, except the collards. Bring the pot likker to a boil and then reduce the heat to a simmer, and let it go for 20 minutes. Add the collards and stir well to make sure all the collards are submerged. Reduce the heat to low, and cover, cook for 2 hours, stirring occasionally. Once done, remove the lid, season if needed, and serve.

Courtesy of Kyle Wilkerson, Sous Chef at Four Square (p. 196) and Executive Chef at *Edible Piedmont* magazine.

Macaroni au Gratin

The walls at Poole's Diner are lined with chalkboard menus that change almost daily depending on what's in season. It's what Chef Ashley Christensen is known for—strong ties to the farming community and show-casing seasonal meats, produce, and seafood on an ever changing menu. Some things, however, are staples, and this mac and cheese recipe is one of them. The use of the different cheeses elevates this simple dish to iconic levels; I truly believe there would be a revolt if it were ever taken off the menu. The plate comes out bubbling hot, and the crusted cheese topping, dripping over the edges, doesn't stand a chance of staying there. If you have an opportunity to visit Poole's, look around at the diners enjoying this dish. The smiles on their faces and the delighted looks in their eyes say it all.

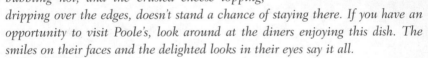

Makes 4 servings

3 cups heavy cream

½ pound of macaroni, cooked al dente and drained

1 cup shredded Jarlsberg, divided

1 cup shredded Grana Padano, divided

3 cups shredded white cheddar, divided

Sea salt, to taste

Cracked black pepper, to taste

Set a rack in the oven about 4 inches from the broiler, and preheat broiler.

In a large sauté pan over medium-high heat, reduce cream by a fourth. Lower the heat to medium. Stir in the macaroni and ¾ cup each of the Jarlsberg, Grana

Padano, and white cheddar. Stir with a wooden spoon while tossing the contents of the pan in a sautéing motion.

Transfer mixture to a baking dish (see Note). Sprinkle the remaining Jarlsberg, Grana Padano, and white cheddar over the top, distributing them evenly.

Place the dish under the broiler. Watch it carefully, as you will need to rotate the dish to create an even crust. This will take from 3 to 5 minutes, depending on the strength of your broiler.

Remove gratin from the oven and season with sea salt and fresh cracked black pepper. Serve immediately.

Note: Chef Christensen suggests that if you wish to add any extra ingredients (such as roasted tomatoes or caramelized onions), they should be layered between the pasta and the cheese topping.

Courtesy of Chef Ashley Christensen of Poole's Downtown Diner (p. 102)

Brinkley Farms Long Island Cheese Pumpkin Soup

Executive Chef Jimmy Reale at the Carolina Crossroads delights his guests with a rotating menu of seasonally inspired dishes. This particular soup, at the height of the fall season, is a perfect start to several courses, or made into a meal with the addition of a green salad and some fresh, crusty French bread. At the restaurant, Jimmy sometimes serves this soup with toasted pumpkinseeds and a drizzle of fig vincotto vinegar. Although this recipe calls for homemade vegetable stock, feel free to substitute reduced-sodium store-bought vegetable or chicken stock.

Yields 1 gallon

- **6 cups roasted Long Island cheese pumpkin (per below; may substitute pie pumpkin)**
- **1 teaspoon olive oil, plus additional for sautéing**
- **Salt and pepper to taste**
- **2 cups peeled and roughly chopped white onions**
- **1 cup roughly chopped celery, leaves removed**
- **1 cup peeled and roughly chopped carrot**
- **2 cups peeled and roughly chopped sweet potatoes**
- **3 cloves garlic, sliced**
- **½ cup brown sugar**
- **Vegetable stock (see recipe below)**
- **½ cup heavy cream**
- **1 tablespoon cider vinegar**

Cut pumpkin in quarters, remove seeds, drizzle with olive oil, and season with salt and pepper. Roast in a 350°F oven for 35 minutes or until soft. Scoop out 6 cups of pumpkin from the shell and reserve.

Heat a large pot, add oil, and sauté onions, celery, carrots, and sweet potato for 5–7 minutes. Add garlic, pumpkin, brown sugar, salt and pepper, then mix well until sugar melts. Add strained vegetable stock and bring to a slow simmer.

Cook for 20 minutes, add heavy cream, and cook an additional 10 minutes. Add cider vinegar, then remove from heat.

Carefully puree hot soup in blender, in batches, until smooth. Taste for proper seasoning. Enjoy!

Vegetable Stock

1 teaspoon oil

1 cup peeled and roughly chopped white onions

1 cup roughly chopped celery, leaves removed

1 cup peeled and roughly chopped carrot

2 teaspoons whole cloves

2 cinnamon sticks

2 teaspoons ground nutmeg

4 dried bay leaves

12 cups water

Heat a large pot, add oil, and sauté onions, celery, and carrots for 5 minutes. Add remaining ingredients and bring to a slow simmer. Cook for 30 minutes. Remove from heat and pour through a fine-mesh strainer.

Courtesy of Executive Chef Jimmy Reale of Carolina Crossroads (p. 240)

English Sweet Pea Salad with Warm Bacon Vinaigrette

Everything is better with bacon, right? And this sweet pea salad by Jim Anile at Revolution is no exception. The smoky bacon flavor is a perfect complement to the sweetness of the peas, tomatoes, and peppers, while the acidity in the dressing brightens the entire dish.

6 servings

4 cups fresh English peas, removed from pod

½ cup applewood-smoked bacon, diced

3 cloves garlic, chopped

1 medium red onion, diced

6 Roma tomatoes, diced

1 yellow pepper, diced

5 tablespoons Dijon mustard

4 tablespoons olive oil

2 tablespoons Worcestershire sauce

½ cup balsamic vinegar

White pepper

Kosher salt

3 ounces tarragon, chopped

In boiling water, blanch peas to just underdone (usually about 3 minutes); drain them and place in ice water. In a large sauté pan, render the bacon to just under crispy, then add garlic, onion, peas, tomato, and yellow pepper. When the vegetables are warm, mix in the mustard, olive oil, and seasonings. Stir in the tarragon and serve warm.

Courtesy of Chef Jim Anile of Revolution (p. 181)

Pamlico Sound Crab Cakes & Shrimp atop Pickled Green Bean & Artichoke Salad

I love a good crab cake, and surprisingly, this is hard to find. There is a definite need of balance when it comes to a good cake—you don't want it to be too bready, nor do you want it falling apart. Chef Pettifer at Margaux's Restaurant has perfected this dish, and I am excited that he has shared it with us. Enjoy!

Makes about 20 1-ounce crab cakes or 6 large crab cakes

5 stalks celery
1 small onion
8 tablespoons (1 stick) butter
1 tablespoon dried thyme
¼ cup white wine
1 pound lump crabmeat
Bread crumbs (add a little at a time until desired consistency is reached, being careful not to dry out the mixture, about 1 cup)

3 tablespoons sour cream
3 tablespoons mayonnaise
Pinch of salt and pepper
1–2 cups bread crumbs for dredging (can be fresh or panko crumbs)
Oil for frying

Finely dice celery and onions, cook in butter until soft. Add herbs and wine and simmer on low heat until almost all liquid is evaporated. Spread vegetables on plate and cool completely. Place crabmeat in a bowl, removing any shell pieces. Add celery/onion mixture, sour cream, mayonnaise, salt, and pepper. Add enough bread crumbs to bind crab mixture (about 1 cup). Form the cakes into desired size (we suggest 2½ ounces) then dredge cake in bread crumbs and refrigerate for 24 hours to set the cakes. Panfry in a small amount of oil until golden brown on all sides and keep warm in low-temperature oven until ready to use. Serve with pickled green beans and artichokes.

Pickled Green Beans & Artichokes

2 cups cider vinegar
1 cup sugar
2 tablespoons salt
3 bay leaves
1 tablespoon mustard seed
1 teaspoon cloves

1 tablespoon dill seed
1 pound fresh green beans, cut into ¼ inch pieces
1 (15 oz.) can artichokes, drained and cut into small pieces

Bring vinegar and remaining ingredients (except vegetables) to a boil, simmer for 5 minutes, then add beans. Simmer until dark green and cut off heat. Add artichokes, stir, and cool completely. This mix will keep for 2 weeks.

Courtesy of Steve Horowitz, Owner, and Andrew Pettifer, Chef, of Margaux's Restaurant (p. 90)

Market's Ketchup

One of the signature dishes Chad McIntyre creates at his restaurant, Market, is actually one of the easiest to re-create in the home kitchen: ketchup. His ketchup is a tangy and flavorful "relish" that works with a wide range of foods. Since this recipe lends itself well to canning, you can enjoy fresh spring and summer tomatoes in the colder parts of the year. The brightness of the apple cider vinegar will dust away the heaviest of winter blues.

Makes about 6–8 cups

- 1 quart peeled, seeded, and diced fresh tomatoes (about 8–10 large tomatoes)
- 2 cups apple cider vinegar
- 1 medium onion, diced
- 1 tablespoons ground black pepper
- 2 tablespoons salt
- ¼ teaspoon cayenne pepper
- 6 cloves of fresh garlic
- 2 cups (packed) light brown sugar

In a large pot start simmering the diced tomatoes in their own juice. In a separate pot, combine the vinegar, onion, pepper, salt, cayenne, and garlic. Reduce by half. Add to the simmering tomatoes along with the brown sugar. Cool to a workable temperature and puree in batches in a blender until smooth. If canning, follow the recommended canning times and temperatures for high acid foods. And as always, follow manufacturer guidelines for the specific jars and lids you use.

Courtesy of Owner Chad McIntyre of Market (p. 91)

Fried Green Tomatoes

Fried green tomatoes are a wonderfully versatile dish. Once you have a plateful, there are numerous ways to serve them. Maybe elevate the classic BLT (my favorite), serve them with your favorite sauce on the side as a delicious appetizer, or use them as a base for a salad: top with fresh pea greens and arugula, sliced grape tomatoes (Sun Golds when they are in season are the best), and shaved Parmesan, then drizzled with a light vinaigrette of your choice. This is an excellent lunch or light dinner. Of course if you don't want to make these at home, just pop on over to ACME in Carrboro and have Chef Kevin Callaghan whip up a batch for you. Note: This was published in Garden and Gun *magazine, June/July 2010.*

Serves 8–10 as appetizer

4 to 6 green tomatoes, sliced (¼-inch thick)

2 cups canola oil mixed with 1 cup (2 sticks) melted unsalted butter (or 1 cup canola oil, 1 cup butter, and 1 cup pork fat)

Wash

2 cups buttermilk (old-fashioned whole buttermilk

that still has fat in it), mixed with 2 large eggs

Dredge

2 cups White Lily (self-rising) flour mixed with:

1 cup stone-ground (medium) cornmeal

½ teaspoon garlic powder

½ teaspoon onion powder

Generous pinch of salt

Generous pinch of freshly ground black pepper

Place sliced tomatoes in a colander. Salt lightly, and let sit for about 5 minutes to help draw out moisture. Rinse under cool water and pat dry with paper towels. Working one at a time, completely coat each tomato slice in the wash and then in the dredge, gently shaking off excess. In a cast-iron skillet over high heat, bring butter and canola oil to 350°F (use a candy thermometer). Reduce heat to stabilize. Working 3 slices at a time, fry the tomatoes until golden brown, turning only once (about 3 to 4 minutes total cooking time). Use a spatula to flip the tomatoes away from you so you don't get splashed. Transfer each batch to drain on brown paper bags.

Courtesy of Chef Kevin Callaghan of ACME (p. 216)

Zwiebelkuchen

An autumn specialty in Germany, Zwiebelkuchen—onion cake, onion pie, or onion tart, depending on which recipe you are using—is an early-fall specialty, usually served with Neuer Wein ("new or young wine"). It is made of sautéed onions with cream, eggs, caraway seeds, and bacon, then baked on dough like a pizza. Because the dough is nice and light, it becomes crispy in the oven and the perfect vessel for the exceptionally flavorful onion topping. I like to serve this with a lightly dressed mixed green salad with (of course, you guessed it) a glass of wine. Please enjoy this rendition from Guglhupf.

Serves 8

- **2 pounds yellow onion, julienned**
- **3 ounces diced bacon (slab preferably)**
- **2 tablespoons clarified butter**
- **2½ ounces all-purpose flour**
- **4 eggs, separated**
- **½ cup sour cream**
- **½ tablespoon caraway seeds**
- **1 teaspoon salt**
- **1 tablespoon unsalted butter**

Pie Dough

- **2 cups all-purpose flour**
- **½ teaspoon kosher salt**
- **3 egg yolks**
- **2 tablespoons heavy cream**
- **9 tablespoons unsalted butter, cubed**

To prepare pie dough, pulse flour and salt in food processor. Add yolks and cream and mix to combine. Add butter and pulse to form dough. Do not overmix. Turn out onto counter and form into a ball. Wrap with plastic wrap and refrigerate for 30 minutes. Roll out to ⅛th of an inch and press into a buttered 10-inch pie pan.

Preheat oven to 400°F.

Sweat onions and bacon in clarified butter over medium-low heat, 7 to 8 minutes. Be careful not to brown the onions. Remove from heat and transfer to a side dish until room temperature. While the onion and bacon mixture is cooling, blend the flour, egg yolks, sour cream, caraway seeds, and salt. Add cooled-off onion mixture and fold in stiffly beaten egg whites. Spread mixture evenly into tart shell and dot the top with nubs of soft unsalted butter. Bake for 35 minutes or until an inserted toothpick comes out clean.

Courtesy of Guglhupf (p. 164).

New Orleans BBQ Shrimp

According to Mel Melton, Chef-Owner of Papa Mojo's Roadhouse, "The food and music of Acadiana have always been inseparable for me." And that is the truth. Not only is "Mojo's" known for great food, but check out the music calendar and you will instantly see the harmonious marriage of the two. Excellent blues, rock, and traditional zydeco become the backdrop to a delectable meal of traditional New Orleans gumbos, jambalaya, and when in season, this "get down and dirty" plate of BBQ shrimp. If you happen to visit the restaurant when this is on the menu, you will not be disappointed. The head-on shrimp reminds one of eating whole crawfish where you pop it off the head and suck out the juices . . . trust me, this is the best part, I swear! You will not want to leave any of the sauce behind, it is that good. It's rich and flavorful and perfect for mopping up with plenty of fresh bread. As with any Cajun Creole cooking, everyone has his own way of stirring things up, so feel free to experiment, just don't leave out the Worcestershire sauce: This is, as far as I am concerned, the key component.

Serves 2 as appetizers

1 pound shrimp, in shell, head
    on (Large 12/16 count)
½ cup Worcestershire sauce
½ cup chopped parsley
10 thin lemon slices
Juice of 1 lemon

2 teaspoons black pepper
2 teaspoons Creole seasoning
1 teaspoon minced garlic
1 tablespoon Tabasco
½ pound butter

Heat shrimp in a skillet on high heat with all seasonings and lemon slices. Cook for 1 minute on each side. Add butter in cubes, stirring constantly. Add each cube of butter after the previous one is melted. Take off the heat, put shrimp in a bowl, and ladle sauce over the top. Serve with plenty of French bread for dipping.

Courtesy of Chef Mel Melton of Papa Mojo's Roadhouse (p. 176).

Mussels with Cranberry—White Balsamic Gastrique

I spoke to Chef John Eisensmith of Six Plates Wine Bar about this dish and I really couldn't say it any better, so I didn't!

"The inspiration for this dish came from the desire to give mussels more dimension and to do something different from the usual 'spicy tomato broth' or 'white wine broth' that traditionally accompanies most mussel dishes. Part of my style of cooking is to try and break the mold of food and then put it back together, adding a few more pieces to the puzzle that you never knew you were missing. Effectively, bringing new flavors and ideas to the table while still being able to recognize the time-honored and well-loved cultural staples from which the idea originated. I believe this mussel dish is a good example of this style. It started simply enough with white wine and cream. Then I added the white beans for sustenance and body, leeks and garlic for background, and cayenne for some earthy heat. Tomatoes give you that little burst of refreshing palate cleansing as you encounter them throughout the dish, while basil brings the anise-herbal notes to round out the palate. Then just a little bit of the gastrique every few bites provides the sweet, sharp acidity that helps cleanse the creamy/earthy/spice of the dish and excite the palate for the next bite. Plenty of bread is always a must with any mussel dish. As you eat the dish, notice the roller coaster effect that you get on the palate; it is one of my favorite characteristics of this mussel dish. I hope you enjoy in good health!"

Serves 2

1 large leek, sliced in rings
3 cloves garlic, thinly sliced
¼ cup olive oil
1 cup white beans, cooked and drained
1 pound mussels, cleaned and debearded
½ cup white wine

1 cup heavy cream
Pinch of cayenne
Salt
1 medium tomato, diced
1 bunch basil, chiffonaded (cut into fine ribbons)
1 baguette or crusty bread

For the Cranberry Gastrique

½ cup dried cranberries
¾ cup white balsamic or Champagne vinegar

¼ cup granulated sugar
¼ cup water

Prepare the gastrique first. Combine all the ingredients for the gastrique in a small saucepan and bring to a boil. Reduce to a simmer and cook for 5 minutes. Cool to room temperature, then puree in a blender and reserve for later.

For the mussels, heat a large sauté pan and sweat the leeks and garlic in the olive oil for 1–2 minutes. Add the beans and the mussels, then the wine. Cook on high for 1 minute or until the wine is reduced by half. Add the cream, cayenne, and salt to taste. Continue cooking on high until all the mussels have opened. Transfer to a bowl and sprinkle with tomatoes and basil. Drizzle the gastrique over the top and serve with plenty of warm bread for the sauce. Enjoy!

Courtesy of Chef John Eisensmith of Six Plates Wine Bar (p. 187).

Raw Vegan "Pad Thai"

Mathew Daniels and Jane Howard Crutchfield, owners of the Triangle Raw Foods truck and weekly delivery service, believe in living a healthy lifestyle, nurturing the mind, body, and soul with fresh, local, and living foods. They love experimenting and creating new recipes to share with others, and their rendition of the classic pad thai made with zucchini and carrots is refreshing and light and makes a very satisfying lunch or dinner.

Serves 4

"Noodles"

2 carrots, peeled and shredded

5 medium to large zucchinis, spiralized (to spiralize, we recommend using a Paderno World Cuisine Spiralize; or thinly slice them with vegetable peeler)

Sauce

2 Thai chiles (add more if you want more heat)

2 cloves garlic

4 reconstituted sun-dried tomatoes (to reconstitute, soak in water for at least an hour)

½ cup sesame oil

¼ cup tamari

3 tablespoons tamarind paste

2 tablespoons chile powder

1 tablespoon paprika

1 tablespoon mirin

1 teaspoon lime juice

Garnish

⅓ cup cilantro

¼ cup crushed raw cashews

Lime, for garnish

In a large mixing bowl, mix shredded carrots and spiralized zucchini until evenly distributed.

To make sauce, in a food processor using the "S" blade (the chopping blade), pulse the Thai chiles, garlic, and sun-dried tomatoes until minced. Add all remaining sauce ingredients and process for about 1 minute on high speed. Pour sauce over noodles and mix until well coated. Garnish with cilantro, cashews, and a slice of lime. Enjoy.

Courtesy of Mathew Daniels and Jane Howard Crutchfield of Triangle Raw Foods (p. 49).

Basil Pesto–Crusted Wild Striped Bass with Elodie Farms Goat Cheese Polenta & Tomato-Caper Sauce

This recipe from the Washington Duke Inn & Golf Club is perfect for spring evenings when the weather is just starting to warm up and dinner is calling for something light but satisfying. The pesto crust offers a delightful crunch to the moist, flaky fish, while the polenta and tomato-caper sauce add a sophisticated element. A perfect meal for entertaining guests alfresco.

Serves 6

6 striped bass fillets with skin intact (6 ounces each)
Salt and pepper
¼ cup olive oil for sautéing
½ cup basil pesto (recipe below)

½ cup panko bread crumbs, seasoned with salt and fresh ground pepper to your taste
½ cup prepared polenta (recipe below)
1 cup tomato caper sauce (recipe below)

Basil Pesto

Makes 1½–2 cups

3 cups basil leaves, tightly packed
2 cloves fresh garlic, minced
1 cup extra-virgin olive oil

Salt and pepper
¼ cup pine nuts, toasted
¼ cup Parmesan cheese, finely grated

Bring a large pot of water to a boil over high heat. Fill a large mixing bowl with ice water. When water boils, add salt. Blanch the basil leaves in the boiling water by immersing them completely. Remove them right away and place directly in the ice water. When thoroughly cooled, drain the basil and squeeze out excess water. Using a food processor, pulse the basil until finely chopped. Add the garlic and pulse again to incorporate. Next drizzle the olive oil little by little into the basil mixture and pulse to incorporate. Once it reaches the consistency of a loose paste transfer the mixture to a mixing bowl. Season lightly with salt and freshly ground pepper, add the pine nuts and the cheese, and mix thoroughly.

Tomato-Caper Sauce

Makes approx. 4 cups

1 tablespoon extra-virgin olive oil

3 cloves garlic, minced

¼ cup minced shallot

1 tablespoon capers

½ cup dry white wine

6 large fresh plum tomatoes, roughly chopped

2 cups V8 Juice

2 sprigs fresh thyme

3 basil leaves

1 tablespoon fresh squeezed lemon juice

Salt and pepper

Heat a medium-size saucepan over medium heat. Add the olive oil, garlic, and shallots and sauté lightly for one minute; add the capers and sauté for one more minute. Add the white wine and bring to a simmer. Allow the wine to reduce by 25 percent. Add fresh tomatoes and the V8 and bring the pot to a simmer. Reduce heat and cook until tomatoes begin to break down. Pick and chop the fresh thyme and the basil. Add them to the sauce and simmer 5 minutes. Remove from heat. Working in small batches, pulse the sauce in a food processor to the *desired consistency and then return the sauce to the stove. Stir in the lemon juice and adjust the seasoning with salt and freshly ground pepper. Serve warm.*

Goat Cheese Polenta

3 cups whole milk
3 tablespoons unsalted butter

1 ½ cups dry polenta, not instant
½ cup fresh chèvre

Bring milk to a simmer over medium-high heat in a heavy saucepan. Add the butter. Whisk in the polenta, bring to a simmer, and reduce heat to low. Cook the polenta for 30–40 minutes until creamy and smooth. Remove from heat and cover until ready to use. When ready to serve, stir the chèvre into the hot polenta until well incorporated.

To Prepare the Bass

Preheat a large sauté pan over medium-high heat and preheat oven to 375°F. Using a very sharp knife, score the skin of the fish, being careful not to cut too deeply into the flesh. Rinse the fillets and pat them dry with a paper towel. Season the fillets with salt and freshly ground pepper. Add just enough olive oil to coat the bottom of the pan (if it smokes immediately, the pan is too hot, so remove from heat for a few moments). When the oil begins to smoke, add the fillets to the pan with the skin side facing down. Cook until the edges of the fish begin to brown, turn them over, and cook until they begin to brown again. Cook about 4 minutes per side. Remove from heat and turn the fish back to skin side down in the sauté pan. Coat the top of the fillets liberally with the pesto, top the pesto liberally with the seasoned bread crumbs, and place the pan in the oven. Cook approximately 8–10 minutes, or until the fish is just cooked through, and remove from the oven.

To Serve

Divide polenta evenly between six plates. Place the fish on top of the polenta and spoon the sauce around the plate as desired. Garnish with fresh thyme leaves and enjoy with a glass of Sauvignon Blanc.

Courtesy of Executive Chef Jason Cunningham
of Fairview Restaurant at Washington Duke Inn & Golf Club (p. 157)

Eastern North Carolina Corned Ham

Since 1992, Bill Smith has been delighting diners with his Southern regional cuisine, at Crook's Corner in Chapel Hill. His interpretations of classic dishes are a little slice of heaven everyone must experience. Summers in the South are made for gatherings, whether it is for a traditional pig pickin' or family picnic. This particular dish lends itself well for a large get-together, any time of year. Although the recipe is time-consuming, the final product is well worth the time and effort.

Serves a crowd

- **15–20 pound fresh ham**
- **Kosher salt**
- **2 green cabbages, finely chopped**
- **4 pounds fresh kale, finely chopped**
- **6 bunches scallions, finely chopped**
- **1 bunch of celery, finely chopped**
- **2 pounds other greens (collards, turnip, spinach, etc.), finely chopped**
- **2 tablespoons celery seed**
- **3 tablespoons whole mustard seed**
- **3 tablespoons red pepper flakes**
- **1 tablespoon black pepper**
- **1 tablespoon salt**

Rinse and dry the ham. Use a sharp boning knife to make a 3- or 4-inch incision at each place that the bone protrudes from the meat. This is usually three places—one at each end and one place on the side. Pack as much salt as possible into each of these incisions then cover the outside of the ham with a thin layer of salt. Place in a nonreactive pan and cover. Keep in the refrigerator for 11 days.

Turn the ham and re-salt the outside if you think about it. On the night of the 11th day rinse the ham and flush the salt out of the pockets that you cut. Soak overnight in cool water.

The ham is ready to cook at this point, and in fact this is the ham that I grew up eating. Just cook in a covered roasting pan with a little water at 325°F for 20 minutes per pound. Uncover for the last hour of cooking so the ham will brown. Ham should be beginning to fall off of the bone. Let it rest a little before serving.

This next part Bill Smith learned last year from Phyllis Richman (formerly of the Washington Post*) by way of the Kitchen Sisters (www.kitchensisters.org).*

Wilt all the vegetables in a little water or oil, then stir in the seasonings. Allow to cool enough to be handled. With the boning knife, cut 2 to 3 inch slits all over the ham, wherever there is room. Stuff as much of the vegetable mixture into these slashes as possible. Pack any leftover stuffing on top of the ham then cook the same as explained above.

Courtesy of Chef Bill Smith of Crook's Corner (p. 241).

Pork Dumplings

The food-truck phenomenon has exploded, and thankfully so. On any given day you can follow the numerous trucks via Twitter or Facebook and find out where your favorite will be parked that day so you can stop by to pick up lunch or dinner. Choose between pizza, Korean, Mexican, or good ol' fashioned burgers— there is always a truck to satisfy your craving. Nothing warms my belly more than a plate of dumplings from the Chirba Chirba Dumpling Truck. There is always a vegetarian option, but I am addicted to their pork dumplings—expertly crafted, tasty, and habit-forming, these are some of the best you will find. Add a side of glass noodles and you are set. Dumplings sound like they are hard to make, but with a little practice, you too can enjoy these little bites of happiness, homemade.

Makes 20–25 dumplings

Dough

1 cup dumpling flour (Found in specialty Asian stores, or substitute all purpose flour)

2 cups water (Note: Use hot water if using all purpose flour)

Option #2: go buy a pack of premade wrappers from your local Asian store

Filling

½ pound ground pork

4½ tablespoons vegetable oil

4 teaspoons sesame oil

4 teaspoons soy sauce

4 teaspoons mushroom soy sauce

¼ teaspoon sugar

½ teaspoon salt

½ teaspoon white pepper powder

1 teaspoon ginger powder

3 teaspoon potato starch

½ cup Chinese celery, chopped

¾ cup Chinese chives, chopped

¼ cup scallion

Chinese rolling pin—a smooth wooden stick (no handles) about 2 to 3 inches in diameter. Some have a bulge in the middle, which helps! Check your local Asian supermarket or get one from a hardware store.

Put one cup of dumpling flour in a mixing bowl. A little at a time, add 2 cups of cold water and stir briskly with chop sticks. The idea is that little dough balls that resemble spaetzle form as you mix. You never want to have wet goopy dough. When all the flour from the sides of the bowl is in dough-ball form, you can knead them all together to make one big dough ball. Knead the ball until you have a smooth, stretchy consistency. Then let it sit for 20 minutes on the counter, covered, while you prepare the filling!

Combine all of the liquid ingredients with the ground pork in a large mixing bowl. Mix well. Next, add sugar, seasonings, and starch and mix well. Lastly, thoroughly combine the celery, chives, and scallion into your meat mixture. Make sure the scallions are the last addition and that you form your dumplings right away as the onions can contribute a slimy texture when marinating in the meat for too long. Now, go wake up your dough!

Roll the dough into a long snake about 1½ inches in diameter. Set it horizontally on a large, well-floured cutting board in front of you. With a knife, cut nuggets about 2 inches long, rotating the snake 90 degrees back and forth after each cut. Start with just a few nuggets at first to see what size you like. Make sure your nuggets are well floured and round. Press them down with the palm of your hand so you have a round, flat disc shape. Next, use three fingers to hold the top edge of the disc so your fingers are pointing toward you. You are going to be rotating the disc counterclockwise after each roll of your rolling pin which starts at the edge of the disc closest to you.

Roll away from you toward your other hand. Do not roll over the entire disc! Stop in the middle. Then, rotate the disc counterclockwise and roll to the middle again. Repeat until your edges are flat but the center has a little soft bulge. This is easier than it sounds! There is a very helpful video on asiandumplingtips.com.

Time to wrap/pleat!

First, grab some friends. This is really fun to do in a group as a dumpling-making party (that is how Chirba Chirba Dumpling Truck began). Assign some people to make wrappers, some to pleat, and then one to boil/steam! For the pleaters: Take a spoonful of filling (start small and work your way up—less filling is easier to pleat) and place it in the center of your wrapper. Here, you've got form and function to consider.

The function of your pleat should be to seal the meat inside of the wrapper so that no filling can escape during the cooking process. You can do this simply by folding the wrapper over the filling in a half circle shape and pinching the edges closed. If you're using homemade wrappers, you shouldn't need a binder. If you're using store-bought wrappers, you'll need a little dish of water to wet the edges in order for the wrapper to stick to itself around the filling.

The form of your pleat is to make it pretty with various pleats and folds. To make this pleat, you fold your wrapper in half around the meat and pinch it on the top. It looks like a taco but sealed at one point at the top. Place the taco round side-up on your index finger, which should be hook-shaped pointing sideways, and hold it steady with your thumb (that has the same curvature as your index finger). Now bring your other hand on the other side of the taco and press the edges of the dumpling against your curved index finger with your two thumbs. The positioning of your thumbs around the edge of the dumplings will feel very awkward at first, but you'll get used to it. If you don't curve your thumbs, then you'll just end up squeezing the meat filling out of the sides and then you have to start over.

Don't be discouraged, practice makes perfect! You can find lots of helpful videos online with different pleating techniques.

Cook!

Steam the dumplings for 10 minutes in a bamboo steamer basket on napa cabbage leaves. Or, drop them into boiling water. When the water returns to a boil, add a cup of cold water. Repeat two more times.

Enjoy with black Chinese vinegar.

Courtesy of Chirba Chirba Dumpling Truck (p. 43).

Butternut Squash Ravioli

At Il Palio, in the Siena Hotel in Chapel Hill, Executive Chef Adam Rose knows a thing or two about pleasing the palates of his customers. Each fall, his customers clamor for the butternut squash ravioli that has been a feature on the fall menu for the last 3 years (now going into its fourth). If he took it off the menu, I swear there would be a picket line in front of the hotel with customers begging (and I'm being kind here) for their return, that is how good they are. All pasta is made in-house, and although I have not included a recipe, there are plenty online.

Filling

2 butternut squash
¼ cup olive oil
¼ cup chopped thyme
3 garlic cloves, chopped
1 teaspoon red pepper flakes

Salt and pepper
1 pound mascarpone
1 teaspoon oregano
¾ cup grated Parmesan
½ teaspoon grated nutmeg

Cut the squash in half lengthwise and rub with olive oil. Sprinkle the thyme, garlic, pepper flakes, salt, and pepper, and roast at 375°F for 30 minutes, or until the squash is soft. Let the squash cool, then scoop the flesh out of the skin and pulse in a food processor until smooth. Fold in the mascarpone, oregano, Parmesan, and nutmeg and season to taste. Fill ravioli and freeze.

Vinaigrette

½ pound unsalted butter

1 cup balsamic vinegar

Melt the butter in a saucepan over medium heat until the white milk solids start to turn into brown bits. The butter will have a nutty aroma. Remove from heat and refrigerate for 10 minutes. Transfer to a squeeze bottle or a quart container, add the vinegar, and shake. Warning: If the vinegar is added when the butter is hot, it may boil over and create a mess.

To Serve

4 sliced shiitake mushrooms **Crushed amaretti cookie**
¼ cup minced chives **Grated Parmesan**

Sauté (pan roast) the mushrooms in butter until crispy, then remove from the pan. Boil the ravioli until the filling is soft, and place into serving bowls. Whisk the vinaigrette together and spoon desired amount over the ravioli. Sprinkle with the crushed amaretti cookie and Parmesan. Top with mushrooms and chives, and enjoy!

Courtesy of Executive Chef Adam Rose of Il Palio (p. 221).

Lemongrass-Grilled Hanger Steak with Cucumber Salad & Spicy Peanut Sauce

These are the components to Jujube's most popular dish, a reconstructed version of the Southeast Asian classic "sate," which amounts to grilled skewers of beef, chicken, or pork, served with peanut sauce and cucumber salad. I do love their version, and it is often the first thing I want to eat at Jujube if I've been out of town for any amount of time.

I love hanger steak and strongly advise that you seek it out for this dish. If, however, you can't find it, either flank or skirt steak make good substitutes. To assemble the dish, grill the steaks as you desire (Chef suggests rare to medium rare), allow to rest briefly, and slice against the grain. Then serve alongside a portion of the cucumber salad with a ramekin of peanut sauce on the side to dip the steak in. This makes a great dish for parties as it lends itself to buffet service, each guest taking as many slices of the steak as they like (and probably coming back for more until it's gone).

Serves 10

Lemongrass Beef Marinade

1 cup fish sauce
¼ cup chile oil
¼ cup sweet chile sauce
½ cup brown sugar

1 stalk lemongrass, finely chopped
5 pounds hanger steak, trimmed

Use only the bottom ⅓ of the lemongrass, avoiding the greener, more fibrous tops. Hanger steak comes with two steaks separated by a layer of silverskin. If you're not adept at butchering, ask your butcher to cut each steak away from the skin for you. There may be some chunks of surface fat remaining and that should be removed.

Combine all marinade ingredients and cover steak. Allow to marinate for several hours to overnight and then remove from marinade. Following your grill's instructions, grill to medium rare or to your liking.

Sweet Chile Cucumbers with Red Onion

2 English cucumbers, thinly sliced on mandoline (not peeled)

1 red onion, peeled and thinly sliced

¼ cup rice vinegar

¼ cup sweet chile sauce (often sold at Asian markets as Chile Sauce for Chicken)

1 teaspoon salt

Zest of 2 lemons

Mix all ingredients and allow to sit for at least 30 minutes.

Peanut Sauce

1 (15-ounce) can coconut milk

1 cup peanut butter

½ onion finely chopped

¼ cup chile garlic sauce

1 tablespoon sugar

1 tablespoon soy sauce

Water to thin to desired thickness

Combine all ingredients and add just enough water to allow you to stir it. Keep in mind, sauce will thin as you heat it, so don't put too much water in to begin with. Heat very slowly and serve warm, but not hot. Sometimes the sauce will separate. If this happens, whisk in a small amount of boiling water to re-emulsify.

Courtesy of Chef Charlie Deal of Jujube (p. 222)

Buttermilk Pie

Jay Pierce, Executive Chef of Lucky 32 Southern Kitchen gets gold stars for this recipe. After featuring lemon chess pie on the menu, he decided he wanted something with a little more nuance and less sweetness. The buttermilk pie was the natural outgrowth, and it is a delightful custard pie, with just enough nutmeg to remind you of eggnog. This is a perfect dessert for any gathering, holiday, or special event, or simply made and served at Sunday dinner.

Makes 1 pie

¼ pound butter
1⅓ cups granulated sugar
4 eggs
3 tablespoons all-purpose flour
½ teaspoon nutmeg
¼ teaspoon salt

1½ cups buttermilk
1 tablespoon lemon juice
1 teaspoon lemon zest
1½ teaspoons vanilla extract
1 prepared pie shell

Preheat oven to 300°F. In a bowl, cream butter and sugar with an electric mixer. Add eggs one at a time, until incorporated. Sift together flour, nutmeg, and salt. Add flour mixture to bowl and mix until just combined. Add remaining ingredients and mix until a homogenous mixture is obtained (less than 2 minutes). Pour into a prepared pie shell. Bake for 55 minutes. Should be done when a toothpick placed in the center comes out clean.

Author Note: If you prefer your pie on the sweeter side, consider serving it with a fruit coulis. If you like a stronger lemon flavor, top with additional lemon zest (also makes for a pretty presentation).

Courtesy of Executive Chef Jay Pierce of Lucky 32 Southern Kitchen (p. 89).

Appendices

Appendix A: Eateries by Cuisine

Pie Bird, 100
Piper's in the Park, 179
Reliable Cheese Company, 210
Remedy Diner, 103
Rick's Diner, 182
Rockford, The, 104
Sandwich, 234
Square Rabbit, The, 110
Straw Valley Cafe, 188
Toast, 190
Wilmoore Cafe, 116

Seafood
Blu Seafood and Bar, 147
Fishmongers Restaurant and Oyster
  Bar, 160
42nd Street Oyster Bar, 121
Margaux's Restaurant, 90
Mura, 94
NC Seafood Restaurant, 94
Squids Restaurant and Oyster
  Bar, 235

Southern
ACME Food & Beverage Co., 216
Big Ed's City Market, 120
Carolina Crossroads, 240

Crook's Corner, 241
Dame's Chicken and Waffles, 155
Farm House Restaurant, The, 242
Four Square, 196
Geer Street Garden, 161
Lucky 32 Southern Kitchen, 89
Mama Dips, 242
Merritt's Store & Grill, 229
Nana's Restaurant, 170
Parker and Otis, 209
Pig, The, 246
Poole's Downtown Diner, 102
Scratch Seasonal Artisan
  Baking, 185
SoCo Farm and Food, 58
Sunrise Biscuit Kitchen, 244
Watts Grocery, 194
Weathervane, 239

Spanish
Tasca Brava, 112

Steak House
Angus Barn, 119
Bin 54, 216
Farm House Restaurant, The, 242
Winston's Grille, 117

Appendix B: Specialties & Purveyors

Index